THE
COMPLETE
PLATE

Kristy & Nat
May food & cooking always
bring you joy ♡

Lauren Kelman

The Complete Plate

▽ **120** Recipes ▽ **30** Meal Plans

A Stronger, Healthier, and Happier You

LAUREN KLUKAS

With Janine Elenko, RD, and Ashlee Gillespie

Figure.1
Vancouver / Berkeley

Copyright © 2018 by Lauren Klukas
Recipes are chef tested.

18 19 20 21 22   5 4 3 2 1

Cataloguing data available from
Library and Archives Canada
ISBN 978-1-77327-015-9 (pbk.)
ISBN 978-1-77327-016-6 (ebook)
ISBN 978-1-77327-017-3 (pdf)

Design and art direction by Natalie Olsen
Photography by Lindsay Nichols
Food styling assistance by Evan Olsen
Ceramics by Kalika Bowlby
Utensils on page 169 and 241 (Antuco 2-Piece Serving Set) and pan on page 135 (CeraStone CeraComm 10-inch Ceramic Fry Pan) courtesy of Crate and Barrel.

Editing by Michelle Meade
Copy editing by Laura Brown
Proofreading by Breanne MacDonald
Indexing by Iva Cheung

Printed and bound in China by C&C Offset Printing Co., Ltd.
Distributed in the U.S. by Publishers Group West

Figure 1 Publishing Inc.
Vancouver BC Canada
figure1publishing.com

RECIPE NOTES

Butter should always be unsalted. / Eggs, vegetables, and fruits are assumed to be medium size, unless otherwise specified. / Milk is always 2%, unless other-wise specified. / Greek yogurt is always 0% MF. / Dark chocolate is always 70%, unless otherwise specified. / All-purpose flour is always unbleached. / Cocoa powder is always unsweetened. / Almond milk is always unsweetened and fortified with calcium. / Tortillas are always low sodium.

Jordan, you are and will always be my anchor.
You have remained strong and steadfast through
this storm. Charlotte, you are my treasure.
Your joy brings me joy, and your delight in
simplicity inspires me.

CONTENTS

Introduction 8

THE COMPLETE PLATE 12

The Basics 14

Nutrition 101 16

How to Use This Book 26

Pantry and Freezer Staples 35

Essential Equipment 36

THE MEAL PLANS 38

1	2	3	4	5	6
7	8	9	10	11	12
13	14	15	16	17	18
19	20	21	22	23	24
25	26	27	28	29	30

Basic Recipes 284

Nutrient Analyses 290

References 296

Acknowledgments 297

Conversion Chart 298

Index 299

Contributors 307

Character cannot be developed in ease and quiet.
Only through experience of trial and suffering can the soul
be strengthened, ambition inspired, and success achieved.

HELEN KELLER

WHAT A WHIRLWIND the past few years have been for this redhead! I became a mom. I created a food blog. I developed an effective eating plan to lose and maintain weight. I launched a pilot for a cooking show, and, if you're reading this, you can see that I also embarked on a journey to write my first cookbook.

The irony is that I only recently discovered a passion for cooking. In fact, if anyone had told me two years ago that I would write a cookbook, I would have laughed out loud. I was one of those people who only had a kitchen because it came with the house. Being very physically active, I felt like I never had to worry about calories, eating out, or enjoying yummy pastry treats high in sugar and trans fats. I would just work it off later. Ergo, I had no reason to use a kitchen or learn how to cook healthy meals at home. When I did venture into this mystery room in the house, I was clueless: "What is braising?" "Seriously, you can make scalloped potatoes from scratch? I thought they only came in a box!" "You don't flip your meat a thousand times while cooking?!" My greatest culinary achievement was pouring cereal into a bowl. So how exactly did I find myself in this paradoxical situation?

Physical activity has always been a priority in my life. In my youth, I was a competitive swimmer, training up to nine times a week. I achieved many significant milestones during my swim career: set club records, obtained qualifying times, and attended high-level training camps with Olympic coaches. A healthy, active lifestyle was intrinsic to me and is what inspired me to attend university and complete my Personal Fitness Trainer (PFT) diploma.

A Life Unrooted

In 2012, my husband and I found out the very exciting news that we were expecting our first baby! But by week 15 of my pregnancy, I was having terrible heart palpitations. Following a multitude of doctors' appointments and tests, and almost a month in the hospital, I was diagnosed with a rare heart condition known as Arrhythmogenic Right Ventricular Cardiomyopathy (ARVC).

The cells of the heart muscle are bound by proteins, but for those with ARVC, our proteins cannot fully develop so the heart muscle cells detach and do not properly repair themselves. This prevents electrical signals from communicating with the bottom of the heart properly, which results in abnormal heart rhythms and improper pumping—the perfect setting for sudden cardiac arrest.

To add to the crazy paradox that is my life, ARVC is genetic and only develops in the perfect environment. Geneticists see a significant correlation between patients who were high-level athletes during their youth and the development of the disease. If doctors knew that I had the genetic code as a child, they would have advised me not to participate in intense physical activity. The active and athletic lifestyle that I had led up to this point was, ironically, the root of my rare and incurable heart condition.

My pregnancy switched from textbook to high risk. At my 36-week checkup, there was concern that my heart might not hold up much longer. I was admitted to the hospital and induced. The delivery was intense, but on May 28, 2013, at 12:15 p.m., our precious baby girl, Charlotte (Charley), was born.

In an attempt to decelerate the damage to my heart and prevent a case of sudden cardiac arrest, I was instructed to cease all physical activity indefinitely. Fitness was my whole life, from swimmer to trainer, so this devastating news turned my world upside down.

I can no longer exercise. My career as a personal trainer is over. I am not allowed to have any more babies because my heart is not strong enough to handle another pregnancy. To add insult to injury, I am not even allowed to have coffee! Grieving the loss of my old life is a dynamic journey with constant ups and downs. However, as I continue to develop new hobbies and skills outside the scope of fitness, I am learning to not only cope with my new reality, but to thrive in it. I'm completely devoted to my role as mother of the most captivating little girl and wife of a supportive and loving husband, but I still sometimes questioned my purpose.

When Life Gives You Lemons...
Bake a Lemon Meringue Pie!

After my diagnosis, I began looking for ways to control my weight without physical activity. In February 2015 I started a blog to share my journey of both weight loss and weight management through proper nutrition. Each week I developed meal plans using a diet analysis program I used in university and shared them, along with lessons learned on my new journey. Seeing the transformation of my body over a year, purely through nutrition, was amazing. And it was encouraging to know that, thanks to a conscientious meal plan, I still had control over my body.

Exercise and Weight Loss

While exercise is necessary for weight maintenance and several important physiological adaptations (like improved cardiovascular and pulmonary health), it is not key for weight loss.[1] Current literature suggests that aerobic training must be frequent and extremely high in intensity for significant weight loss to occur.[2] Nutrition is a fundamental factor in weight loss and one variable in my life that I can control. (See more on Nutrition on page 16.)

I would never recommend a sedentary lifestyle or suggest someone give up their exercise routine, but a large portion of the population is not meeting the minimum guidelines of physical activity to receive any health benefits. Studies support that current minimum physical activity guidelines for adults—two and a half hours of moderate- to vigorous-intensity physical activity per week—is sufficient for reducing the risk of chronic diseases.[3] However, in the United States, less than 5 percent of adults get 30 minutes of physical activity a day[4] and only one in three adults get the recommended amount of physical activity each week.[5]

While campaigns promoting a healthy lifestyle continue to find more efficient and effective ways to encourage the long-term adoption of physical activity, a balanced meal plan—including whole foods with proper micro- and macronutrient composition—can also provide positive health benefits and prevention of chronic diseases. (See more on Micro- and Macronutrients, starting on page 16.)

The Beautiful Paradox of Adversity

ARVC has redefined my life in a way that many would consider calamitous, but there is a beautiful paradox with adversity. The painful refining process of trials and tribulations can lead to profound personal growth and create opportunities that never would have emerged otherwise. Weight loss is only a small chapter of this story. Weight loss and a particular body image are not, by any means, a reflection of successfully establishing a healthy lifestyle. My journey has simply highlighted the importance of meal planning, nutrition, and cooking in the attaining of food wellness and has led to the design and implementation of a successful lifestyle for weight management that works with my sedentary life.

The Mission

My mission for *The Complete Plate* is to redefine people's understanding of nutrition. Life would be easier if food's only purpose was to nourish our bodies. Food is at the center of our celebrations, times of fellowship, religious ceremonies, and cultural festivities. The relationship between joy and food has been fused together since the beginning of time, and that is why to establish sustainable healthy eating habits we need to rediscover joy in eating and abandon the mind-set of good foods versus bad foods (the mentality of eat this, not that). For healthy eating to be sustainable, it needs to be more than chicken, quinoa, and vegetables for the rest of your life. I don't want to bully anyone into eating healthily. I want to encourage critical thinking and provide a resource that presents sound nutritional information so anyone can develop healthy and positive associations with food. My hope is that *The Complete Plate* will be a valuable tool in this transition to a sustainable, healthy new lifestyle. Now let's get cooking!

VITAMIN B12 76%
1 Tbsp nutritional yeast

VITAMIN D 5%
1 egg yolk

VITAMIN B5 56%
1 avocado

ZINC 32%
¼ cup wheat germ

FOLATE 15%
1 cup spinach

OMEGA-3 140%
1 Tbsp flaxseeds

POTASSIUM 21%
1 avocado

THE COMPLETE PLATE

These analyses were determined using NutriBase©Personal Plus Edition, v.11.73.

OMEGA-6 71%
¼ cup pumpkin seeds

VITAMIN B2 35%
1 cup milk

MAGNESIUM 16%
¼ cup peanuts

VITAMIN B3 64%
75 g chicken

VITAMIN A 59%
½ cup carrots

CALCIUM 13%
2 Tbsp tahini

VITAMIN E 47%
⅓ cup almonds

VITAMIN B6 16%
½ cup water chestnuts

PHOSPHORUS
12%
1/3 cup edamame

VITAMIN C
94%
1 kiwi fruit

MANGANESE
68%
1/4 cup pumpkin seeds

VITAMIN K1
228%
1/2 cup kale

VITAMIN B1
14%
1/4 cup sunflower seeds

SELENIUM
33%
1/2 cup shiitake mushrooms

IRON
13%
1/2 cup hearts of palm

THE BASICS

WEIGHT MAINTENANCE, and weight loss, can be achieved through a balanced diet made up of ingredients that come together to meet both nutritional and caloric demands. In the process of creating a perfectly balanced daily diet, I quickly discovered that compiling this information involved a significant amount of time, research, energy, and patience. I wondered if there was a tool or book to help people like myself map everything out. Surprisingly, there wasn't. And this is how the idea for *The Complete Plate* was conceived.

What Is The Complete Plate?

The Complete Plate attempts to bridge the gap between nutrition and flavor. It provides 30 daily meal plans for caloric requirements of 1500, 2000, and 2500 calories per day. Each day is perfectly balanced to provide 100% of your micro- and macronutrient needs, based on current Dietary Reference Intake (DRI) values.

How It Works

The Complete Plate is not a program or a diet. It is a lifestyle made up of three components: nutrition, meal planning, and cooking. Together, these three elements create a union of food wellness and healthy eating habits.

Food wellness is a term we created to describe the ideal state for making healthy eating habits a part of your busy day-to-day life. The hope is that when food wellness is achieved, your mind and body will be able to perform at peak performance. But if one of the three components is missing, it is almost impossible to establish sustainable healthy eating habits and achieve food wellness.

Nutrition is the fuel you put into your body, and it impacts performance and mood. With the overwhelming amount of unscientifically based nutrition information available, it can be difficult to discern what is true and what is trendy. This is why having insight into sound nutritional information is a key foundation for obtaining food wellness.

Organized meal planning is essential for successfully executing and maintaining healthy eating habits. Meal planning reduces stress, saves money, and helps prevent consuming calorie-dense convenience foods.

Cooking your meals helps foster healthy eating habits. You may be incredibly organized and have immense nutritional insight, but you need to get all that wonderful knowledge onto a plate.

What Can I Eat?

I'm often asked, "What foods do I need to eliminate on this program?" The answer is simple: none! This book is NOT a program, it is a lifestyle. One that does not label foods as good or as bad. Some recipes will include ingredients such as bacon, bread, and cheese; *The Complete Plate* does not demonize whole nutrients like fat or sugar. Nutrients work best in a food ecosystem. Eliminating certain foods, or single ingredients, prevents whole foods from doing their job. *The Complete Plate* promotes a balanced diet that does not deprive the user of specific foods.

Why It Works

This approach to eating works because it is not revolutionary—wait, what?! We have been conditioned to believe that a diet must be extreme, radical, and sexy in order for it to work. We do not give our bodies enough credit! Sure, there are situations that warrant a more creative approach, but for the general healthy population, our bodies are more than capable of handling the food we put into it within moderation. This plan is going back to the basics. It is not overcomplicating science, it is rooted in context and solid research, and it is fostering healthy relationships with food.

While other programs are prohibitive or eliminatory, *The Complete Plate* encourages balanced eating, which leads to optimal nutrition and satiation. And because you are eating a variety of foods, including the occasional treat, you never feel the need to cheat. This way of eating celebrates delicious and healthy food consumed in moderation.

Best of all, *The Complete Plate* works because it's sustainable. Since each meal plan is perfectly balanced for your DRI values, you don't have to follow the meal plans in order. If you are still becoming comfortable in the kitchen, keep it simple by choosing a few of your favorite meal plans and enjoy them over and over again. If variety is your spice of life, feel free to choose a different plan for every day of the week. With this book, I want you to feel empowered to make choices suited to your lifestyle needs.

Say Goodbye to Cravings

A little anecdotal plug. Once I started fulfilling my body's daily micro- and macronutrient needs, my sugar cravings stopped. Essentially, by following my meal plans, my body is in a continually content state because it receives everything it needs to function at its peak performance on a daily basis. It is important to clarify that I would never label treats as bad, or a form of "cheating," but when I get my DRI values from food, I simply lose my desire for those foods.

Additionally, a balanced meal plan that provides your body with all its recommended intake values tends to reduce mindless snacking—a prime culprit for empty calories that add up quickly. But don't worry, we don't demonize snacking in *The Complete Plate*. Each meal plan provides a list of delicious and healthy snacks to curb hunger.

NUTRITION 101

by Janine Elenko, RD

I BELIEVE THAT EVERYONE should have access to reliable nutrition information to help them make decisions about their health. What we eat impacts us throughout our lives, from our mother's diet during our fetal development to our golden years. My interest in nutrition started when I met my husband, back when we were still kids. He was diagnosed with type 1 diabetes mellitus at the age of 12, and I was fascinated with how food had such an immediate impact on his health. This sparked my journey to become a dietitian so I could help equip people to meet their health and nutrition goals.

Making a change is not a simple process because not only do we eat for physical nourishment, but also for social, psychological, and cultural reasons. Time, busy schedules, and finances impact our food choices, as well as the myriad of dietary preferences and requests of the people we are cooking for. Then, there is the flurry of information about nutrition from television, the Internet, and social circles (social media anyone?) that we try to sort through to make the best choices we can. What a process! Everyone should have access to trustworthy nutrition information; however, one of the challenges in the Information Age is being able to navigate, interpret, and trust the overwhelming amount of information at our fingertips.

Our body is a complex system of organs (large scale) made up of many types of individualized cells (small scale). The foods that we eat provide the essential building blocks for these cells and organs to function, of which our understanding continues to evolve. The body relies on macronutrients—carbohydrates, protein, and fat—along with micronutrients—vitamins and minerals—to carry out life-giving functions. *The Complete Plate* is in no way a comprehensive lesson on nutrition, but I hope to clarify some of the foundations of nutrition as you embark on your healthy lifestyle adventure.

Macronutrients

Carbohydrates, protein, and fat act as the main building blocks in our body and are the components of food that contribute calories. Now here is a significant question: how much do calories count? When looking at weight management, the number of calories you consume makes a difference, as this is the amount of energy we are feeding our body, and that energy either needs to be used or stored. However, it is more important to put the emphasis on choosing foods that are "nutrient dense" versus "calorie dense." This means your calories should come from foods that provide many nutrients important to our health (nutrient dense), rather than foods that have few nutrients but are high in energy (calorie dense). The body needs energy to function, but as with other concepts in nutrition, moderation is key—we want to give our body the energy it needs, not a lot of extra energy to store.

Carbohydrates are the primary fuel source for our body, in particular for our brain, and provide fiber and multiple vitamins and minerals.[6] A healthy diet should get 45–65 percent of its calories from complex carbohydrates,[7] not refined (highly processed) carbohydrates and free sugars (see next paragraph). Whole grains, starchy vegetables, and legumes are considered complex carbohydrates, meaning they are high in fiber and require more work for our body to digest, helping us feel fuller for longer and stabilizing blood sugar and cholesterol levels. Refined carbohydrates are grains that have been processed (think of turning grain kernels into flour) and have had most of the fiber removed. Examples include white flour and white pasta. These foods are digested faster by our body, which impacts our hunger, blood sugar, and heart health. If you enjoy refined carbohydrates, try to make a shift to include them as treats, not as a staple part of your diet.

Sugars that are found in whole fruit and dairy products are also part of a healthy diet in moderation, as these foods are nutrient dense. Free sugars, on the other hand, are found in treat foods such as candy, cakes, sweetened yogurt, and ice cream, as well as in sugar-sweetened beverages (think pop), honey, syrup, and fruit juice. Yes, even 100 percent fruit juice! Limiting free sugars is beneficial for our overall health and helps with weight management and in reducing the risk for associated chronic diseases.[8]

Protein is the key building block of all structures in our body, including organs, muscles, and skin, as well as things we cannot see like enzymes and hormones. It is recommended that protein account for 10–35 percent of our caloric intake or 0.8–1.0 grams of protein for every kilogram of body weight (you will also need more protein if you are very active or have certain medical conditions).[9]

Typically, when we think of protein, we think of animal products such as meat and poultry, eggs, and dairy products. These protein sources are complete proteins, meaning they contain all of the amino acids (protein components) that our bodies need but cannot make, and therefore must get from food. It is possible to get too much protein, although this is often achieved through supplemental protein intake rather than diet alone. Excess protein intake leads to protein being stored as fat and puts extra stress on the kidneys.

Grains, nuts and seeds, and legumes also contribute protein to our diet. But since plants (except quinoa and soy) are missing some of the amino acids our body needs, eating a variety of plant-based foods is important. Adding more plant sources of protein also helps cut back on the fats we get from animal products and increase our fiber intake, which improves overall health. Really, it is all about variety and moderation.

Fat also has important roles in our body, including insulation, protecting our organs, maintaining nerve and brain function, and providing energy stores needed in moderation. Fat should account for 20–35 percent of our caloric intake, with an emphasis on unsaturated fats (not all fats are equal in their health effects).[10]

There are three main categories of fat: saturated, unsaturated, and trans. Saturated fats come primarily from animal sources, with the exception of coconut oil and palm oil. These fats are known to raise cholesterol levels, which is related to cardiovascular disease, though more research is being done on whether the source of the saturated fat impacts health outcomes. Unsaturated fats are plant oils and omega-3 fats from certain fish, and are known to be beneficial to our health, especially cardiovascular health. Omega-3 fats come from fatty fish such as salmon, mackerel, and trout, and plant sources such as flaxseeds, walnuts, and canola, but since our body inefficiently converts plant-source omega-3s to the form found in fish, eating at least two servings of fatty fish a week is important for cardio-vascular health.[11] Trans fats are plant oils that have been chemically altered to act as an animal fat in baking and are the most detrimental to our health. Store-bought treats like cookies, pies, croissants, and fried foods may contain trans fats like partially hydrogenated or hydrogenated oil, although this is changing as consumers pressure the food industry to remove it.

FIBER

There is a lot of hype about fiber, but what is it beyond a dietitian's buzzword? Well, it's the parts of plants that the human body cannot break down and digest. There are two general groups of fiber: soluble (acts like a sponge, helping with cholesterol and glucose control) and insoluble (acts as roughage, promoting colon health). The typical North American pattern of eating is low in fiber; increasing your intake of fruits, vegetables, beans and legumes, nuts and seeds, and whole grains increases your fiber intake and acts as an investment in your health. Make sure you increase your fluid intake with your fiber intake to keep everything moving smoothly! (See page 284 for fun flavored water ideas.)

Micronutrients are broken down into vitamins and minerals. We often hear these terms, but do you know what the difference is? Remember learning about the periodic table in school? Minerals are the micronutrients found on the periodic table. Think iron, sodium, iodine, magnesium, and calcium. Vitamins are *organic* compounds, and no, that does not mean that they are made without fertilizer! It means they are compounds that contain carbon, along with other types of atoms. Our body is capable of making vitamin D (although this is limited by many factors), but otherwise we need to get vitamins from food. One thing I have learned, and am reminded of continuously in my practice, is that our bodies are complex and there is no miracle nutrient! So I have decided to go through the different body systems and explain what micronutrients are essential to their functioning to hopefully help you discover the incredible relationship between nutrients and the importance of taking a food-first approach instead of relying on supplements.

Let's start with our largest organ: skin. I don't have the secret to everlasting youth, but vitamin A, vitamin C, riboflavin, and zinc are all micronutrients that help keep skin healthy and intact. You may take this for granted, but frail skin that tears easily makes an ideal entrance point for germs into your body.

Bones and muscles are the framing of our body that allows us to do both day-to-day activities and the fun activities that bring quality to our life. Perhaps it makes sense that since bones and muscles work together, they need similar nutrients to function. Vitamin D, potassium, magnesium, and calcium are involved in both muscle and bone health, but in different mechanisms. In bones, these nutrients are used for the end goal of creating a strong, durable structure. Bones also require vitamin C for collagen production and vitamin K to bind calcium. Muscles use calcium, magnesium, and potassium to contract, and require iron to supply and store oxygen.

The nervous system is the electrical system in our body that allows us to perceive and respond to what's around us. There are many nutrients needed for the electrical impulses to occur, including calcium (and consequently vitamin D to regulate calcium levels), magnesium, potassium, and zinc. Neurotransmitters is the fancy name for the chemicals sent between neurons—or neurons and muscle cells—that allow the electrical signal to continue. Many of the B vitamins, as well as vitamin C, are involved in making neurotransmitters.

The cardiovascular system includes our heart and blood vessels, and with the rise in heart attacks and strokes, has become an organ system of focus. Many people are familiar with sodium (salt) impacting blood pressure, but did you know that potassium, magnesium, and calcium all have a role in blood-pressure regulation? These nutrients are also

important for the heart to contract properly. In a different capacity, vitamins B6,
B9, and B12 are involved in clearing
homocysteine (a toxic by-product of bodily
functions) from the blood, decreasing
inflammation in blood vessels and
consequently lowering the risk of cardiovascular disease.

We often overlook how nutrients other
than iron impact the function of our blood,
but there are many nutrients needed for
blood to work its best. Vitamin A and B
vitamins are needed to incorporate iron
into the red blood cells, and vitamin C
is a secondary helper by promoting iron
absorption from plant sources. Another
important life-necessitating function is
blood clotting, in which vitamin K plays a
crucial role.

Immune function is a hot topic, both
in terms of protecting the body from
infectious diseases, but also protecting
the body from autoimmune diseases such
as type 1 diabetes and celiac disease.
Vitamin A, vitamin D, B vitamins, and
iron are all involved in immune function.
A different, but still relative, mechanism
is preventing oxidation, which causes
damage and inflammation to the body.
Riboflavin (vitamin B2), vitamin C, and
vitamin E are powerful antioxidants,
protecting our cells from oxidation.

Now, you may be wondering why there
is a recommended intake for sodium when
a lot of attention has been paid on how it
negatively impacts our health (especially
blood pressure). But the truth is, our body
needs sodium for life-sustaining processes,

VITAMIN D

If you look at the nutrient
analysis in this book
(page 290), the vitamin D
level is frequently low. Our
body produces vitamin D from
sunlight exposure, but if you
live at high latitudes (like
Canada!), spend most of your
day indoors, protect yourself
from sunlight when you are
outside, or a combination of all
three, your body is likely not
producing adequate vitamin D.
Milk and some brands of milk
alternatives (for example,
almond or soy milk) have
been fortified with vitamin D.
Fish with small bones are
also a significant source of
dietary vitamin D. Vitamin D
supplementation is generally
recommended to help meet
our recommended intake.
Otherwise, if you are eating a
balanced diet, most people do
not need additional vitamin or
mineral supplements. Check
with your health care provider
prior to starting any vitamin
or mineral supplementation.[13]

including metabolism and nerve and muscle function. However, the typical North American diet that relies heavily on highly processed foods provides too much sodium, which can lead to negative health consequences, including high blood pressure. Again, moderation is key. Reducing our intake of highly processed foods, and cooking more from scratch, gives us control over the amount of sodium in our food, providing us with what our bodies need while also promoting health.

I want to address metabolism and micronutrients. First, I need to clarify that when I talk about metabolism I am not referring to the ability to use energy and consequently lose weight, but rather to the ability to break down the food we eat and turn it into energy that the cells in our body can then use to function. B vitamins are central to the metabolism of macronutrients (carbohydrates, protein, and fat) into energy, but magnesium and iron also play a key role in this process.

Lastly, we may forget to think about how nutrients impact our genes, but even DNA needs vitamins and minerals to perform the functions essential to our survival. B vitamins are needed to create and repair DNA, while magnesium, iron, and zinc are needed for DNA production.

It is incredible how the food we eat impacts our body's ability to function all the way from the essential creation of DNA to being able to jump on a trampoline and have strong skin. Nutrients work as a team, not individuals, in allowing our body to function.

Multivitamins

It's a common misconception that taking a multivitamin will help provide "nutrient insurance" if you are busy and not always eating a healthy diet; however, there are several reactions that occur with micronutrients and food that cannot be replicated in a supplement, like how the lactose in milk helps our body absorb the calcium. Unless it's vitamin D, it is best to make an effort to get key vitamins and minerals from food.

Dietary Reference Intakes (DRI)

Developed by American and Canadian experts after an extensive research review process, Dietary Reference Intakes (DRI) are a set of values used to explain the amount of a nutrient needed by most healthy individuals.[14] Using the DRI as a guide for The Complete Plate, we have analyzed ingredients, put recipes together, and created a plan that ensures you get a complete set of macro- and micronutrients each day.

To cover the largest demographic possible (male and female aged 19–50 years old), we accounted for the highest DRI values for each group. However, even when considering the highest DRI values, intakes still fall below set upper limits. If you would like an in-depth diet analysis for each meal plan, please refer to page 290.

CHOLESTEROL

Cholesterol is often an area of confusion. Cholesterol, which has functional roles in our body, is both produced in our body and obtained from food. Some bodies have a hard time regulating cholesterol, and excess LDL cholesterol in our blood can cause plaque to build up in our arteries, which can then lead to cardio-vascular disease. It used to be common practice to restrict cholesterol-containing foods; however, there is not enough evidence to recommend low-cholesterol diets. Rather, once again, we need to focus on a healthy eating pattern that is rich in nutrient-dense foods and keeps treat foods as treats.

Weight Loss

WEIGHT LOSS 101: caloric deficit leads to weight loss, calorie surplus leads to weight gain. A caloric deficit of 3500 kcal equals 1 pound lost. A loss of 1–2 pounds per week is argued to be the most sustainable rate of weight loss to keep it off long-term. To attain this, you want to aim for a caloric deficit of approximately 500 kcal per day: 250 caloric deficit from food, 250 caloric deficit from exercise. The 3500-calorie rule works as a good rule of thumb.

While the core concept of weight loss appears simple, and these numbers work well for the first stages of weight loss, the 3500-calorie rule eventually falls short because it is not capable of accounting for the drop in metabolic rate as body mass decreases. In other words, the amount of energy that your body expends while at rest decreases as you lose weight. Metabolic rate is an extremely important variable for weight loss because it accounts for 60–75 percent of daily calorie expenditure.

With this being said, while metabolic slowdown is a factor for plateauing early in the weight-loss journey, it is more often related to individuals not consistently adhering to a reduced-calorie meal plan.[15]

Additionally, several confounding factors impact weight loss—including genetics, environment, medical conditions, age, and gender— which are often out of our control.

There are also day-to-day barriers that prevent us from losing weight. Once we are aware of these obstacles, which can be easily managed, weight control becomes easier. Some tips to consider when navigating these barriers are:

MAKE HEALTHY EATING A PRIORITY

The busyness of life is the main reason so many of us cannot sustain long-term healthy eating habits. Time is one of our most valuable commodities, and the reality is, adopting a healthy lifestyle takes effort and time. But if establishing healthy eating habits becomes a priority, then tasks like cooking a healthy meal will become a joy rather than an inconvenience.

FIND SUSTAINABILITY IN A DIET

Countless scientifically unsupported and anecdotally based weight-loss concepts tell us what (and what not) to eat, and we as consumers are overwhelmed by the options. As there is no governing body to review content and monitor the distribution of weight-loss information, anyone can present a sexy, new weight-loss method without scientific support or testing. Consequently, essential foods and nutrients, like fat, are irresponsibly eliminated from a diet without any repercussions or accountability. As we have said before, nutrients do not work alone; they work in an ecosystem with other nutrients. Fad diets are unsustainable, and the weight will return eventually. Sustainability is the key to success.

ESTABLISH A HEALTHY RELATIONSHIP WITH FOOD

All the uncontrolled diet fads on the market have damaged our relationship with food. Words like clean eating, detox, and cleanse give the illusion that certain foods should be put on a pedestal, while other foods will cause long-term irreparable damage. All the misinformation and fear mongering surrounding what is considered "healthy" is becoming more than just a marketing tactic to make more money; there are now serious consequences with the lack of accountability to erroneous nutritional claims.

This new trend of fear over facts has led to the concern of a potentially new form of disordered eating called Orthorexia Nervosa. It is an unhealthy obsession of being so fixated on righteous eating that people become paralyzed by fear, afraid to eat anything because it may cause cancer, or it may contain "bad fat," or it isn't a complete protein and so on. They become so focused on a perfect orthorexics' diet that they develop malnourishment. While it is not considered an official diagnosis, it does highlight a growing concern about the fear-based nutrition environment we are living in.

The psychological connection we have with our food, if not addressed, could be more dangerous than a rogue sugar or fat molecule. Building healthy relationships with food means taking away the food labels of good and bad, it means taking away the feeling of guilt or shame with having a treat, it means tossing out the concept of "cheating," and it means finding joy in food and eating patterns. *The Complete Plate* celebrates delicious and healthy food in moderation. We give people permission to enjoy food.

CREATE REALISTIC GOALS AND EXPECTATIONS

Sustainable, healthy eating habits and weight loss require realistic goals. If you expect to look a certain way after eating one salad, you will be disappointed. Behavioral changes cannot be done overnight. Sustainability means making changes slowly to break long-term habits. Eventually, these slow and steady changes will result in healthier new habits. The goal of any lifestyle change should be to improve your overall health and wellness.

EMBRACE VARIETY

Resenting the process is the main reason people give up at making lifestyle changes. If you feel healthy eating means just consuming chicken, quinoa, and veggies the rest of your life, it will get old quickly. As you make changes to your eating habits, consider adding foods to your diet rather than eliminating foods.

HOW TO USE
THIS BOOK

Determine Your Caloric Intake

How does one determine which caloric level to follow? It is important to check with your health care provider, but if you do not have any medical conditions, you can start with some general guidelines.

If you are physically active, you will need more calories. Also, males tend to need more calories, based on the same level of physical activity, than females. There have been many equations developed to attempt to predict caloric requirements, each with their own strengths and limitations. The Mifflin-St Jeor equation is one of the more reliable ways to estimate caloric requirements in healthy individuals, and you can find Mifflin-St Jeor calculators online.[16] Caloric estimation is not an exact science; you are unique and calculating your estimated energy requirements is just a place to start. Use your experience (how full you feel, weight changes) to provide feedback on which calorie level to follow and consult your health care provider. An additional note of encouragement: weight is not the end-all-be-all to health; the health benefits of eating a well-balanced diet go well beyond the scale.

If you follow a plan lower than 1500 kcal, you require very specific instructions from a medical professional. Additionally, if you require any more than 2500 calories, you are likely a high-level athlete and require a very specific dietary plan.

Make a Plan

Every single daily meal plan in the book provides a perfect balance for your DRI values. If you follow the daily meal plan for your caloric intake and eat all of the meals and snacks for the day, you will receive all your daily nutrients just from what you eat. With 30 balanced days in total, you can design a meal strategy that best suits your flavor preferences, eating patterns, and family dynamic. This flexibility promotes sustainability because it allows you to adapt meals to fit your lifestyle.

The adaptability allows you to create a realistic schedule. You may decide that you want to adopt a Complete Plate seven days of the week. Or you may just start with a few days of the week. Additionally, you may decide that you want to try new recipes every single day. Or you may choose to pick one or two days and double or triple each recipe, batch cooking the same recipes for the whole week. The options are endless.

Shopping

Everyone has their own grocery-shopping preferences. For myself, I like to shop on Sunday and get everything I need for the week. Others prefer to use produce when it is at its freshest, so they shop every other day. Whatever your inclination, there is an ingredient list provided at the beginning of each day to help you quickly build your grocery list.

Pantry and Freezer Staples (page 35) features a list of regularly used items that you should always have in your pantry or freezer. It makes weekly shopping more manageable!

Portion Control

Each recipe includes the number of servings as well as the number of portions to be served for each calorie plan. Portions are intended for healthy males and females, aged 19–50 years old, based on current DRI values. Some people may be surprised by actual portion sizes, and it may take some time to adjust to eating proper portion sizes. A gram weight is often included next to the volume measure. You don't need to live life worrying about every single gram you eat, but weight does have an impact on the caloric range of certain types of foods. For example, 3 cups of spinach or ½ cup of shredded cheddar will vary depending on how tightly they're packed into measuring cups. Invest in a digital scale to get the most accurate measurements (see Essential Equipment, page 36).

Please be aware that meal plan portions are not suitable for children, but kids can still eat the same meal. Just be sure to give them their usual portions.

Snacks

I've included a snack list for each meal plan. Consume all the snacks within your caloric plan to keep you satiated throughout the day and to ensure you meet your DRI requirement. I recommend spreading them out over the course of the day.

Hydration

Males require 15½ cups of water per day and females require 11½ cups. This number includes drinking water, water from beverages, and water from food. While you receive some water from food, you definitely do not receive all of it. Your water intake should come from tap water, tea and coffee (with no additional cream or sugar), and sparkling water. If your sparkling water is sweetened, be sure it is sweetened naturally (e.g., with fresh lime juice) and not with an artificial sweetener. Water is vital with this plan as your fiber intake will most likely be much higher than you are used to. (See page 284 for fun flavored water ideas!)

Five Days Planned, Two Days Smart

Meal planning reduces stress during the busy work week and protects you from consuming energy-dense convenience foods. Being prepared and organized is essential for establishing positive relationships with food and for being successful in the execution of maintaining healthy eating habits.

The book is designed so that no matter what plan you choose (page 38), you will consume a complete set of nutrients for the day, purely through dietary means. As someone who loves to organize, I find meal planning an effective tool for weight management—especially when I eat Five Days Planned, Two Days Smart. Why five days and not seven? The common theme you will find throughout this book is that success is all about sustainability. Planning meals for seven days of the week is not realistic for everyone. Breaks from cooking are important, planning for leftovers, making a simple grilled cheese, or eating out for a night is all a part of fostering a healthy relationship with food.

One approach that I've found to be successful is what I call Five Days Planned, Two Days Smart. For five days I eat specific to the meal plan portions. I am considerate of portion sizes and measure everything out. I do not estimate my portion sizes, because when I am hungry estimating 1 Tbsp turns into a ¼ cup. For the two days that I don't have a meal plan, I make sensible eating decisions. Whether it's having some of the leftovers from the week or dining out with my husband and daughter, I appreciate the freedom that comes with making wise eating decisions. If I have a hankering for French fries, so be it. If I want the chocolate-almond croissant at my local patisserie, I'll indulge. We all have favorite comfort foods and so long as we make considered choices and consume in moderation, we can establish a healthy relationship with food.

Five Days Planned, Two Days Smart requires a bit of pre-planning and the process may seem slow at first, but with routine and habit, it's something you can easily incorporate into your life.

Anatomy of a Meal Plan

Organization is key to successful meal plans and weight management. Here, I show you how a week-long meal plan might look with recipes and strategies for planning ahead.

I like to have fish one day of the week, a slow-cooker recipe on a busier day, and a few days of variety. (If you're just starting out, I recommend choosing two or three of your favorite meal plans and spreading them out across the week.)

When I plan I also look at how I can use leftover ingredients in multiple recipes. For example, leftover chicken on day 1 can be used for lunch on day 2. Some of the other meal plans that require precooked chicken include Meal Plans 8, 15, 16, 22, and 30. Therefore, it would work well to combine Meal Plans 1, 6, and 13 with the former meal plans so you already have your chicken prepared.

MEAL PLAN				
1	**2**	**3**	**4**	**5**
BREAKFAST				
Southwest Crustless Quiche and Tropical Green Smoothie	*Vanilla Blueberry Chia Pudding*	*Eggs in a Ring*	*Coconut and Flaxseed French Toast*	*Goat Cheese and Avocado Toast*
LUNCH				
Grilled Vegetable and Hummus Flatbread	*Bocconcini Salad*	*Portobello and Prosciutto Pizza*	*Quinoa, Buckwheat, and Bean Salad*	*Berry and Boursin® Salad*
DINNER				
Thai Chicken, Quinoa, and Veggie Bowl	*Potato and Leek Soup with Buckwheat Salad*	*Bison, Spinach, and Sweet Potato Salad*	*Slow-Cooked Chicken Fajitas*	*Arctic Char with Wild Rice, Corn Salad, and Beet Greens*

A Shopping List

Once you have a well-stocked pantry and freezer (Pantry and Freezer Staples on page 35), you only need to shop once each week for the necessities. At the beginning of the week, go through and see which groceries you already have and which ones you need to pick up. (Online grocery shopping—which is so common and convenient these days—saves me a lot of time as well.) For this sample meal plan, my shopping list would look like this:

PRODUCE
3 red bell peppers
2 yellow bell peppers
2 orange bell peppers
1 cucumber
2¼ lbs cherry tomatoes
4 avocados
1 zucchini
1 (2-lb) bag carrots
2 heads broccoli
1 lemon
1 lime
1 bunch kale
2 bunches Swiss chard
2 bunches collard greens
1 bunch green onions
14 bananas
2 pints strawberries
2 pints blackberries
2 pints raspberries
2–3 pints blueberries
2 mangos
4 oranges
1 lb grapes
6 Portobello mushrooms
8–10 white mushrooms
3 (1-lb) containers spinach
1 (8-oz) package sugar snap peas
1 (5-oz) container arugula
3 leeks
1 acorn squash
1 large butternut squash
3–4 sweet potatoes
3 Russet potatoes
3 shallots
2 large yellow onions
1 head garlic
1 small root ginger
1 (32-fl oz) carton orange juice

BAKERY
1 bag whole wheat pita
1 loaf whole grain, high-fiber bread
1 bag corn tortillas

DELI
1 (10-oz) container hummus
1 (5-oz) package prosciutto

MEAT AND FISH
1 whole broiler chicken
2–3 boneless skinless chicken breasts
1 (37-g) pack bacon, thick cut
10½ oz fillet Arctic char

FROZEN
1 bag pineapple
1 bag blueberries
1 bag papaya
1 bag peas

DAIRY
18 eggs
1 (8-oz) container sour cream
1 (16-oz) container plain Greek yogurt
1 (16-oz) container vanilla Greek yogurt
1 (17½-oz) container fruit-bottom yogurt, <1% fat
1 small container plain kefir
7 oz cheddar cheese
1 (4-oz) container Parmesan cheese
1 (7-oz) container feta cheese
1 (5-oz) package soft goat cheese
1 (5-oz) package Boursin® Garlic & Fine Herbs
1 (7-oz) container bocconcini
1 stick butter

DRY GOODS
1 (18-oz) can diced tomatoes with green chilies in lime juice
1 (18-oz) can lentils
1 (18-oz) can chickpeas
1 (18-oz) can small white beans
1 (13½-oz) can hearts of palm
¼ cup pine nuts
¼ cup slivered almonds
¼ cup whole almonds
1 cup cashews
½ cup hemp seeds
½ cup oat bran
1 cup buckwheat
¼ cup coconut flour
1 (1½-oz) bottle pure lemon extract
½ cup brown sugar
1 small container cashew butter
1 small bottle Thai sweet chili sauce
1 (32-fl oz) carton chocolate almond milk
1 container coconut oil
1 jar whole grain mustard
½ cup milk chocolate chips

Plan for the Week

And lastly, in an effort to prepare as much as possible in advance of the week and ensure I'm operating at an optimal level, I review all my recipes and make note of simple things I can make ahead. For this week, I might:

PREPARE SOME DISHES IN ADVANCE

Southwest Quinoa Quiche, Buckwheat Quinoa Salad, or Chia Pudding can all be made ahead of time and refrigerated until I need them. When a dish needs to be served warm, I simply reheat it in the microwave or on the stovetop.

BATCH COOK

Batch cooking is another great time-saving technique to promote sustainability. Select 2–3 meal plans for the week and when you prepare the first meal, double the recipe so you have enough for two full days. Repeat for the other 1–2 meal plans so you are only cooking every second or third day.

PRE-COOK GRAINS

If an ingredient, like quinoa or buckwheat, is used more than once during the week, cooking a big batch at the beginning of the week and portioning it out cuts down on daily prep time.

FREEZE SMOOTHIES

I place ingredients for each smoothie, except juice, milk, or water, into individual freezer bags and label each bag. When I'm ready to make the smoothie, I simply put the ingredients into the blender, add the liquids, and blend until smooth.

REFER TO "GRAB AND GO" NOTES

These tips help me prepare the meals I need to eat when I'm away from home.

Mindful Eating

MIND THE SAUCE

Prepared sauces often contain added sugar, salt, and fat and have minimal vitamins and minerals. Be mindful of the portion sizes and use nutrient-dense options such as hummus and tomato paste. When eating out, ask for dressings or sauces on the side so you can control how much is added.

MEASURE HIGH-CALORIE INGREDIENTS

Nutrient-dense ingredients such as cheese and nuts are also high in calories. Measuring these ingredients either by weight or measuring cups a few times will give you a better sense of portions.

ENJOY GOOD FLAVOR

Eat slowly and enjoy the dining experience. Taking time to savor food will help you feel more satisfied and satiated.

PACK WISELY

When eating out, ask for a to-go box to come with your meal. Immediately split your meal into the portion that you want to eat now and the portion you want to save for later—this gives you greater confidence to dine out.

SHARE THE LOVE

When eating a treat, share it with a friend. This decreases the portion size you consume, but in an enjoyable way that adds to the eating experience.

INDULGE YOURSELF

Stop defining foods as good or bad. Instead, indulge only in treats that you really enjoy and listen to your body's feedback system for cues that you're full.

FIND ACTIVITIES YOU ENJOY

We often eat for reasons other than hunger, including stress or boredom. Engage in fun, easy-to-do activities (such as bubble baths, sketching, reading) to replace eating in these situations.

SELF-CONTROL

Your body is full, your sweet tooth is satisfied, but you can't stop eating. Try a strong mint or even go and brush your teeth—mint suppresses the need for munchies—plus the thought of orange juice after brushing your teeth is an instant turnoff!

FILL UP ON FIBER

Are you going to an event where you know there will be a beautiful assortment of yummy goodies? Control your urges by consuming a high-fiber, protein-rich snack like half a banana with a nut butter before you head out.

PANTRY AND FREEZER STAPLES

A well-stocked kitchen will have you whipping up your favorite meals in no time.
To reduce time and save money (through bulk shopping), be sure your
pantry and freezer are always filled with these must-haves.

CANNED GOODS
Black beans
Coconut milk
Coconut water
Tomato paste
Vanilla almond milk

SEEDS, GRAINS, NUTS
Chia seeds
Flaxseeds
Pistachios
Pumpkin seeds
Quinoa
Sunflower seeds
Toasted sesame seeds
Wheat germ
Wild rice

BAKING
All-purpose flour
Almond flour
Baking powder
Baking soda
Blackstrap molasses
Cocoa powder
Cornstarch
Honey
Pure maple syrup
Unsweetened shredded
  coconut
Vanilla extract
Whole grain flour

DRIED HERBS AND SPICES
Basil
Black pepper
Chili powder
Chipotle powder
Cinnamon
Coarse garlic salt
Coriander
Cumin
Dry mustard
Fennel seed
Garlic powder
Ground ginger
Nutmeg
Onion powder
Oregano
Paprika
Rosemary
Salt
Taco Seasoning (page 286)
Thyme
Turmeric

VINEGARS AND OILS
Balsamic Reduction (page 286)
Balsamic vinegar
Grapeseed oil
Natural rice vinegar
Safflower oil
Sesame oil
Sunflower oil
Truffle oil
Vegetable oil

MISCELLANEOUS
Chicken Stock (page 287)
Cooking spray
Dark chocolate
Dried apricots
Low-sodium soy sauce
Mayonnaise
Nutritional yeast
Popcorn kernels
Sun-dried tomatoes, dry-packed
Sriracha

FROZEN
Corn
Mango
Strawberries

ESSENTIAL EQUIPMENT

Sure every home is stocked with the basics: knife sets, food processors, and common pots and pans, but setting up your kitchen with these appliances and tools will make the cooking process all the more fun and efficient.

HOT AIR POPCORN MAKER

Air-popped popcorn is a regular snack in the meal plans, and the hot air popcorn maker allows you to prepare popcorn without oil. If you don't own a hot air popcorn maker, see page 287 for how-to instructions.

HOT/COLD TRAVEL MUG

Smoothies are a regular snack in the meal plans. A 12-hour hot/cold travel mug will keep your smoothie cold while you're at work or away from the house.

MANDOLINE

A mandoline helps to cut ingredients evenly and helps save time when there is a lot of chopping to do.

RICE COOKER

The rice cooker can be used to prepare quinoa as well as rice. Most rice cookers have a delayed start time so you can have perfectly prepared rice when you walk in the door at the end of the day.

SCALE

Invest in a scale to help control your portions. You can often find a simple and inexpensive digital scale at your local grocery store.

SLOW COOKER

Plan your slow-cooker day for nights that you know are going to be busy. Whether you need to work late or you have three kids who all have different activities in the opposite ends of the city, there is always that one night a week when we default to eating out—simply out of convenience and haste. If you can better prepare at home, you can enjoy your restaurant meals on far less hectic occasions.

What Are You in the Mood For?

For the more adventurous spirit, peruse the pages and find inspiration in the recipes and photographs. Or utilize this guide to help create the perfect custom meal plan for you; one that is unique to your flavor preferences and dynamic schedule. Let your cravings inspire what is on the menu. What are you in the mood for today?

	DISH	MEAL PLAN
BREAKFAST	Cereal, oatmeal, or parfait	20, 22, 30
	Chia	2, 8, 16, 28
	Crepes or pancakes	12, 15, 18, 24, 26
	Eggs	1, 3, 5, 9, 11, 13, 17, 19, 21, 23, 25, 27, 29
	French toasts	4, 10
	Grab and go	1, 2, 6, 7, 14, 16, 22, 27, 28, 29
	Savory	1, 3, 5, 7, 9, 11, 13, 15, 17, 19, 21, 23, 25, 27, 29
	Scones	7, 14
	Sweet	2, 4, 6, 8, 10, 12, 14, 16, 18, 20, 22, 24, 26, 28, 30
	Vegetarian	1, 2, 3, 4, 5, 6, 8, 9, 10, 12, 13, 14, 15, 16, 17, 18, 20, 21, 22, 24, 26, 27, 28, 29, 30
LUNCH	Baked potato	11
	Bowls	19, 29
	Chicken	2 (2000, 2500), 8, 15, 22, 27, 30
	Fish	21
	Grab and go	4, 8, 10, 12, 13, 19, 29
	Pizza	1, 3, 15, 28
	Roll or wrap	8, 14, 20, 23
	Salad	2, 4, 5, 7, 9, 12, 13, 15, 16, 24, 25, 30
	Sandwich	6, 17, 18, 22, 26, 27
	Soup	10
	Vegetarian	1, 2 (1500), 4, 5, 6, 7, 11, 12, 13, 14, 18, 19, 23, 25, 26, 29
DINNER	Chicken	1, 4, 6, 10, 12, 13, 16, 21, 23, 26
	Fish	5, 9, 11, 17, 22, 29
	Pork	8, 14, 18, 25
	Red meat	3, 27, 30
	Salad	1, 3, 21, 27
	Slow cooker	4, 8, 14, 23
	Soup	2, 14, 16, 28
	Turkey	7, 15, 20, 28
	Vegetarian	2, 19, 24

THE MEAL PLANS

MEAL PLAN

1
PAGE 42

Southwest Crustless Quiche *and Tropical Green Smoothie*
Grilled Vegetable and Hummus Flatbread
Thai Chicken, Quinoa, and Veggie Bowl

2
PAGE 50

Vanilla Blueberry Chia Pudding
Bocconcini Salad
Potato and Leek Soup *with Buckwheat Salad*

3
PAGE 58

Eggs in a Ring
Portobello and Prosciutto Pizza
Bison, Spinach, and Sweet Potato Salad

4
PAGE 66

Coconut and Flaxseed French Toast
Quinoa, Buckwheat, and Bean Salad
Slow-Cooked Chicken Fajitas

5
PAGE 74

Goat Cheese and Avocado Toast
Berry and Boursin® Salad
Arctic Char *with Wild Rice, Corn Salad, and Beet Greens*

6
PAGE 82

Breakfast Summer Roll
Tomato, Ricotta, and Pesto Toast
Roast Chicken *with Vegetables and Cauliflower Mash*

7
PAGE 92

Prosciutto, Cheese, and Caramelized Onion Scones
Roasted Vegetable Salad
Cauliflower Cottage Pie *with Quinoa Salad*

8
PAGE 100

Strawberry-Mango Chia Jam
Chicken and Mango Summer Roll
Slow-Cooked Pork and Bean Chili

9
PAGE 108

Breakfast Quesadilla
Warm Green Bean Salad
Coconut and Lemongrass Poached Halibut *with Collard Greens, Quinoa, and Wild Rice*

10
PAGE 116

Carrot Cake French Toast *with Cream Cheese Syrup*
Instant Noodles
Roasted Butternut Squash and Spinach Salad *with Chicken, Prosciutto, and Pomegranate*

11
PAGE 124

Cheese and Onion Crustless Quiche
Baked Potato *with Spinach Salad*
Fish Tacos *with Kale Slaw and Mango Salsa*

12
PAGE 132

Vanilla Chia Crepes *with Cream Cheese Syrup*
White Bean and Kale Salad
Chicken Fingers *with Fries and Tzatziki*

13
PAGE 140

Breakfast Sandwich
Green Bean, Feta, and Pomegranate Salad
Roast Chicken *with Baby Potatoes, Baby Carrots, and Spinach Salad*

14
PAGE 148

Mango, Ginger, and White Chocolate Scones
Greek Wrap
Creamy Corn, Ham, and Roasted Red Pepper Chowder

15
PAGE 156

Butternut Squash Pancakes
Mango BBQ Chicken Pizza
Stuffed Squash *with Tahini Sauce*

16
PAGE 164

Chocolate Chia Pudding *with Strawberry Sauce*
Spinach and Egg Salad
Chicken Noodle Soup

17
PAGE 172

Britt's Brussels
Turkey Crepe Sandwich
Sole en Papillote *with Roasted Vegetables*

18
PAGE 180

Lemon-Ricotta Crepe
Spicy Egg Salad on a Chia-Flax Bagel
Stuffed Pork Roast

19
PAGE 188

Prosciutto Cup
Quinoa Taco Bowl
Spaghetti Squash Bowl *with Sun-Dried Tomatoes, Mozzarella, and Pesto*

20
PAGE 196

Creamy Berry Farina Cereal
Asian Lettuce Wraps
Turkey Sausage and Zucchini Pizza Loaf *with Spinach Salad*

21
PAGE 204

Soft-Boiled Egg and Soldiers
Tuna Quinoa Bake
Watermelon, Goat Cheese, and Beet Salad

22
PAGE 212

Banana Parfait
Chicken-Gruyère Crepe *with Shiitake-Truffle Sauce*
Poached Halibut *with Baked Quinoa and Collard Greens*

23
PAGE 220

Sweet Potato Breakfast Stack
Lentil Taco Lettuce Wraps
Slow-Cooked Chicken Pot Pie

24
PAGE 228

Tropical Dollar Pancakes *with Mango Syrup*
Not-Your-Average Cobb Salad
Vegetable Bake

25
PAGE 236

Breakfast Pizza
Grilled Squash Salad
Pork Schnitzel *with Asparagus and Shiitake-Truffle Pilaf*

26
PAGE 244

Pop-up Pancakes
Portobello Mushroom Sandwich
Chimichurri Chicken *with Beans and Squash*

27
PAGE 252

Sweet Potato Frittata
Chicken Chimichurri Melt
Bison Taco Salad

28
PAGE 260

Apple Pie Chia Pudding
Spicy Hawaiian Pizza
Turkey Sausage Soup in an Acorn Squash Bowl

29
PAGE 268

Breakfast Burrito
Roasted Balsamic Tomato Bowl
Spicy Maple Salmon *with Grilled Vegetables and Wild Rice*

30
PAGE 276

Mulberry Puffed Quinoa Cereal
BBQ Chicken Salad
Slow-Cooked Bison Stew

▽

Southwest Crustless Quiche and Tropical Green Smoothie

▽

Grilled Vegetable and Hummus Flatbread

▽

Thai Chicken, Quinoa, and Veggie Bowl

MEAL PLAN

CHECKLIST*

PRODUCE
Apple (2500)
Bananas
Broccoli
Carrots
Cherry tomatoes
Collard greens
Garlic
Ginger
Green onions
Kale
Orange juice (2500)
Spinach
Strawberries
Sugar snap peas
Swiss chard
White mushrooms
Zucchini

BAKERY
8-inch whole wheat pita

MEAT
Broiler chicken, 2½ lbs

DAIRY
Butter
Cheddar cheese
Eggs
Feta cheese
Hummus (page 287)
Plain Greek yogurt

FROZEN
Pineapple

DRY GOODS
Brown sugar
Canned diced tomatoes with
    green chilies and lime juice
Hemp seeds
Oat bran
Thai sweet chili sauce

This list assumes that all basic ingredients (see Pantry and Freezer Staples, page 35) have been stocked.

Southwest Crustless Quiche
and Tropical Green Smoothie

MAKES 9 QUICHES	1500	2000	2500
For the quiche	2 quiches	2 quiches	2 quiches
Eggs, large	4 (200 g)	4 (200 g)	4 (200 g)
Plain Greek yogurt	2 Tbsp	2 Tbsp	2 Tbsp
Canned diced tomatoes	1 cup (260 g)	1 cup (260 g)	1 cup (260 g)
Canned black beans	¼ cup (43 g)	¼ cup (43 g)	¼ cup (43 g)
Cheddar cheese, shredded	½ cup + 2 Tbsp (50 g)	½ cup + 2 Tbsp (50 g)	½ cup + 2 Tbsp (50 g)
Corn, frozen	¼ cup (41 g)	¼ cup (41 g)	¼ cup (41 g)
Green onions, chopped	¼ cup (25 g)	¼ cup (25 g)	¼ cup (25 g)
Cooked Quinoa (page 286)	½ cup (69 g)	½ cup (69 g)	½ cup (69 g)
Cooking spray			
SERVES 1			
For the smoothie			
Banana	/ / / / / / / /	1 small (101 g)	1 small (101 g)
Spinach	2 cups (60 g)	1 cup (30 g)	1 cup (30 g)
Kale	½ cup (33 g)	½ cup (33 g)	½ cup (33 g)
Swiss chard	½ cup (18 g)	/ / / / / / / /	/ / / / / / / /
Mango, frozen	½ cup (82 g)	1 cup (65 g)	1 cup (65 g)
Pineapple, frozen	⅓ cup (52 g)	½ cup (77 g)	½ cup (77 g)
Wheat germ	1½ Tbsp	2 Tbsp	2 Tbsp
Coconut water	1½ cups	1¼ cups	/ / / / / / / /
Orange juice	/ / / / / / / /	/ / / / / / / /	½ cup
Water	/ / / / / / / /	/ / / / / / / /	1 cup
Ice	1 cup	1 cup	1 cup
CALORIES	389 KCAL	537 KCAL	671 KCAL

❶ Preheat the oven to 350°F. Spray a 12-cup muffin tin with cooking spray and set aside.

❷ In a medium bowl, combine eggs and yogurt and whisk together. Fold in tomatoes, black beans, cheddar, corn, green onions, and quinoa. Spoon ⅓-cup portions into 9 compartments of the prepared muffin tin and bake for 20–25 minutes, until tops are golden and a skewer inserted into the center comes out clean.

❸ While quiches are baking, prepare the smoothie by placing all ingredients in a blender and blending until smooth. If the smoothie is too thick, add water (not coconut water or orange juice). If you prefer a thicker texture, add more ice and blend until smooth.

❹ Serve smoothie with warm quiche.

Healthy Choices: Greek yogurt has double the protein than regular yogurt. Make sure you choose Greek yogurt, not Greek-style yogurt, which is made using a different process and does not have the same protein punch.

Freezer Friendly: Leftover quiche can be frozen in a resealable bag for up to a month. Simply reheat in the microwave for 30 seconds to 1 minute.

Snacks

SERVES 1	1500	2000	2500
Yogurt Parfait 1	recipe below	recipe below	recipe below
Hot Chocolate 1	recipe below	recipe below	recipe below
Carrot sticks	½ cup (64 g)	½ cup (64 g)	¾ cup (96 g)
Hummus (page 287)	////////	////////	2 Tbsp
Apple, sliced	////////	////////	½ (106 g)
Dark chocolate	////////	////////	20 g

Yogurt Parfait ①

SERVES 1	1500	2000	2500
Plain Greek yogurt	¼ cup	½ cup	½ cup
Banana, sliced	⅓ cup (75 g)	⅓ cup (75 g)	⅓ cup (75 g)
Strawberries, sliced	½ cup (83 g)	¾ cup (124 g)	¾ cup (124 g)
Flaxseeds	2 tsp	2 tsp	1 Tbsp
Pumpkin seeds	2 tsp	1 Tbsp	1 Tbsp
Hemp seeds	1½ tsp	1½ Tbsp	1½ Tbsp
Oat bran	////////	2 Tbsp	2 Tbsp
Honey	1 tsp	1 tsp	1½ tsp
CALORIES	253 KCAL	412 KCAL	441 KCAL

Put yogurt in a medium bowl. Layer bananas and strawberries overtop, sprinkle with seeds and oat bran (if using), and drizzle with honey.

Hot Chocolate ①

SERVES 1	1500	2000	2500
Vanilla almond milk	1 cup	1 cup	1 cup
Cocoa powder	2 tsp	2 tsp	1 Tbsp
Honey	////////	////////	1 tsp
CALORIES	99 KCAL	99 KCAL	124 KCAL

In a large microwave-safe mug, mix together cocoa powder with 1–2 Tbsp of almond milk until smooth and pasty. Add remaining milk and honey (if using) and stir to combine. Place the mug in the microwave, cover with a microwave-safe lid, and heat on high for 2 minutes.

Grilled Vegetable and Hummus Flatbread

SERVES 1	1500	2000	2500
Zucchini, thinly sliced into rounds	¼ cup (28 g)	¼ cup (28 g)	¼ cup (28 g)
Grapeseed oil	¼ tsp	¼ tsp	¼ tsp
Whole wheat pita	1 (57 g)	1 (57 g)	1 (57 g)
Hummus (page 287)	3 Tbsp	3 Tbsp	3 Tbsp
Cherry tomatoes, halved	⅓ cup (85 g)	⅓ cup (85 g)	⅓ cup (85 g)
Feta cheese, crumbled	2 tsp	2 tsp	2 tsp
Balsamic Reduction (page 286)	1 tsp	1 tsp	1 tsp
CALORIES	310 KCAL	310 KCAL	310 KCAL

❶ Preheat the oven to 350°F. Line a baking sheet with parchment paper.

❷ Heat a cast-iron grill pan or skillet over medium-high heat. Toss zucchini with grapeseed oil in a small bowl and place in pan or skillet. Cook for about 3 minutes on each side, until golden brown. Remove from heat.

❸ Put pita on the prepared baking sheet and spread hummus overtop. Layer with zucchini and tomatoes and sprinkle with feta. Bake for 10–12 minutes, until golden brown. Drizzle balsamic reduction over flatbread and serve.

Grab and Go: Prepare flatbread the night before, allow to cool, and store in a resealable container. The next day, warm in toaster oven for 3–5 minutes or reheat in microwave for 30 seconds to 1 minute.

Thai Chicken, Quinoa, and Veggie Bowl

SERVES 6	1500	2000	2500
For the chicken	75 g chicken	113 g chicken	113 g chicken
Broiler chicken	1	1	1
Butter	1 Tbsp	1 Tbsp	1 Tbsp
Brown sugar, packed	¼ cup	¼ cup	¼ cup
Black pepper	¼ tsp	¼ tsp	¼ tsp
Thai sweet chili sauce	4 tsp	4 tsp	4 tsp
SERVES 1			
For the veggie bowl			
Grapeseed oil	1 tsp	1 tsp	1½ tsp
Ginger, grated	½ tsp	1 tsp	1 tsp
Garlic, finely chopped	1 clove	1 clove	1 clove
Water	¼ cup	¼ cup	¼ cup
Broccoli florets	½ cup (44 g)	½ cup (44 g)	½ cup (44 g)
White mushrooms, quartered	½ cup (54 g)	½ cup (54 g)	½ cup (54 g)
Sugar snap peas, chopped	½ cup (49 g)	½ cup (49 g)	½ cup (49 g)
Carrots, sliced	¼ cup (32 g)	¼ cup (32 g)	¼ cup (32 g)
Swiss chard, stems removed, leaves roughly chopped	1½ cups (54 g)	1 cup (36 g)	1 cup (36 g)
Collard greens, stems removed, leaves roughly chopped	1½ cups (54 g)	1½ cups (54 g)	1½ cups (54 g)
Spinach	2 cups (60 g)	////////	////////
Sesame oil	1 tsp	1 tsp	1½ tsp
Cooked Quinoa (page 286)	¼ cup (17 g)	¼ cup (17 g)	⅓ cup (46 g)
Sunflower seeds	1 Tbsp	1 Tbsp	1½ Tbsp
CALORIES	489 KCAL	611 KCAL	687 KCAL

❶ Preheat the oven to 350°F. Insert a rack into a roasting pan.

❷ Butterfly chicken. Using a pair of kitchen scissors, cut chicken through the ribs, along one side of the backbone. Repeat along the other side and remove the backbone entirely (it can be used to make stock). Place the chicken on a flat surface, breast-side up, and flatten with the heel of your hand. (Alternatively, ask your butcher to butterfly the chicken for you.)

❸ Rub 1½ tsp of butter between skin and breast of chicken. Sprinkle sugar evenly over entire bird and season with pepper. Put chicken on rack in roasting pan, with wings lying on top of chicken breasts. (They will burn if they are tucked under the chicken.)

❹ Fill a roasting pan with just enough water to cover the bottom and cook for 1 hour and 15 minutes, or until chicken reaches an internal temperature of 165°F and juices run clear.

❺ Brush chicken with chili sauce and roast for another 5–10 minutes, until skin has browned and sauce has glazed.

❻ While sauce is glazing, heat oil in a skillet over medium-high heat. Add ginger and garlic and cook for 1 minute, until fragrant. Add water, broccoli, mushrooms, sugar snap peas, and carrots. Cover and steam for 3 minutes, until vegetables are vibrant and slightly al dente.

❼ Add Swiss chard, collard greens, and spinach (if using) to skillet, cover, and cook for 1–2 minutes, until greens are tender. Stir in sesame oil and remove from heat.

❽ To serve, in a bowl, put portion of quinoa on one side, stir-fried ingredients on the other, and fan chicken overtop. Garnish with sunflower seeds.

▽

*Vanilla Blueberry
Chia Pudding*

▽

*Bocconcini
Salad*

▽

*Potato and Leek
Soup with Buckwheat
Salad*

MEAL
PLAN
2

CHECKLIST*

PRODUCE
Avocado
Banana
Basil
Blueberries
Butternut squash
Cherry tomatoes
Cremini mushrooms
Cucumber
Leeks
Lemon
Orange
Orange juice
Raspberries
Russet potatoes
Spinach
Sugar snap peas

BAKERY
Whole grain bread

MEAT
Cooked boneless skin-
  less chicken breast
Thick-cut bacon

DAIRY
Bocconcini pearls
Butter
Kefir
Soft goat cheese
Vanilla Greek yogurt

FROZEN
Blueberries
Papaya

DRY GOODS
Buckwheat
Cashew butter
Chocolate almond milk
Milk chocolate
Oat bran
Pure lemon extract

* This list assumes that all basic ingredients (see Pantry and Freezer Staples, page 35) have been stocked.

Vanilla Blueberry Chia Pudding

SERVES 2	1500	2000	2500
For the pudding	1 serving	1 serving	1 serving
Vanilla almond milk	1 cup	1 cup	1 cup
Vanilla Greek yogurt	¼ cup (75 g)	¼ cup (75 g)	¼ cup (75 g)
Chia seeds	3 Tbsp	3 Tbsp	3 Tbsp
Pure lemon extract	1 tsp	1 tsp	1 tsp
Blueberries, frozen	3 cups (396 g)	3 cups (396 g)	3 cups (396 g)
Honey	1½ tsp	1½ tsp	1½ tsp
Lemon zest	1 tsp	1 tsp	1 tsp
Lemon juice	1½ Tbsp	1½ Tbsp	1½ Tbsp
Cornstarch	½ tsp	½ tsp	½ tsp
Blueberries, to garnish	½ cup (66 g)	½ cup (66 g)	////////
CALORIES	314 KCAL	314 KCAL	273 KCAL

❶ In a medium bowl, combine almond milk, yogurt, chia seeds, and lemon extract. Cover and place in the fridge overnight, or for at least 3 hours, to let chia seeds gel.

❷ Put blueberries, honey, and lemon zest in a small saucepan and bring to a gentle simmer over medium heat. In a small bowl, combine lemon juice and cornstarch and mix until smooth. Add mixture to blueberries and cook for about 5 minutes, until thickened. (Try to keep blueberries full and intact.)

❸ Remove chia seed mixture from the fridge and give it a good stir. Divide between two bowls and top each with half of the blueberry mixture. Add fresh blueberries (if using) overtop. Leftover portion will keep for up to a week in the refrigerator.

Mix It Up: This is a great recipe for those who are new to the kitchen and want to experiment working with different flavors. Have fun trying new and unusual flavor combinations, such as blood orange and dark chocolate, and using different extracts, yogurts, and fruits.

Bocconcini Salad

SERVES 1	1500	2000	2500
For the salad			
Spinach	3 cups (90 g)	3 cups (90 g)	3 cups (90 g)
Avocado, diced	¼ (43 g)	⅓ (58 g)	⅓ (58 g)
Cucumber, diced	⅓ cup (40 g)	⅓ cup (40 g)	⅓ cup (40 g)
Cherry tomatoes, halved	⅓ cup (85 g)	⅓ cup (85 g)	⅓ cup (85 g)
Bocconcini pearls, halved	10 (15 g)	13 (20 g)	13 (20 g)
Cooked Quinoa (page 286)	⅓ cup (46 g)	½ cup (69 g)	½ cup (69 g)
Cooked chicken breast, diced	////////	½ cup (70 g)	½ cup (70 g)
For the dressing	1½ tsp serving	1 Tbsp serving	1 Tbsp serving
Balsamic vinegar	2 tsp	2 tsp	2 tsp
Honey	½ tsp	½ tsp	½ tsp
Basil leaves, chopped	1 Tbsp	1 Tbsp	1 Tbsp
Sunflower oil	1 Tbsp	1 Tbsp	1 Tbsp
Basil leaves, whole	to taste	to taste	to taste
CALORIES	212 KCAL	277 KCAL	408 KCAL

❶ Make a bed of spinach in a salad bowl or on a large plate. Top with avocado, cucumber, tomatoes, bocconcini, quinoa, and chicken (if using).

❷ In a small bowl, whisk together vinegar, honey, and chopped basil leaves. Whisking continuously, gradually pour in oil until emulsified. Drizzle portion over salad. Reserve remaining dressing for dinner.

❸ Garnish with basil leaves, if desired.

Life Made Easier: To quickly ripen an avocado, place it in a bowl or a brown paper bag with a banana and it will be ripe enough to eat the next day. But watch out, the avocado will ripen fast, so if left for more than a day it will start to go brown.

Grab and Go: Make recipe as directed, but keep cherry tomatoes whole, put dressing in a separate resealable container, and store in the refrigerator. When you are ready to eat, drizzle dressing over salad and enjoy.

Snacks

SERVES 1	1500	2000	2500
Tropical Smoothie 1	recipe below	recipe below	recipe below
Warm Chocolate Steamer	recipe below	recipe below	recipe below
Dried apricots	/ / / / / / / /	¼ cup (63 g)	¼ cup (63 g)
Orange	1 (96 g)	/ / / / / / / /	/ / / / / / / /
Raspberries	/ / / / / / / /	/ / / / / / / /	½ cup (63 g)
Air-Popped Popcorn (page 287)	/ / / / / / / /	2 cups	2 cups
Sugar snap peas	/ / / / / / / /	/ / / / / / / /	1 cup (63 g)
Toasted whole grain bread	/ / / / / / / /	/ / / / / / / /	1 slice (29 g)
Cashew butter	/ / / / / / / /	/ / / / / / / /	1½ tsp

Tropical Smoothie ①

SERVES 1	1500	2000	2500
Banana	1 large (150 g)	1 (115 g)	1 (115 g)
Strawberries, fresh or frozen	½ cup (110 g)	⅓ cup (74 g)	1 cup (221 g)
Papaya, fresh or frozen	/ / / / / / / /	½ cup (70 g)	½ cup (70 g)
Wheat germ	3 Tbsp	3 Tbsp	2 Tbsp
Oat bran	/ / / / / / / /	/ / / / / / / /	2 Tbsp
Kefir	⅓ cup	½ cup	⅓ cup
Coconut water	1 cup	1½ cups	/ / / / / / / /
Orange juice	/ / / / / / / /	/ / / / / / / /	½ cup
Water	/ / / / / / / /	/ / / / / / / /	1½ cups
CALORIES	344 KCAL	371 KCAL	408 KCAL

Put all ingredients into a blender and blend until smooth.
If the smoothie is too thick, add water (not coconut water
or orange juice). If you prefer a thicker texture, add ice
and blend until smooth.

Warm Chocolate Steamer

SERVES 1	1500	2000	2500
Chocolate almond milk	1 cup	1½ cups	1¼ cups
Blackstrap molasses	1 tsp	/ / / / / / / /	/ / / / / / / /
Cocoa powder	1 tsp	1 tsp	1 tsp
Dark chocolate	2.5 g	/ / / / / / / /	5 g
Milk chocolate	/ / / / / / / /	/ / / / / / / /	5 g
CALORIES	155 KCAL	184 KCAL	211 KCAL

Put all ingredients into a microwave-safe mug and
mix well. Cover and microwave on high for 1 minute.
Stir and microwave for another 30–45 seconds.

Potato and Leek Soup
with Buckwheat Salad

MAKES 5 CUPS	1500	2000	2500
For the soup	¾ cup (217 g)	1½ cups (435 g)	1½ cups (435 g)
Butter	½ tsp	½ tsp	½ tsp
Bacon	2 slices	2 slices	2 slices
Leeks, halved lengthwise and sliced	2 (134 g)	2 (134 g)	2 (134 g)
Salt	1 tsp	1 tsp	1 tsp
Butternut squash, peeled and cubed	2 cups (280 g)	2 cups (280 g)	2 cups (280 g)
Russet potatoes, peeled and cubed	2 (168 g)	2 (168 g)	2 (168 g)
Coconut milk	½ can (7 oz)	½ can (7 oz)	½ can (7 oz)
Water	2½ cups	2½ cups	2½ cups
Black pepper	to taste	to taste	to taste
SERVES 1			
For the salad			
Cremini mushrooms, sliced	121 g	121 g	121 g
Balsamic vinegar	1½ tsp	1 Tbsp	1 Tbsp
Spinach	3 cups (90 g)	3 cups (90 g)	3 cups (90 g)
Cooked Buckwheat (page 286)	½ cup (84 g)	½ cup (84 g)	½ cup (84 g)
Pumpkin seeds	1 Tbsp	1 Tbsp	2 Tbsp
Sunflower seeds	1 Tbsp	1½ tsp	////////
Soft goat cheese, crumbled	2 tsp (10 g)	1½ tsp (7 g)	2 tsp (10 g)
Balsamic Dressing (from Lunch)	1½ tsp	1 Tbsp	1 Tbsp
CALORIES	467 KCAL	602 KCAL	886 KCAL

❶ In a large stockpot, melt butter over medium-high heat. Add bacon, leeks, and salt and stir for 7–10 minutes, until leeks are caramelized and bacon is browned. Add butternut squash and sauté for 5 minutes. Add potatoes, coconut milk, and water and bring to a boil. Cook for 25–30 minutes, until potatoes and squash are tender.

❷ During the last 10 minutes of soup cooking time, heat a skillet over medium-high heat. Add mushrooms and brush with balsamic vinegar. Cook for 3 minutes, flip, and cook for another 2–3 minutes, until nicely browned.

❸ Once mushrooms are done, assemble salad. Make a bed of spinach in a salad bowl or on a large plate. Top with buckwheat, mushrooms, pumpkin seeds, sunflower seeds, and goat cheese. Drizzle dressing overtop.

❹ Transfer soup, in batches, to a blender and blend until smooth. (Alternatively, use an immersion blender.) Season with black pepper and serve with salad.

Life Made Easier: To clean leeks, cut them in half lengthwise, then into half-moon slices, and then wash in a colander. To reduce food waste, use the less edible dark green part of the leek to add flavor to roasts or stocks.

Healthy Choices: Portobello mushrooms make a great meat substitute; eating two or more vegetarian meals a week is helpful for increasing your fiber intake and decreasing your saturated fat intake.

▽ **Eggs in a Ring** ▽ **Portobello and Prosciutto Pizza** ▽ **Bison, Spinach, and Sweet Potato Salad**

MEAL PLAN 3

CHECKLIST*

PRODUCE
Acorn squash
Arugula
Banana
Blueberries
Carrots
Grapes
Green onions
Onion
Orange
Portobello mushroom(s)
Raspberries
Red bell pepper
Shallots
Spinach
Sugar snap peas
Sweet potato

DELI
Hummus (page 287)
Sliced prosciutto

MEAT
Bison top sirloin steak

DAIRY
Boursin® Garlic & Fine Herbs
Butter
Eggs
Fruit-bottom yogurt
Plain Greek yogurt
Soft goat cheese

FROZEN
Papaya

DRY GOODS
Almonds
Cashew nuts

This list assumes that all basic ingredients (see Pantry and Freezer Staples, page 35) have been stocked.

Eggs in a Ring

SERVES 1	1500	2000	2500
Acorn squash, unpeeled, cut into ½-inch rings and deseeded	2 rings (75 g)	2 rings (75 g)	2 rings (75 g)
Grapeseed oil	1 tsp	1 tsp	1 tsp
Egg	1 (50 g)	1 (50 g)	1 (50 g)
Egg white	1 (33 g)	1 (33 g)	1 (33 g)
Onion powder	¼ tsp	¼ tsp	¼ tsp
Black pepper	dash	dash	dash
CALORIES	183 KCAL	183 KCAL	183 KCAL

❶ Preheat the oven to 400°F. Line a baking sheet with parchment paper.

❷ Place squash rings on the prepared baking sheet and brush with oil. Bake for 15–20 minutes, or until fork tender. Crack whole egg into one ring and pour egg white into the other. Season with onion powder and pepper.

❸ Bake for 10 minutes, until egg whites are fully cooked and no longer glossy. Remove ring with egg white to a plate and continue cooking ring with whole egg until yoke is cooked to your preferred doneness (another 2–5 minutes for medium). Serve hot.

Mix It Up: This recipe works with many different kinds of squash. Try the delicata variety, which has a very thin skin and is easy to eat. Sweet dumpling and red kuri squash are also just as delicious. All winter squash (with the exception of spaghetti squash) have an edible skin, and the longer you roast squash, the more tender the skin becomes.

Healthy Choices: Acorn squash is high in vitamin A and potassium. Most people know that vitamin A is needed for your eyesight, but did you know that your body also needs vitamin A for your immune system?

Snacks

SERVES 1	1500	2000	2500
Vanilla Green Smoothie	recipe below	recipe below	recipe below
Cashew nuts, dry roasted	¼ cup (34 g)	¼ cup (34 g)	¼ cup (34 g)
Fruit-bottom yogurt, <1% fat	½ cup (122 g)	½ cup (122 g)	////////
Almonds, dry roasted	////////	////////	¼ cup (21 g)
Air-Popped Popcorn (page 287)	2 cups (16 g)	2 cups (16 g)	3 cups (24 g)
Raspberries	⅓ cup (41 g)	½ cup (61 g)	½ cup (61 g)
Grapes	⅓ cup (51 g)	1 cup (154 g)	1 cup (154 g)
Orange	////////	1 large (184 g)	1 large (184 g)
Dark chocolate	////////	////////	20 g
Blueberries	////////	////////	½ cup (72 g)
Carrot sticks	////////	////////	¾ cup (96 g)
Sugar snap peas	////////	////////	1 cup (63 g)
Hummus (page 287)	////////	////////	2 Tbsp

Vanilla Green Smoothie

SERVES 1	1500	2000	2500
Banana	1 small (101 g)	1 large (169 g)	1 (136 g)
Spinach	2⅓ cups (70 g)	1½ cups (45 g)	////////
Papaya, fresh or frozen	½ cup (70 g)	½ cup (70 g)	¾ cup (105 g)
Mango, fresh or frozen	////////	////////	¾ cup (124 g)
Plain Greek yogurt	1½ Tbsp	2 Tbsp	⅓ cup + 2 Tbsp
Blackstrap molasses	1 tsp	1 Tbsp	////////
Flaxseeds	1 Tbsp	2 tsp	¾ Tbsp
Vanilla almond milk	½ cup	¾ cup	1 cup
Coconut water	½ cup	¾ cup	////////
Ice	½ cup	½ cup	////////
Water	////////	////////	⅔ cup
CALORIES	286 KCAL	396 KCAL	453 KCAL

Put all ingredients into a blender and blend until smooth. If the smoothie is too thick, add water (not almond milk or coconut water). If you prefer a thicker texture, add ice and blend until smooth.

Portobello and Prosciutto Pizza

SERVES 1	1500	2000	2500
Prosciutto	1 slice (15 g)	1 slice (15 g)	2 slices (30 g)
Portobello mushroom(s), stem and gills removed	1 (85 g)	1 (85 g)	2 (170 g)
Tomato paste	2 Tbsp	1 Tbsp	2 Tbsp
Red bell pepper, deseeded and chopped	1 Tbsp	1 Tbsp	2 Tbsp
Shallots, thinly sliced	1 tsp	1 tsp	2 tsp
Soft goat cheese, crumbled	2 tsp (10 g)	2 tsp (10 g)	4 tsp (20 g)
Arugula	¼ cup (5 g)	¼ cup (5 g)	½ cup (5 g)
CALORIES	122 KCAL	109 KCAL	218 KCAL

❶ Preheat the oven broiler to 450°F. Line a baking sheet with parchment paper.

❷ Heat a skillet over medium-high heat. Add prosciutto and cook for 30 seconds on one side, flip and cook for another 30 seconds to 1 minute, until prosciutto is crispy and golden brown. Remove from heat and set aside.

❸ Place mushroom cap(s), top-side down, on the prepared baking sheet. Evenly spread tomato paste on the inside of cap(s). Crumble prosciutto and sprinkle evenly over tomato paste. Top with red pepper, shallots, and goat cheese.

❹ Broil for 7–10 minutes, until cheese begins to bubble and turn golden brown. Remove from oven, top with fresh arugula, and serve.

Grab and Go: Prepare pizza(s) ahead of time, keeping arugula separate. When ready to eat, cook in toaster oven for 3–5 minutes, until cheese is golden brown, or heat in microwave for 1–2 minutes, until warm. Add arugula and serve.

Bison, Spinach, and Sweet Potato Salad

SERVES 1	1500	2000	2500
For the salad			
Bison top sirloin steak	75 g	150 g	150 g
Sweet potato, scrubbed clean and diced	1 large (225 g)	1 large (225 g)	1 large (225 g)
Salt	⅛ tsp	⅛ tsp	////////
Butter	1 tsp	2 tsp	2 tsp
Onion, halved and sliced	½ (50 g)	1 (100 g)	1 (100 g)
Spinach	2 cups (60 g)	2 cups (60 g)	2 cups (60 g)
Boursin® Garlic & Fine Herbs	1 tsp	2 tsp	2 tsp
Sunflower seeds, dry roasted	1½ tsp	1½ tsp	1½ tsp
Green onions, chopped	1 Tbsp	2 Tbsp	2 Tbsp
Cooking spray			
For the dressing	1 Tbsp serving	1 Tbsp serving	1 Tbsp serving
Balsamic vinegar	2½ Tbsp	2½ Tbsp	2½ Tbsp
Honey	2 tsp	2 tsp	2 tsp
Dried basil	½ tsp	½ tsp	½ tsp
Sunflower oil	¼ cup	¼ cup	¼ cup
CALORIES	514 KCAL	720 KCAL	720 KCAL

❶ Preheat the oven to 350°F. Line a baking sheet with parchment paper.

❷ Remove steak from fridge and allow it to come to room temperature, about 20 minutes. (This step helps meat cook more evenly).

❸ Meanwhile, place sweet potato in an even layer on the prepared baking sheet. Spray with cooking spray and sprinkle with salt (if using). Place sweet potato in oven and roast for 25–30 minutes, or until golden and fork tender.

❹ Melt butter in an ovenproof skillet over medium heat. Add onions to skillet (working in batches if necessary to avoid overcrowding) and sauté for 7 minutes, until translucent. Reduce heat to low and cook for another 10–15 minutes, until caramelized. Once onions are finished cooking, transfer to a plate and set aside.

❺ Put skillet back on stove and over high heat. Add steak and sear, untouched, for 1 minute. Flip and sear for another minute. Place skillet in oven and cook until preferred doneness.

For medium-rare (my preference), cook steak in oven for 3–4 minutes, until steak reaches an internal temperature of 110°F. For medium, cook for 5–6 minutes, until steak reaches an internal temperature of 115°F.

❻ Remove steak from heat and let it rest for 3–5 minutes before cutting. Slice into even strips.

❼ To prepare the dressing, whisk together vinegar, honey, and basil in a small bowl. Whisking continuously, gradually add oil until emulsified.

❽ Make a bed of spinach in a salad bowl or on a large plate. Arrange roasted sweet potato and fan steak, top with caramelized onions and crumbled Boursin®, and sprinkle with sunflower seeds and green onions.

❾ Drizzle with dressing and serve.

Mix It Up: Steak and creamy cheese can still have its place in a healthy lifestyle. Bison is a lean alternative for beef and adds more variety (and iron!) to your diet.

▽
Coconut and Flaxseed
French Toast

▽
Quinoa, Buckwheat,
and Bean Salad

▽
Slow-Cooked
Chicken Fajitas

MEAL PLAN 4

CHECKLIST*

PRODUCE
Avocado
Banana
Bell peppers
  (orange, red, and yellow)
Blackberries
Blueberries
Cherry tomatoes
Cucumber
Lime
Onion
Raspberries
Shallot
Spinach

BAKERY
Corn tortillas
Whole grain loaf

MEAT
Boneless skinless chicken
  breast

DAIRY
Cheddar cheese
Egg(s)
Parmesan cheese
Sour cream
Vanilla Greek yogurt

FROZEN
Peas

DRY GOODS
Buckwheat
Chickpeas, canned
Coconut oil
Lentils, canned
Pine nuts
Small white beans, canned
Whole grain mustard

* *This list assumes that all basic ingredients (see Pantry and Freezer Staples, page 35) have been stocked.*

Coconut and Flaxseed French Toast

SERVES 1	1500	2000	2500
Egg(s)	1 large (50 g)	1 large (50 g)	2 large (100 g)
Vanilla Greek yogurt	1 Tbsp	1 Tbsp	2 Tbsp
Shredded coconut, unsweetened	1 Tbsp	1 Tbsp	2 Tbsp
Flaxseeds	1½ tsp	1½ tsp	1 Tbsp
Vanilla extract	1 tsp	1 tsp	2 tsp
Coconut oil	1 tsp	1 tsp	2 tsp
Whole grain loaf	2 slices (50 g)	2 slices (50 g)	4 slices (100 g)
Blackberries	¼ cup (36 g)	¼ cup (36 g)	⅓ cup (48 g)
Blueberries	¼ cup (36 g)	½ cup (72 g)	⅓ cup (48 g)
Raspberries	¼ cup (31 g)	½ cup (61 g)	⅓ cup (41 g)
Pure maple syrup	////////	1½ tsp	1 Tbsp
CALORIES	363 KCAL	426 KCAL	745 KCAL

❶ In a medium shallow bowl, whisk together egg(s), yogurt, coconut, flaxseeds, and vanilla.
❷ Melt coconut oil in a skillet over medium-low heat. Dip bread into egg mixture until saturated on both sides. Place bread in skillet and cook for 2–3 minutes, until golden. Flip and cook for another 2–3 minutes.
❸ Top with berries and maple syrup (if using).

Healthy Choices: *Flaxseeds can be used whole or ground. While whole flaxseeds provide great fiber, ground flaxseeds allow your body to also access the omega-3 fatty acids and protein.*

Quinoa, Buckwheat, and Bean Salad

SERVES 2–3	1500	2000	2500
For the salad	Serves 1	Serves 1½	Serves 1½
Peas, frozen	½ cup (80 g)	½ cup (80 g)	½ cup (80 g)
Cooked Quinoa (page 286)	½ cup (69 g)	½ cup (69 g)	½ cup (69 g)
Cooked Buckwheat (page 286)	½ cup (84 g)	½ cup (84 g)	½ cup (84 g)
Lentils, drained and rinsed	¼ cup (50 g)	¼ cup (50 g)	¼ cup (50 g)
Chickpeas, drained and rinsed	¼ cup (41 g)	¼ cup (41 g)	¼ cup (41 g)
Small white beans, drained and rinsed	¼ cup (45 g)	½ cup (90 g)	½ cup (90 g)
Cucumber, sliced	½ cup (52 g)	½ cup (52 g)	½ cup (52 g)
Cherry tomatoes, halved	5 (85 g)	5 (85 g)	5 (85 g)
Sunflower seeds, to serve	1½ Tbsp	////////	////////
For the dressing			
Shallot, skin removed and ends trimmed	1 (10 g)	1 (10 g)	1 (10 g)
Grapeseed oil, divided	2 Tbsp	2 Tbsp	2 Tbsp
Pine nuts	2 Tbsp (17 g)	2 Tbsp (17 g)	2 Tbsp (17 g)
Whole grain mustard	1½ tsp	1½ tsp	1½ tsp
Balsamic vinegar	½ tsp	½ tsp	½ tsp
Parmesan cheese, shredded	2 Tbsp (10 g)	2 Tbsp (10 g)	2 Tbsp (10 g)
CALORIES	304 KCAL	422 KCAL	422 KCAL

❶ Preheat the oven to 350°F. Line a baking sheet with parchment paper.

❷ Place shallot on a sheet of aluminum foil. Brush shallot with a ¼ tsp of grapeseed oil, wrap in foil, and roast for 12–15 minutes, until fragrant.

❸ Meanwhile, evenly spread pine nuts on the prepared baking sheet. During the last 2 minutes of the shallot cooking, add pine nuts to the oven. Remove pine nuts and shallot from oven.

❹ To make the dressing, combine shallot, pine nuts, mustard, vinegar, and Parmesan in a food processor or blender. Turn on, gradually add remaining oil, and blend until emulsified. Set aside.

❺ Put peas in a microwave-safe bowl with 1 Tbsp of water and microwave for 1 minute. Stir and heat for another 45 seconds to 1 minute, until defrosted.

❻ In a large bowl, combine quinoa, buckwheat, lentils, chickpeas, and white beans. Add cucumber, tomatoes, and peas to salad. Gently toss salad with the dressing and serve. Add sunflower seeds (if using).

Slow-Cooked Chicken Fajitas

SERVES 2	1500	2000	2500
For the filling			
Red bell pepper, deseeded and sliced	1 (119 g)	1 (119 g)	1 (119 g)
Orange bell pepper, deseeded and sliced	1 (186 g)	1 (186 g)	1 (186 g)
Yellow bell pepper, deseeded and sliced	1 (186 g)	1 (186 g)	1 (186 g)
Onion, halved and sliced	1 (75 g)	1 (75 g)	1 (75 g)
Chicken breast	1 (181 g)	1 (181 g)	1 (181 g)
Taco Seasoning (page 286)	1½ Tbsp	1½ Tbsp	1½ Tbsp
To serve	1 serving	1½ servings	2 servings
Corn tortillas	2 (98 g)	2 (98 g)	3 (147 g)
Avocado, cubed	2 Tbsp (19 g)	3 Tbsp (28 g)	3 Tbsp (28 g)
Cheddar cheese, shredded	1½ Tbsp (10 g)	2 Tbsp (15 g)	1½ Tbsp (10 g)
Sour cream, 14% fat	1 Tbsp	1½ Tbsp	1½ Tbsp
CALORIES	485 KCAL	650 KCAL	829 KCAL

❶ Place peppers, onions, chicken, and taco seasoning in a slow cooker and cook on low for at least 5 hours.

❷ Divide the filling equally among tortillas. Top with avocado, cheddar, and sour cream and serve.

Snacks

SERVES 1	1500	2000	2500
Coconut Water with Lime 1	recipe below	recipe below	recipe below
Chocolate-Banana Smoothie 1	recipe below	recipe below	recipe below
Dried apricots	¼ cup (62 g)	¼ cup (62 g)	////////
Air-Popped Popcorn (page 287)	////////	////////	2 cups (16 g)

Coconut Water with Lime ①

SERVES 1	1500	2000	2500
Coconut water	1⅔ cups	1½ cups	¾ cup
Lime juice	1 Tbsp	1 Tbsp	1 Tbsp
CALORIES	80 KCAL	72 KCAL	38 KCAL

Pour coconut water and lime juice into a glass
filled with ice and stir to mix well.

Chocolate-Banana Smoothie ①

SERVES 1	1500	2000	2500
Banana	½ small (51 g)	1 small (101 g)	1 large (136 g)
Spinach	2½ cups (75 g)	2½ cups (75 g)	1 cup (30 g)
Blackstrap molasses	1½ tsp	////////	////////
Flaxseeds	½ tsp	1 tsp	////////
Wheat germ	1 Tbsp	1 Tbsp	1 Tbsp
Cocoa powder	1 tsp	2 tsp	1 tsp
Honey	////////	////////	2 tsp
Vanilla almond milk	1¼ cups	1½ cups	1¼ cups
Ice	1 cup	1 cup	1 cup
CALORIES	275 KCAL	338 KCAL	351 KCAL

Put all ingredients into a blender and blend until smooth.
If the smoothie is too thick, add water (not almond milk).
If you prefer a thicker texture, add ice and blend until smooth.

▽

**Goat Cheese and
Avocado Toast**

▽

**Berry and Boursin®
Salad**

▽

**Arctic Char with
Wild Rice, Corn Salad,
and Beet Greens**

MEAL
PLAN
5

CHECKLIST*

PRODUCE
Avocado
Banana
Beet greens
Blackberries
Blueberries (2500)
Garlic
Grapes (2000, 2500)
Lemon
Lime
Portobello mushrooms
Raspberries
Red bell pepper
Shallot
Spinach
Strawberries (2500)
Sugar snap peas

BAKERY
Whole grain bread

FISH
Arctic char, skin on

DAIRY
Boursin® Garlic & Fine Herbs
Eggs
Feta cheese
Soft goat cheese

DRY GOODS
Almonds, slivered (2500)
Chocolate almond milk
Coconut flour
Hearts of palm (1500)
White vinegar

This list assumes that all basic ingredients (see Pantry and Freezer Staples, page 35) have been stocked.

Goat Cheese and Avocado Toast

SERVES 1	1500	2000	2500
White vinegar	1 Tbsp	1 Tbsp	1 Tbsp
Egg	1 small (38 g)	1 large (50 g)	1 small (38 g)
Egg white	////////	1 large (33 g)	1 large (33 g)
Whole grain bread	1 slice (43 g)	1 slice (43 g)	2 slices (86 g)
Avocado, sliced	¼ (43 g)	½ (87 g)	1 (174 g)
Lemon juice	½ tsp	½ tsp	1½ tsp
Soft goat cheese	1½ tsp (7.5 g)	2 tsp (10 g)	2 tsp (10 g)
Sriracha	½ tsp	½ tsp	½ tsp
Mango, cubed	⅔ cup (110 g)	⅔ cup (110 g)	1 cup (165 g)
CALORIES	347 KCAL	442 KCAL	750 KCAL

❶ Bring a large pot of water to a boil. When water begins to simmer, mix in vinegar. When the water reaches a boil, gently stir water in a circular motion to create a little whirlpool. While whirlpool is spinning, crack egg into the pot. Leave egg to cook for 3–5 minutes. Remove with a slotted spoon. Repeat for remaining egg white (if using). Set aside.

❷ Toast bread. Transfer to a plate.

❸ Spread goat cheese on toast, add avocado, and sprinkle lemon juice overtop.

❹ Gently place poached egg and egg white (if using) on top of avocado, dollop with Sriracha, and serve with mango.

Note: *Poach egg according to your preferred doneness, but I recommend soft to medium.*

Berry and Boursin® Salad

SERVES 1	1500	2000	2500
For the salad			
Spinach	3½ cups (105 g)	3½ cups (105 g)	3½ cups (105 g)
Blackberries	½ cup (72 g)	½ cup (72 g)	½ cup (72 g)
Raspberries	½ cup (61 g)	½ cup (61 g)	½ cup (61 g)
Strawberries, thinly sliced	////////	////////	⅓ cup (55 g)
Shallot, sliced	1½ tsp	1½ tsp	1½ tsp
Hearts of palm, thinly sliced	¼ cup (36 g)	////////	////////
Boursin® Garlic & Fine Herbs	1½ tsp (7.5 g)	2 tsp (10 g)	2 tsp (10 g)
Flaxseeds	1½ tsp	1½ tsp	1½ tsp
Sunflower seeds	1½ Tbsp	1½ Tbsp	1½ Tbsp
Almonds, slivered	////////	////////	1 Tbsp
For the dressing	2½ tsp	4 tsp	4 tsp
Balsamic vinegar	½ tsp	1 tsp	1 tsp
Honey	½ tsp	1 tsp	1 tsp
Garlic powder	⅛ tsp	¼ tsp	¼ tsp
Onion powder	⅛ tsp	¼ tsp	¼ tsp
Safflower oil	////////	1½ tsp	1½ tsp
Grapeseed oil	1½ tsp	////////	////////
CALORIES	272 KCAL	318 KCAL	375 KCAL

❶ Make a bed of spinach in a salad bowl or on a large plate. Top with blackberries, raspberries, strawberries (if using), shallot, and hearts of palm (if using). Crumble Boursin® overtop and sprinkle with flaxseeds, sunflower seeds, and almonds (if using).

❷ In a small bowl, whisk together vinegar, honey, garlic powder, and onion powder. Whisking continuously, gradually add oil until emulsified.

❸ Drizzle dressing over salad and serve.

Healthy Choices: Berries are a powerhouse of nutrients, including flavonoids, which give berries their rich color, and also improve our heart health.

Grab and Go: Keep salad fresh and crisp by storing berries and hearts of palm (if using) in a separate resealable container from your greens, seeds, nuts (if using), and cheese. Additionally, place your dressing in a different resealable container. At lunch, mix all together.

Arctic Char

with Wild Rice, Corn Salad, and Beet Greens

SERVES 2	1500	2000	2500
For the Arctic char	75 g char	75 g char	75 g char
Almond flour	6 Tbsp	6 Tbsp	6 Tbsp
Coconut flour	2 Tbsp	2 Tbsp	2 Tbsp
Wheat germ	2 Tbsp	2 Tbsp	2 Tbsp
Coconut milk	2 Tbsp	2 Tbsp	2 Tbsp
Dried basil	¼ tsp	¼ tsp	¼ tsp
Dried rosemary, lightly chopped	¼ tsp	¼ tsp	¼ tsp
Dried oregano	¼ tsp	¼ tsp	¼ tsp
Fennel seeds	⅛ tsp	⅛ tsp	⅛ tsp
Arctic char, skin on	150 g	150 g	150 g
For the roasted corn salad	½ serving	1 serving	1 serving
Corn, frozen	1¼ cups (205 g)	1¼ cups (205 g)	1¼ cups (205 g)
Red bell pepper, deseeded and diced	½ cup (75 g)	½ cup (75 g)	½ cup (75 g)
Salt	¼ tsp	¼ tsp	¼ tsp
Garlic, finely chopped	1 clove	1 clove	1 clove
Grapeseed oil	1 tsp	1 tsp	1 tsp
Feta cheese	15 g	15 g	15 g
For the wild rice	1 serving	1 serving	1 serving
Portobello mushrooms, gills removed, sliced thick	⅔ cup (80 g)	⅔ cup (80 g)	1 cup (121 g)
Cooked Wild Rice (page 286)	1⅓ cup (218 g)	1⅓ cup (218 g)	1 cup (164 g)
Cooked Quinoa (page 286)	////////	////////	1 cup (139 g)
Truffle oil	¼ tsp	½ tsp	½ tsp
For the beet greens	1 serving	1 serving	1 serving
Safflower oil	1 tsp	1 tsp	1 tsp
Garlic, minced	1 tsp	1 tsp	1 tsp
Beet greens, roughly chopped	4 cups (152 g)	4 cups (152 g)	4 cups (152 g)
CALORIES	522 KCAL	599 KCAL	662 KCAL

❶ Preheat the oven to 350°F. Line two baking sheets with parchment paper.

❷ In a medium bowl, mix together almond and coconut flours, wheat germ, coconut milk, basil, rosemary, oregano, and fennel until the consistency is similar to a crumble topping. Lay fish, skin-side down, on a prepared baking sheet. Firmly coat the skinless side of the fish.

❸ Place fish on middle rack of oven and bake for 20–25 minutes, or until fish is opaque and flaky, but still moist. (Safe internal temperature for fish is 158°F.) Remove skin.

❹ Meanwhile, in a bowl, mix together corn, pepper, salt, garlic, and oil and spread on the second prepared baking sheet. Crumble feta over the corn and place on top rack of oven.

Roast for 10–15 minutes, until golden brown.

❺ Meanwhile, warm a cast-iron grill pan or skillet over medium-high heat. Add mushrooms and cook for 2–3 minutes, until golden brown. Flip and cook for 2–3 minutes, until tender. Remove from heat and place mushrooms in a serving bowl.

❻ Add wild rice, quinoa (if using), and truffle oil to serving bowl with mushrooms and stir gently to combine.

❼ Put skillet back on stove over medium-high heat. Add safflower oil and garlic and cook 1–2 minutes, until slightly golden brown and fragrant. Add beet greens and sauté for 2–3 minutes, until greens are tender.

❽ Serve fish with corn, rice blend, and beet greens.

Snacks

SERVES 1	1500	2000	2500
Sugar snap peas	1 cup (63 g)	1½ cups (95 g)	1½ cups (95 g)
Air-Popped Popcorn (page 287)	////////	2½ cups (20 g)	2½ cups (20 g)
Blueberries	////////	////////	⅔ cup (97 g)
Grapes	////////	1½ cups (231 g)	1½ cups (231 g)
Banana	1 large (136 g)	1 large (136 g)	1 large (136 g)
Coconut Water with Lime 2	recipe below	recipe below	recipe below
Hot Chocolate 2	recipe below	recipe below	recipe below

Coconut Water with Lime ②

SERVES 1	1500	2000	2500
Coconut water	1½ cups	1¼ cups	1 cup
Lime juice	1 Tbsp	1 Tbsp	1 tsp
CALORIES	72 KCAL	61 KCAL	47 KCAL

Pour coconut water and lime juice into a glass filled
with ice and stir to mix well.

Hot Chocolate ②

SERVES 1	1500	2000	2500
Chocolate almond milk	1¼ cups	1½ cups	1½ cups
Blackstrap molasses	¼ Tbsp	////////	////////
Cocoa powder	1 tsp	1 tsp	1 tsp
Dark chocolate	5 g	////////	////////
Honey	////////	1 tsp	1 tsp
CALORIES	216 KCAL	364 KCAL	364 KCAL

In a large microwave-safe mug, mix together milk,
molasses (if using), cocoa powder, chocolate (if using),
and honey (if using). Place the mug in the microwave,
cover with a microwave-safe lid, and heat on high for
1 minute. Stir, mixing in all of the melted chocolate,
and then heat for another 30–45 seconds.

▽
**Breakfast
Summer Roll**

▽
**Tomato, Ricotta,
and Pesto Toast**

▽
**Roast Chicken
with Vegetables and
Cauliflower Mash**

MEAL PLAN

6

CHECKLIST*

PRODUCE
Asparagus
Banana
Blueberries (2500)
Cantaloupe (1500)
Carrots
Cauliflower
Cherry tomatoes
Chives
Kiwi
Mango
Onion
Orange (2500)
Passion fruit
Pineapple
Pure carrot juice
Shiitake mushrooms
Spinach (1500, 2000)
Strawberries
Sugar snap peas (2500)
Zucchini

BAKERY
Whole grain baguette

MEAT
Broiler chicken, 4–5 lbs

DAIRY
Butter
Ricotta cheese, part skim
Soft goat cheese
Vanilla Greek yogurt

FROZEN
Papaya
Raspberries

DRY GOODS
Basil Pesto (page 286)
Coconut milk beverage
  (not canned coconut milk)
Hemp seeds
Milk chocolate chips
Rice paper
Slivered almonds

This list assumes that all basic ingredients (see Pantry and Freezer Staples, page 35) have been stocked.

Breakfast Summer Roll

MAKES 4	1500	2000	2500
For the rolls	1 roll	1 roll	1 roll
Quinoa, uncooked	½ cup (85 g)	½ cup (85 g)	½ cup (85 g)
Coconut milk beverage	1 cup	1 cup	1 cup
Vanilla extract	½ tsp	½ tsp	½ tsp
Ground cinnamon	¼ tsp	¼ tsp	¼ tsp
Sesame seeds, toasted	1 Tbsp	1 Tbsp	1 Tbsp
Shredded coconut, unsweetened	2 Tbsp	2 Tbsp	2 Tbsp
Hemp seeds	2 Tbsp	2 Tbsp	2 Tbsp
Rice paper	4 sheets	4 sheets	4 sheets
Kiwis, thinly sliced	2 large (182 g)	2 large (182 g)	2 large (182 g)
Mango, thinly sliced	1 (207 g)	1 (207 g)	1 (207 g)
Pineapple, thinly sliced	¼ (118 g)	¼ (118 g)	¼ (118 g)
Strawberries, thinly sliced	½ cup (83 g)	½ cup (83 g)	½ cup (83 g)
Raspberries, frozen	1 cup (123 g)	1 cup (123 g)	1 cup (123 g)
Honey	1 Tbsp	1 Tbsp	1 Tbsp
Passion fruit	1	1	1
CALORIES	287 KCAL	287 KCAL	287 KCAL

❶ Put quinoa, coconut beverage, vanilla, and cinnamon in a medium saucepan and bring to a boil over high heat. Reduce heat to medium-low, cover, and simmer for about 15 minutes (quinoa is cooked when grain is fluffy and coconut beverage has been fully absorbed). Stir every 5 minutes to prevent the coconut beverage from burning, but avoid keeping the lid off for too long. Remove from heat. Stir in sesame seeds, coconut, and hemp seeds. Set aside.

❷ Line a plate with two damp paper towels and set aside. Lay rice paper sheets in a casserole dish and add just enough warm water to cover. Soak for 5 seconds, then remove from dish and place on cutting board. (The water makes the rice paper more pliable and flexible.)

❸ Layer kiwi, mango, pineapple, and strawberries along one edge of the rice paper. Top fruit with ½ cup of the quinoa mixture. Fold in the sides of the rice paper perpendicular to the fruit and quinoa. Roll fruit and quinoa over from the bottom to encase filling. Continue rolling until roll is sealed. Place rolls under a damp paper towel to keep rice paper from drying out while making remaining 3 rolls.

❹ Put raspberries and honey into a small saucepan and warm over low heat for 3–5 minutes, until thickened into a sauce. Set aside to cool slightly.

❺ Meanwhile, use a mortar and pestle to squeeze all the juice out of each passion fruit seed pod. Strain contents of mortar through a sifter into a small bowl, making sure to get all the juice. (While passion fruit seeds are edible, the texture can be slightly unpleasant.) Add passion fruit juice to raspberry sauce and serve as a dip with rolls.

Note: Store leftover rolls in a resealable container. Rolls will keep for up to 5 days refrigerated.

Tomato, Ricotta, and Pesto Toast

SERVES 1	1500	2000	2500
Whole grain baguette	1 slice (32 g)	1 slice (32 g)	2 slices (64 g)
Ricotta cheese, part skim	2 Tbsp (31 g)	½ cup (61 g)	1 cup (128 g)
Basil Pesto (page 286)	1 tsp	1 tsp	2 tsp
Cherry tomatoes, halved	¼ cup (68 g)	¼ cup (68 g)	½ cup (136 g)
Balsamic Reduction (page 286)	½ tsp	1 tsp	2 tsp
CALORIES	170 KCAL	220 KCAL	444 KCAL

❶ Toast bread.
❷ Put ricotta and pesto in a small bowl and stir until only slightly mixed. Spread mixture on toast, top with tomatoes, and drizzle balsamic reduction overtop.

Roast Chicken
with Vegetables and Cauliflower Mash

SERVES 6		1500	2000	2500
For the chicken		85 g chicken	110 g chicken	165 g chicken
Broiler chicken		1	1	1
Butter, softened, divided		2 Tbsp	2 Tbsp	2 Tbsp
For the seasoning				
Paprika		1½ tsp	1½ tsp	1½ tsp
Onion powder		1½ tsp	1½ tsp	1½ tsp
Garlic powder		1½ tsp	1½ tsp	1½ tsp
Rosemary		1 tsp	1 tsp	1 tsp
Ground ginger		½ tsp	½ tsp	½ tsp
Salt		½ tsp	½ tsp	½ tsp
Black pepper		½ tsp	½ tsp	½ tsp
Thyme		½ tsp	½ tsp	½ tsp
Turmeric		½ tsp	½ tsp	½ tsp
Coriander		½ tsp	½ tsp	½ tsp
Cumin		½ tsp	½ tsp	½ tsp
Nutmeg		¼ tsp	¼ tsp	¼ tsp
Dry mustard		¼ tsp	¼ tsp	¼ tsp
For the vegetables		157 g serving	157 g serving	235 g serving
Butter, melted		1 Tbsp	1 Tbsp	1 Tbsp
Safflower oil		1 Tbsp	1 Tbsp	1 Tbsp
Onion, coarsely chopped		1 large (150 g)	1 large (150 g)	1 large (150 g)
Carrots, halved lengthwise		7 (288 g)	7 (288 g)	7 (288 g)
Zucchini, chopped		1 (196 g)	1 (196 g)	1 (196 g)
Shiitake mushrooms		½ cup (36 g)	½ cup (36 g)	½ cup (36 g)
Asparagus spears, cut into 1-inch lengths		10 (160 g)	10 (160 g)	10 (160 g)
For the cauliflower mash		215 g serving	215 g serving	215 g serving
Cauliflower		1½ heads (1260 g)	1½ heads (1260 g)	1½ heads (1260 g)
Nutritional yeast		6 Tbsp (22.5 g)	6 Tbsp (22.5 g)	6 Tbsp (22.5 g)
Chives, chopped		3 Tbsp	3 Tbsp	3 Tbsp
SERVES 1				
To serve				
Soft goat cheese		1½ tsp (7.5 g)	1 Tbsp (15 g)	1 Tbsp (15 g)
Balsamic Reduction (page 286)		/ / / / / / / /	1 tsp	1 tsp
CALORIES		384 KCAL	491 KCAL	675 KCAL

❶ Preheat the oven to 375°F. Fill a roasting pan with just enough water to cover bottom.

❷ Using paper towel, pat chicken dry. Check cavity of chicken for giblets and remove if there are any. Place butter between meat and skin 1½ tsp at a time. (Take care to leave the skin attached between the two chicken breasts.)

❸ Combine seasoning ingredients in a small bowl and mix well. Massage entire chicken with mixture. Put chicken on rack in the roasting pan, with wings lying on top of chicken breasts. (They will burn if they are tucked under the chicken.) Add any remaining dry rub seasoning to the roasting pan (for a boost of flavor). Cover and roast, on lowest oven rack, for 90 minutes.

❹ Meanwhile, prepare the vegetables. Combine butter and oil in a casserole dish, add onions, carrots, zucchini, mushrooms, and asparagus, and toss to coat. After chicken has roasted for 30 minutes, add vegetables to oven on top rack. Roast both for 1 hour, stirring the vegetables every 15–20 minutes, until they are golden brown and fork tender and chicken is cooked through. (Safe internal temperature for chicken is 165°F.)

❺ Meanwhile, prepare the mash. Fill a large pot with 1 inch of water, cover, and bring to a boil over high heat. Gently lower cauliflower, stem-sides down, into pot. Cover and steam for 10–15 minutes, until fork tender.

❻ Drain cauliflower, transfer to a cutting board, and set aside for 5 minutes. When cool enough to handle, roughly chop and place in a clean dish towel. Bring the four corners of the dish towel together and twist to wring out as much water as possible from the cauliflower. Transfer to a food processor and purée until smooth. Stir in nutritional yeast and chives.

❼ Evenly spread cauliflower mash into a baking dish, place in oven alongside vegetables, and roast for 15–20 minutes.

❽ Plate chicken with vegetables and mash. Sprinkle goat cheese and balsamic reduction over the vegetables and serve.

Note: *Any leftover chicken can be reserved for other recipes such as Chicken and Mango Summer Rolls (page 104). Leftover roasted vegetables can be used in Roasted Vegetable Salad (page 96). Leftovers will keep for up to 2 days refrigerated. Any leftovers after 2 days can be frozen.*

Healthy Choices: *Are you new to nutritional yeast? It has a cheesy flavor and is a great source of vitamin B12, making it ideal for vegetarian dishes.*

Snacks

SERVES 1	1500	2000	2500
Carrot Juice Smoothie	recipe below	recipe below	recipe below
Popcorn Trail Mix	recipe below	recipe below	recipe below
Hot Chocolate 3	recipe below	recipe below	recipe below
Cantaloupe, chopped	½ cup (80 g)	////////	////////
Orange	////////	////////	1 large (184 g)
Dark chocolate	////////	////////	15 g
Sugar snap peas	////////	////////	1 cup (63 g)
Blueberries	////////	////////	1 cup (145 g)

Carrot Juice Smoothie

SERVES 1	1500	2000	2500
Spinach	2 cups (60 g)	2 cups (60 g)	////////
Strawberries, fresh or frozen	⅓ cup (74 g)	////////	////////
Banana	1 small (101 g)	1 large (136 g)	1 large (136 g)
Mango, fresh or frozen	////////	1 cup (165 g)	1 cup (165 g)
Papaya, fresh or frozen	////////	½ cup (70 g)	½ cup (70 g)
Flaxseeds	2¼ tsp	2 tsp	2 tsp
Wheat germ	2 Tbsp	2 Tbsp	////////
Vanilla Greek yogurt	¼ cup	////////	////////
Coconut water	1¼ cups	1 cup	1¼ cups
Pure carrot juice	½ cup	½ cup	½ cup
CALORIES	378 KCAL	447 KCAL	393 KCAL

Put all ingredients into a blender and blend until smooth.
If the smoothie is too thick, add water (not coconut water
or carrot juice). If you prefer a thicker texture, add ice
and blend until smooth.

Popcorn Trail Mix

SERVES 1	1500	2000	2500
Almonds, slivered	1 Tbsp	////////	////////
Sunflower seeds	1 Tbsp	1 Tbsp	1 Tbsp
Pumpkin seeds	1 Tbsp	1 Tbsp	1 Tbsp
Air-Popped Popcorn (page 287)	1 cup (8 g)	2 cups (16 g)	2 cups (16 g)
Dried apricots, chopped	////////	¼ cup (62 g)	⅓ cup (83 g)
Dark chocolate, roughly chopped	////////	10 g	5 g
CALORIES	198 KCAL	323 KCAL	322 KCAL

❶ Put almonds and seeds in a skillet and sauté for 1-3 minutes over medium heat, stirring or shaking the skillet frequently, until golden. Set aside to cool completely.
❷ In a medium bowl, combine all ingredients and mix well.

Hot Chocolate ③

SERVES 1	1500	2000	2500
Vanilla almond milk	1 cup	1½ cups	1½ cups
Blackstrap molasses	2½ tsp	////////	////////
Cocoa powder	1 tsp	1 tsp	1 tsp
Milk chocolate chips	1 tsp	////////	////////
Honey	////////	1 tsp	////////
CALORIES	154 KCAL	162 KCAL	141 KCAL

In a large microwave-safe mug, mix together milk, molasses (if using), cocoa powder, chocolate chips (if using), and honey (if using). Place the mug in the microwave, cover, and heat on high for 1 minute. Stir, mixing in all of the melted chocolate, and then heat for another 30–45 seconds.

▽ **Prosciutto, Cheese, and Caramelized Onion Scones**

▽ **Roasted Vegetable Salad**

▽ **Cauliflower Cottage Pie with Quinoa Salad**

MEAL PLAN 7

CHECKLIST*

PRODUCE
Arugula
Banana
Basil paste
Blueberries (2000, 2500)
Cantaloupe
Carrots
Cauliflower
Garlic
Grapes (2500)
Leeks
Lime (1500, 2000)
Onion
Orange (2500)
Plum tomatoes
Raspberries (1500)
Shiitake mushrooms
Spinach
Sugar snap peas
Zucchini

DELI
Sliced prosciutto

MEAT
Ground turkey

DAIRY
Butter
Buttermilk
Egg
Mozzarella cheese
Plain Greek yogurt
Soft goat cheese

DRY GOODS
Coconut oil (2500)
Dried mango (2000, 2500)
Natural peanut butter
Sugar

PREMADE
Roasted Vegetables
  (page 88)

* This list assumes that all basic ingredients (see Pantry and Freezer Staples, page 35) have been stocked.

Prosciutto, Cheese, and Caramelized Onion Scones

MAKES 7 SCONES	1500	2000	2500
For the scones	1 scone	1 scone	1 scone
Butter, chilled and diced	½ cup + 1 Tbsp	½ cup + 1 Tbsp	½ cup + 1 Tbsp
Onion, sliced	1 large (150 g)	1 large (150 g)	1 large (150 g)
Sugar	1 Tbsp	1 Tbsp	1 Tbsp
Buttermilk	1 cup + 2 Tbsp	1 cup + 2 Tbsp	1 cup + 2 Tbsp
All-purpose flour	2½ cups	2½ cups	2½ cups
Baking powder	2 tsp	2 tsp	2 tsp
Baking soda	1¼ tsp	1¼ tsp	1¼ tsp
Flaxseeds	¼ cup	¼ cup	¼ cup
Prosciutto, finely chopped	4 slices (60 g)	4 slices (60 g)	4 slices (60 g)
Mozzarella cheese, shredded	½ cup (56 g)	½ cup (56 g)	½ cup (56 g)
SERVES 1			
Cantaloupe, chopped	1 cup (160 g)	1 cup (160 g)	1 cup (160 g)
Hard-boiled egg	1 small (38 g)	1 large (50 g)	1 large (50 g)
CALORIES	500 KCAL	515 KCAL	515 KCAL

❶ Preheat the oven to 325°F. Line a baking sheet with parchment paper.

❷ Melt 1 Tbsp butter in a skillet over medium heat, add onions to skillet (avoid overcrowding), and cook for 5–7 minutes, until translucent. Reduce to low heat and cook for another 15–20 minutes, until caramelized and brown.

❸ In a large bowl, add remaining ½ cup chopped butter, sugar, buttermilk, flour, baking powder, and baking soda. Using a stand mixer fitted with the paddle attachment, mix on medium speed until ingredients are just barely combined. Add flaxseeds and mix for another 5 seconds. The dough should be wet to the touch.

❹ Add prosciutto, mozzarella, and caramelized onions to the dough and mix for no more than 5 seconds. Transfer dough to a floured surface and gently flatten with your hand until 1-inch thick. Cut dough into 7 equal portions and place, spaced evenly apart, on prepared baking sheet. Bake for 20–25 minutes, or until golden brown on top.

Freezer Friendly: Put unbaked scones onto a baking sheet and freeze. Once solid, place them in an airtight container or freezer bag and store for up to 2 months. To serve, bake them according to instructions, adding another 3-4 minutes.

Roasted Vegetable Salad

SERVES 1	1500	2000	2500
For the salad			
Spinach	1½ cups (45 g)	1½ cups (45 g)	1 cup (30 g)
Arugula	1 cup (20 g)	1 cup (20 g)	1 cup (20 g)
Roasted Vegetables (page 88)	1 serving	2 servings	2 servings
Soft goat cheese	1 tsp (5 g)	2 tsp (10 g)	1 Tbsp (15 g)
For the dressing	2 tsp serving	1 Tbsp serving	1 Tbsp serving
Balsamic vinegar	2 tsp	2 tsp	2 tsp
Honey	½ tsp	½ tsp	½ tsp
Basil, dried or fresh	¼ tsp	¼ tsp	¼ tsp
Sunflower oil	1 Tbsp	1 Tbsp	1 Tbsp
CALORIES	162 KCAL	287 KCAL	297 KCAL

❶ If you prefer a warm salad, reheat the roasted vegetables in a skillet over medium heat, until just warmed through. Make a bed of spinach and arugula in a salad bowl or on a large plate, top with roasted vegetables, and crumble goat cheese overtop.

❷ In a small bowl, whisk together vinegar, honey, and basil. Gradually pour in oil, whisking vigorously, until emulsified. Drizzle over salad and serve.

Snacks

SERVES 1	1500	2000	2500
Peanut Butter and Almond Smoothie	recipe below	recipe below	recipe below
Coconut Water with Lime 3	recipe below	recipe below	////////
Air-Popped Popcorn (page 287)	2 cups (16 g)	2 cups (16 g)	////////
Cinnamon-Sugar Popcorn 1	////////	////////	recipe below
Sugar snap peas	1 cup (63 g)	1 cup (63 g)	½ cup (32 g)
Raspberries	1 cup (123 g)	////////	////////
Blueberries	////////	½ cup (72 g)	1 cup (145 g)
Dried mango	////////	5 pieces (33 g)	6 pieces (40 g)
Grapes	////////	////////	1¼ cups (193 g)
Orange	////////	////////	1 large (184 g)

Peanut Butter and Almond Milk Smoothie

SERVES 1	1500	2000	2500
Blackstrap molasses	1½ tsp	////////	////////
Natural peanut butter	1 tsp	1½ tsp	1 Tbsp
Banana	1 (118 g)	1 large (136 g)	1 large (136 g)
Wheat germ	1 Tbsp	1 Tbsp	1 Tbsp
Flaxseeds	1½ tsp	1½ tsp	2 tsp
Plain Greek yogurt	////////	½ cup	½ cup
Vanilla almond milk	1¼ cups	1½ cups	1½ cups
Honey	////////	1½ tsp	1½ tsp
CALORIES	325 KCAL	476 KCAL	530 KCAL

Put all ingredients into a blender and blend until smooth.
If the smoothie is too thick, add water (not almond milk).
If you prefer a thicker texture, add ice and blend until smooth.

Coconut Water with Lime ③

SERVES 1	1500	2000	2500
Coconut water	1½ cups	1½ cups	////////
Lime juice	1½ tsp	1 tsp	////////
CALORIES	70 KCAL	69 KCAL	

Pour coconut water and lime juice into a glass filled with ice
and stir to mix well.

Cinnamon-Sugar Popcorn ①

SERVES 1	1500	2000	2500
Air-Popped Popcorn (page 287)	////////	////////	3 cups (24 g)
Coconut oil, melted	////////	////////	1 tsp
Ground cinnamon	////////	////////	½ tsp
Sugar	////////	////////	1 tsp
CALORIES			151 KCAL

Put popcorn in a large bowl, drizzle coconut oil overtop,
sprinkle with cinnamon and sugar, and gently stir to combine.

Cauliflower Cottage Pie
with Quinoa Salad

SERVES 8	1500	2000	2500
For the cottage pie	1 serving	1 serving	2 servings
Safflower oil, divided	1½ tsp	1½ tsp	1½ tsp
Onions, diced	2 small (165 g)	2 small (165 g)	2 small (165 g)
Ground turkey	1 lb (454 g)	1 lb (454 g)	1 lb (454 g)
Cauliflower	1 head (840 g)	1 head (840 g)	1 head (840 g)
Carrots, chopped	3 large (216 g)	3 large (216 g)	3 large (216 g)
Leeks, halved lengthwise and sliced	1 (45 g)	1 (45 g)	1 (45 g)
Garlic, minced	4 large cloves	4 large cloves	4 large cloves
Plum tomatoes, chopped	6 (372 g)	6 (372 g)	6 (372 g)
Basil paste	1½ Tbsp	1½ Tbsp	1½ Tbsp
Salt, divided	½ tsp	½ tsp	½ tsp
Nutritional yeast	½ cup	½ cup	½ cup
SERVES 1			
For the salad			
Spinach	1½ cups (45 g)	1½ cups (45 g)	1 cup (30 g)
Arugula	1 cup (20 g)	1 cup (20 g)	1 cup (20 g)
Cooked Quinoa (page 286)	½ cup (69 g)	½ cup (69 g)	½ cup (69 g)
Sunflower seeds	////////	1½ tsp	1½ tsp
Shiitake mushrooms, halved	½ cup (72 g)	½ cup (72 g)	⅓ cup (48 g)
For the dressing	1½ tsp serving	1 Tbsp serving	1 Tbsp serving
Balsamic vinegar	2 tsp	2 tsp	2 tsp
Honey	½ tsp	½ tsp	½ tsp
Basil, dried or fresh	¼ tsp	¼ tsp	¼ tsp
Sunflower oil	1 Tbsp	1 Tbsp	1 Tbsp
CALORIES	340 KCAL	398 KCAL	547 KCAL

❶ Preheat the oven to 375°F.

❷ In a Dutch oven, heat ¾ tsp oil over medium heat. Add onions, reduce heat to medium-low, and cook for 2–3 minutes, or until translucent. Add ground turkey and cook for another 10–12 minutes, until meat is no longer pink. Set aside.

❸ Fill a large pot with 2 inches of water, cover, and bring to a boil over high heat. Gently lower cauliflower, stem-side down, into pot. Cover and cook for 10 minutes, until fork tender. Drain in a colander and set aside to cool.

❹ In a skillet, heat remaining ¾ tsp of oil over medium-high heat. Add carrots, leeks, and garlic and cook for 10–12 minutes, until carrots are al dente (cooked but slightly firm to the touch). Add tomatoes, basil paste, and ¼ tsp salt. Stir, cover, and simmer over low heat for 10 minutes, until tomatoes have thickened. Add this mixture to the skillet of turkey. Stir well.

❺ Roughly chop cauliflower, add to a food processor, and process until smooth. Transfer mixture to a large bowl, stir in nutritional yeast and ¼ tsp salt. In a casserole dish, spread meat mixture in an even layer and top with an even layer of cauliflower mash. (Alternatively, divide mixture between 8 individual ramekins.) Bake for 15–20 minutes.

❻ Meanwhile, in a medium bowl, combine spinach, arugula, quinoa, and sunflower seeds. Add dressing and toss. Add 2 Tbsp water and shiitake mushrooms to a skillet and sauté over medium-high heat for 3–5 minutes, until tender. Mix mushrooms into quinoa salad.

❼ Serve the cottage pie with salad.

Note: *Leftover cottage pie should be consumed within 2 days. Any leftovers after 2 days can be frozen in individual portions. To reheat, warm in a covered ovenproof dish at 350°F for 30–45 minutes, then remove cover and cook for an additional 10–15 minutes, until heated through.*

▽ **Strawberry-Mango Chia Jam**   ▽ **Chicken and Mango Summer Roll**   ▽ **Slow-Cooked Pork and Bean Chili**

MEAL PLAN

8

CHECKLIST*

PRODUCE
Avocado
Banana
Blueberries (2000, 2500)
Cantaloupe (1500)
Carrots
Cilantro
Green onions
Kale
Mango
Orange (2000, 2500)
Raspberries (1500)
Red cabbage
Spinach
Sugar snap peas (1500, 2500)

BAKERY
Whole grain bread

MEAT
Cooked chicken breast
Pork sirloin
Thick-cut bacon

DAIRY
Egg (1500)
Plain Greek yogurt

DRY GOODS
Brown sugar
Cashews, dry roasted
  (2000, 2500)
Hearts of palm (1500)
Hemp seeds (2500)
Navy beans, dry
Pinto beans, dry
Rice noodles
Rice paper
Tomato sauce, canned
Vegetable broth

This list assumes that all basic ingredients (see Pantry and Freezer Staples, page 35) have been stocked.

Strawberry-Mango Chia Jam

MAKES 3½ CUPS	1500	2000	2500
For the jam	2 Tbsp serving	3 Tbsp serving	3 Tbsp serving
Strawberries, fresh or frozen	1¾ cups (290 g)	1¾ cups (290 g)	1¾ cups (290 g)
Mango, fresh or frozen	1½ cups (247 g)	1½ cups (247 g)	1½ cups (247 g)
Blackstrap molasses	1 Tbsp	1 Tbsp	1 Tbsp
Honey	1 Tbsp	1 Tbsp	1 Tbsp
Chia seeds	6 Tbsp	6 Tbsp	6 Tbsp
SERVES 1			
To serve			
Whole grain loaf	1 slice (26 g)	2 slices (52 g)	2 slices (52 g)
Hard-boiled egg	1 small (38 g)	////////	////////
CALORIES	166 KCAL	202 KCAL	202 KCAL

❶ Place strawberries, mango, molasses, and honey in a large bowl and, using an immersion blender, blend until well combined but still slightly chunky. Add chia seeds and mix well. Cover and refrigerate overnight, to let chia seeds gel.

❷ Toast bread. Evenly spread jam over toast and serve with an egg (if using).

Freezer Friendly: Chia jam is delicious on top of ice cream or in a yogurt parfait. Leftover chia jam will keep for up to a week refrigerated or can be frozen in individual portions.

Chicken and Mango Summer Roll

MAKES 2 ROLLS	1500	2000	2500
For the roll	1½ rolls	2 rolls	2 rolls
Rice paper	2 sheets (18 g)	2 sheets (18 g)	2 sheets (18 g)
Sesame seeds, toasted	////////	1 Tbsp	1 Tbsp
Mango, thinly sliced	½ cup (82 g)	½ cup (82 g)	½ cup (82 g)
Avocado, thinly sliced	½ cup (74 g)	½ cup (74 g)	½ cup (74 g)
Spinach	½ cup (16 g)	½ cup (16 g)	½ cup (16 g)
Chicken breast, cooked	½ cup (70 g)	½ cup (70 g)	½ cup (70 g)
Rice noodles, cooked	½ cup (88 g)	½ cup (88 g)	½ cup (88 g)
Carrots, sliced thinly lengthwise	¼ cup (32 g)	¼ cup (32 g)	¼ cup (32 g)
Green onions, sliced lengthwise	2 (10 g)	2 (10 g)	2 (10 g)
Red cabbage, shredded	¼ cup (18 g)	¼ cup (18 g)	¼ cup (18 g)
SERVES 1			
Natural rice vinegar, to serve	1 Tbsp	1 Tbsp	2 Tbsp
CALORIES	354 KCAL	494 KCAL	494 KCAL

❶ Arrange all ingredients on a cutting board for easy assembly. Line a plate with two damp paper towels and set aside.

❷ Lay rice paper sheets in a casserole dish and add just enough warm water to cover. Soak for 5 seconds, then remove from dish and place on cutting board. (The water makes the rice paper more pliable and flexible.)

❸ Sprinkle sesame seeds (if using) over each rice paper.

❹ In the center of the rice paper, layer mango, avocado, spinach, chicken, rice noodles, carrots, green onions, and red cabbage. Fold over and roll, leaving ends open. Place roll under a damp paper towel to keep rice paper from drying out while making second roll.

❺ Refrigerate for about 5–10 minutes, until rice papers become tacky.

❻ Remove rolls from fridge and tuck in the ends. (The rice paper will stick easily to the ends.) Cut rolls in half and serve with vinegar for dipping.

Snacks

SERVES 1	1500	2000	2500
Chocolate-Banana Smoothie 2	recipe below	recipe below	recipe below
Cantaloupe, chopped	¾ cup (120 g)	////////	////////
Raspberries	½ cup (61 g)	////////	////////
Sugar snap peas	1 cup (63 g)	////////	1 cup (63 g)
Orange	////////	1 (131 g)	1 (131 g)
Blueberries	////////	½ cup (72 g)	½ cup (72 g)
Cashews, dry roasted	////////	¼ cup (34 g)	¼ cup (34 g)
Air-Popped Popcorn (page 287)	////////	1 cup (8 g)	3 cups (24 g)

Chocolate-Banana Smoothie ②

SERVES 1	1500	2000	2500
Plain Greek yogurt	1 Tbsp	1 Tbsp	¼ cup
Blackstrap molasses	1½ tsp	////////	////////
Wheat germ	1 Tbsp	1 Tbsp	1 Tbsp
Flaxseeds	1 tsp	1 tsp	1 tsp
Vanilla extract	½ tsp	½ tsp	½ tsp
Cocoa powder	1 Tbsp	1 Tbsp	1½ tsp
Dark chocolate	5 g	5 g	10 g
Banana	½ (59 g)	1 small (101 g)	1 (118 g)
Coconut water	1 cup	1 cup	1 cup
Vanilla almond milk	1 cup	1 cup	1 cup
CALORIES	315 KCAL	329 KCAL	402 KCAL

Put all ingredients into a blender and blend until smooth.
If the smoothie is too thick, add water (not coconut water
or almond milk). If you prefer a thicker texture, add ice
and blend until smooth.

Slow-Cooked Pork and Bean Chili

SERVES 6	1500	2000	2500
For the chili	177 g beans + 75 g pork	355 g beans + 75 g pork	355 g beans + 75 g pork
Pinto beans, dry, soaked overnight and drained	1 cup (193 g)	1 cup (193 g)	1 cup (193 g)
Navy beans, dry, soaked overnight and drained	1 cup (208 g)	1 cup (208 g)	1 cup (208 g)
Bacon, roughly chopped	6 slices (228 g)	6 slices (228 g)	6 slices (228 g)
Pork sirloin	450 g	450 g	450 g
Tomato sauce	1 can (14 oz)	1 can (14 oz)	1 can (14 oz)
Vegetable broth	4 cups	4 cups	4 cups
Brown sugar	½ cup (110 g)	½ cup (110 g)	½ cup (110 g)
Chili powder	1 Tbsp	1 Tbsp	1 Tbsp
Cumin	1½ tsp	1½ tsp	1½ tsp
Chipotle powder	1½ tsp	1½ tsp	1½ tsp
Garlic powder	1½ tsp	1½ tsp	1½ tsp
Cilantro, to garnish (optional)			
SERVES 1			
For the slaw			
Spinach	1⅔ cups (50 g)	1½ cups (45 g)	1 cup (30 g)
Kale, stems removed, leaves chopped	1 cup (67 g)	1 cup (67 g)	1 cup (67 g)
Red cabbage, shredded	½ cup (35 g)	½ cup (35 g)	¼ cup (17 g)
Carrots, shredded	¼ cup (32 g)	¼ cup (32 g)	¼ cup (32 g)
Hearts of palm, sliced	⅓ cup (49 g)	////////	////////
Sunflower seeds	1½ Tbsp	1 Tbsp	1 Tbsp
Pumpkin seeds	1½ tsp	1 Tbsp	1 Tbsp
Hemp seeds	////////	////////	1½ tsp
For the dressing	2 tsp serving	2½ tsp serving	1 Tbsp serving
Balsamic vinegar	½ tsp	1 tsp	1 tsp
Honey	½ tsp	////////	////////
Garlic powder	////////	¼ tsp	¼ tsp
Onion powder	////////	¼ tsp	¼ tsp
Grapeseed oil	1 tsp	////////	////////
Safflower oil	////////	1½ tsp	1½ tsp
CALORIES	661 KCAL	943 KCAL	984 KCAL

❶ Warm skillet over medium-high heat. Add bacon and cook for 5–7 minutes, until it starts to turn golden brown. Transfer to a paper towel–lined plate.

❷ In the same pan with bacon grease, carefully place pork sirloin and sear for 2½ minutes. (Do not move the meat during this time; you want it to develop a golden brown sear.) Flip pork and sear for another 2½ minutes, until golden brown. Transfer pork to a slow cooker.

❸ Add bacon, beans, tomato sauce, vegetable broth, sugar, chili powder, cumin, chipotle powder, and garlic powder to the slow cooker and cook on low for 8–10 hours.

❹ Meanwhile, in a medium bowl, mix together spinach, kale, cabbage, carrots, hearts of palm, sunflower seeds, pumpkin seeds, and hemp seeds.

❺ In a small bowl, whisk together vinegar, honey, garlic powder, and onion powder. Gradually pour in oil, whisking constantly until emulsified. Drizzle over salad and toss to combine.

❻ Measure out a portion of pork and cut into ½-inch cubes. Put beans in a bowl, add pork, and garnish with chopped cilantro, if desired. Serve with salad.

▽

Breakfast Quesadilla

▽

Warm Green Bean Salad

▽

Coconut and Lemongrass Poached Halibut with Collard Greens, Quinoa, and Wild Rice

MEAL PLAN 9

CHECKLIST*

PRODUCE
Banana
Cantaloupe
Collard greens
Garlic
Grapes (2500)
Green beans
Kale
Lemongrass
Mango (1500, 2500)
Orange (2000, 2500)
Pure carrot juice (2500)
Red bell pepper
Red cabbage
Red chili pepper
Shallot
Shiitake mushrooms

BAKERY
8-inch whole wheat tortilla

DELI
Sliced prosciutto

FISH
Halibut

DAIRY
Eggs
Feta cheese
Plain Greek yogurt
Soft goat cheese

FROZEN
Raspberries

DRY GOODS
Hearts of palm
Oat bran (1500)

This list assumes that all basic ingredients (see Pantry and Freezer Staples, page 35) have been stocked.

Breakfast Quesadilla

SERVES 1	1500	2000	2500
Kale, stems removed, leaves chopped	1 cup (67 g)	1 cup (67 g)	1 cup (67 g)
Shiitake mushrooms, halved	¼ cup (37 g)	¼ cup (37 g)	¼ cup (37 g)
Red bell pepper, deseeded and chopped	¼ cup (37 g)	¼ cup (37 g)	¼ cup (37 g)
Egg	1 large (50 g)	1 large (50 g)	1 large (50 g)
Egg white	1 large (33 g)	1 large (33 g)	1 large (33 g)
Plain Greek yogurt	1 Tbsp	1 Tbsp	1 Tbsp
Whole wheat tortilla	1 (48 g)	1 (48 g)	1 (48 g)
Feta cheese, divided	1½ tsp (7.5 g)	1½ tsp (7.5 g)	1½ tsp (7.5 g)
Cooking spray			
To serve			
Cantaloupe, chopped	¾ cup (120 g)	1 cup (160 g)	1 cup (160 g)
Mango, chopped	¾ cup (124 g)	////////	1 cup (165 g)
CALORIES	436 KCAL	369 KCAL	476 KCAL

❶ Warm a large non-stick skillet over medium-high heat, add 1 Tbsp water, kale, mushrooms, and red pepper, and sauté for 3–5 minutes, until tender. Transfer to a plate and set aside.

❷ Return skillet to stovetop and reduce heat to medium.

❸ In a small bowl, stir together egg, egg white, and yogurt, add to pan, and sauté for 2–3 minutes, until cooked through.

❹ Place tortilla on a plate. Sprinkle half the feta on one side of the tortilla. Top with vegetable mixture, eggs, and the remaining cheese. Fold in half. Lightly spray each side of the quesadilla with cooking spray, place in skillet, and cook for 2–3 minutes, until feta is melted and tortilla is browned. Flip and cook for another 2–3 minutes, until browned. Cut into wedges and serve with fruit.

Snacks

SERVES 1	1500	2000	2500
Red Smoothie	recipe below	recipe below	recipe below
Hot Chocolate 4	recipe below	recipe below	recipe below
Pistachios	////////	////////	¼ cup (31 g)
Orange	////////	1 (131 g)	1 (131 g)
Grapes	////////	////////	¾ cup (116 g)
Dark chocolate	////////	15 g	15 g
Air-Popped Popcorn (page 287)	////////	2½ cups (20 g)	3 cups (24 g)

Red Smoothie

SERVES 1	1500	2000	2500
Red cabbage, roughly chopped	1 cup (70 g)	1 cup (70 g)	1 cup (70 g)
Raspberries, frozen	½ cup (61 g)	½ cup (61 g)	½ cup (61 g)
Strawberries, frozen	¾ cup (166 g)	1 cup (221 g)	1 cup (221 g)
Banana	½ small (51 g)	1 (118 g)	1 large (136 g)
Hearts of palm	¼ cup (36 g)	⅓ cup (49 g)	⅓ cup (49 g)
Wheat germ	2 Tbsp	2 Tbsp	2 Tbsp
Oat bran	1 Tbsp	////////	////////
Flaxseeds	1½ tsp	1½ tsp	1½ tsp
Plain Greek yogurt	1 Tbsp	////////	////////
Coconut water	1⅓ cup	1 cup	1 cup
Pure carrot juice	////////	////////	¼ cup
CALORIES	331 KCAL	373 KCAL	412 KCAL

Put all ingredients into a blender and blend until smooth.
If the smoothie is too thick, add water (not coconut water
or carrot juice). If you prefer a thicker texture, add ice
and blend until smooth.

Hot Chocolate ④

SERVES 1	1500	2000	2500
Vanilla almond milk	1¼ cups	1½ cups	1½ cups
Cocoa powder	2 tsp	2 tsp	2 tsp
Dark chocolate	5 g	5 g	////////
Blackstrap molasses	2 tsp	////////	////////
CALORIES	184 KCAL	174 KCAL	145 KCAL

In a large microwave-safe mug, mix together milk, cocoa powder,
chocolate (if using), and molasses (if using). Place mug in
microwave, cover, and heat on high for 2 minutes. Stir, mixing in
all of the melted chocolate, and then heat for another minute.

Warm Green Bean Salad

SERVES 3	1500	2000	2500
For the salad	1 serving	1½ servings	2 servings
Grapeseed oil	2 tsp	2 tsp	2 tsp
Garlic, finely chopped	1 clove	1 clove	1 clove
Shallot, chopped	1 (15 g)	1 (15 g)	1 (15 g)
Green beans, cut into 1-inch lengths	2 cups (220 g)	2 cups (220 g)	2 cups (220 g)
Prosciutto, roughly chopped	3 slices (45 g)	3 slices (45 g)	3 slices (45 g)
Pistachios, dry roasted and chopped	¼ cup (31 g)	¼ cup (31 g)	¼ cup (31 g)
Balsamic vinegar	¼ cup	¼ cup	¼ cup
Soft goat cheese, crumbled	2 Tbsp (50 g)	2 Tbsp (50 g)	2 Tbsp (50 g)
SERVES 1			
Pumpkin seeds, dry roasted	1½ tsp	1 Tbsp	1 Tbsp
Sunflower seeds, dry roasted	1 Tbsp	1½ tsp	1½ tsp
CALORIES	298 KCAL	419 KCAL	525 KCAL

❶ Heat oil in a large skillet over medium heat. Add garlic and shallots and sauté for 1–2 minutes, until fragrant.

❷ Add beans, prosciutto, and pistachios to the pan and sauté for 3–5 minutes, until beans are al dente. Remove from heat and drizzle with balsamic vinegar.

❸ Transfer to a plate, top with goat cheese, pumpkin seeds, and sunflower seeds, and serve. Leftover salad will keep for up to 5 days refrigerated.

Life Made Easier: When dry-roasting nuts, remove pan from the heat as soon as nuts become fragrant. This prevents them from burning because the nuts will continue to brown in the pan.

Grab and Go: Prepare the salad the night before, omitting goat cheese. Allow to cool and store in a microwave-safe resealable container in the fridge. When ready to serve, heat in microwave for 30–45 seconds, stir, and top with goat cheese. (This salad is also delicious served cold.)

Coconut and Lemongrass Poached Halibut

with Collard Greens, Quinoa, and Wild Rice

SERVES 1	1500	2000	2500
For the fish			
Halibut fillet, with or without skin	1 (100 g)	1 (150 g)	1 (150 g)
Coconut milk, canned	½ cup	½ cup	½ cup
Lemongrass, snapped in a few spots along the stalk	2	2	2
Red chili, sliced	½	½	½
For the collard greens			
Grapeseed oil	1 tsp	½ tsp	½ tsp
Garlic, minced	1 clove	1 clove	1 clove
Collard greens, stems removed, leaves roughly chopped	3 cups (108 g)	2 cups (72 g)	2 cups (72 g)
For the wild rice and quinoa			
Cooked Wild Rice (page 286)	⅓ cup (55 g)	½ cup (82 g)	½ cup (82 g)
Cooked Quinoa (page 286)	⅓ cup (46 g)	½ cup (69 g)	½ cup (69 g)
CALORIES	333 KCAL	433 KCAL	433 KCAL

❶ Preheat the oven to 350°F.

❷ Place halibut in an ovenproof skillet. Add coconut milk, lemongrass, and chilies to the skillet.

❸ Cut parchment into a circle 1-inch wider than skillet. Carefully cut 5 small slits in the center of parchment circle and place on top of skillet (this allows for steam to vent). Bake for 10–15 minutes, or until fish is opaque, flaky, and cooked through. (Safe internal temperature for fish is 158°F.)

❹ Meanwhile, make the collard greens. Heat oil in a large skillet over medium-high heat, add garlic, and sauté for 1 minute, until fragrant. Add collard greens and sauté for 2–3 minutes, until tender.

❺ In a medium bowl, mix together wild rice and quinoa.

❻ To serve, make a bed of the rice mixture on a plate, top with collard greens, and place fish on top. Drizzle 1 Tbsp of coconut lemongrass sauce overtop and serve.

▽
**Carrot Cake
French Toast with
Cream Cheese Syrup**

▽
Instant Noodles

▽
**Roasted Butternut Squash
and Spinach Salad
with Chicken, Prosciutto,
and Pomegranate**

MEAL PLAN 10

CHECKLIST*

PRODUCE
Banana (2500)
Blackberries (2000, 2500)
Butternut squash
Cantaloupe
Carrot
Green onions
Kale
Lemon
Lime (1500, 2000)
Mango
Mint (1500, 2000)
Orange (2000, 2500)
Pomegranate arils
Raspberries
Red bell pepper
Snow peas
Spinach
Sugar snap peas

BAKERY
Whole grain baguette

DELI
Sliced prosciutto

MEAT
Cooked boneless skinless
  chicken breast

DAIRY
Cream cheese
Eggs
Soft goat cheese
Vanilla Greek yogurt (2500)

FROZEN
Edamame

DRY GOODS
Almonds (2000)
Hearts of palm
Poppy seeds
Thin rice noodles
Vegetable bouillon, low sodium

This list assumes that all basic ingredients (see Pantry and Freezer Staples, page 35) have been stocked.

Carrot Cake French Toast

with Cream Cheese Syrup

MAKES ABOUT ¼ CUP	1500	2000	2500
For the cream cheese syrup	1½ tsp serving	1½ Tbsp serving	3 Tbsp serving
Cream cheese	2 Tbsp (29 g)	2 Tbsp (29 g)	2 Tbsp (29 g)
Vanilla extract	¼ tsp	¼ tsp	¼ tsp
Pure maple syrup	1½ tsp	1½ tsp	1½ tsp
Vanilla almond milk	1 Tbsp	1 Tbsp	1 Tbsp
MAKES 12 SLICES			
For the French toast	3 slices	3 slices	5 slices
Whole grain baguette	200 g	200 g	200 g
Eggs	4 large (200 g)	4 large (200 g)	4 large (200 g)
Vanilla Greek yogurt	1 Tbsp	1 Tbsp	1 Tbsp
Vanilla extract	1 tsp	1 tsp	1 tsp
Carrot, grated	⅓ cup (43 g)	⅓ cup (43 g)	⅓ cup (43 g)
Ground cinnamon	1 tsp	1 tsp	1 tsp
Pumpkin seeds	⅓ cup (76 g)	⅓ cup (76 g)	⅓ cup (76 g)
Sunflower seeds	3 Tbsp (24 g)	3 Tbsp (24 g)	3 Tbsp (24 g)
Flaxseeds	3 Tbsp (29 g)	3 Tbsp (29 g)	3 Tbsp (29 g)
Poppy seeds	3 Tbsp (26 g)	3 Tbsp (26 g)	3 Tbsp (26 g)
Cooking spray			
To serve			
Cantaloupe, chopped	1¼ cup (200 g)	1 cup (160 g)	1 cup (160 g)
Mango, chopped	⅓ cup (55 g)	1 cup (165 g)	1 cup (165 g)
CALORIES	554 KCAL	645 KCAL	982 KCAL

❶ Preheat the oven to 200°F. Line a baking sheet with parchment paper and place in the oven.

❷ In a small bowl, whisk together cream cheese, vanilla, maple syrup, and almond milk until smooth. Set aside.

❸ Slice baguette into 12 equal-size pieces. In a medium shallow bowl, whisk together eggs, yogurt, vanilla, carrot, and cinnamon. In a separate shallow bowl, combine pumpkin seeds, sunflower seeds, flaxseeds, and poppy seeds.

❹ Heat a skillet over medium-low heat and spray with cooking spray. Soak bread in egg mixture about 30–45 seconds, until fully saturated on both sides. Transfer bread to seed mixture and lightly press down on bread so seeds stick. Flip and coat opposite side.

❺ Place bread in skillet and cook for 2–3 minutes, until egg mixture is cooked and seeds turn golden. Flip and cook the other side for another 2–3 minutes. Place on the baking sheet in the oven to keep warm. Repeat with the remaining slices.

❻ Place French toast on a plate, drizzle syrup on top, and serve with fruit. Leftover syrup will keep for up to 5 days refrigerated.

Snacks

SERVES 1	1500	2000	2500
Coconut-Lime Mojito 1	recipe below	recipe below	////////
Hot Chocolate 5	recipe below	recipe below	recipe below
Orange	////////	1 large (184 g)	1 large (184 g)
Banana	////////	////////	1 large (136 g)
Raspberries	⅔ cup (82 g)	½ cup (61 g)	½ cup (61 g)
Blackberries	////////	½ cup (72 g)	½ cup (72 g)
Sugar snap peas	////////	½ cup (32 g)	1 cup (63 g)
Vanilla Greek yogurt	////////	////////	½ cup
Almonds, dry roasted	////////	¼ cup (21 g)	////////
Air-Popped Popcorn (page 287)	////////	2 cups (16 g)	3 cups (24 g)

Coconut-Lime Mojito ①

SERVES 1	1500	2000	2500
Mint leaves	small handful	small handful	////////
Lime juice	1 tsp	1 Tbsp	////////
Coconut water	1½ cups	1½ cups	////////
CALORIES	72 KCAL	73 KCAL	

Muddle mint leaves with lime juice in bottom of
a glass. Add ice and pour in coconut water.

Hot Chocolate ⑤

SERVES 1	1500	2000	2500
Vanilla almond milk	1 cup	1½ cups	1½ cups
Cocoa powder	1 tsp	1 tsp	2 tsp
Honey	////////	////////	1 tsp
CALORIES	95 KCAL	141 KCAL	166 KCAL

In a large microwave-safe mug, mix together milk,
cocoa powder, and honey (if using). Place the mug in
the microwave, cover, and heat on high for 2 minutes.
Stir and heat for another minute.

Instant Noodles

SERVES 1	1500	2000	2500
Sriracha	½ tsp	½ tsp	½ tsp
Ground ginger	¼ tsp	¼ tsp	¼ tsp
Onion powder	½ tsp	½ tsp	½ tsp
Garlic powder	½ tsp	½ tsp	½ tsp
Vegetable bouillon	1 tsp	1 tsp	1 tsp
Blackstrap molasses	1 tsp	1 tsp	1 tsp
Thin rice noodles, uncooked	45 g	45 g	45 g
Kale, chopped	¼ cup (17 g)	¼ cup (17 g)	¼ cup (17 g)
Carrots, thinly sliced	¼ cup (32 g)	¼ cup (32 g)	¼ cup (32 g)
Edamame, prepared	2 Tbsp (19 g)	2 Tbsp (19 g)	2 Tbsp (19 g)
Snow peas, chopped	¼ cup (24 g)	¼ cup (24 g)	¼ cup (24 g)
Hearts of palm, sliced	¼ cup (36 g)	¼ cup (36 g)	¼ cup (36 g)
Green onions, chopped	2 Tbsp (12 g)	2 Tbsp (12 g)	2 Tbsp (12 g)
Hot water	2 cups	2 cups	2 cups
CALORIES	299 KCAL	299 KCAL	299 KCAL

❶ In a medium heat-proof bowl with a lid, combine Sriracha, ginger, onion powder, garlic powder, bouillon, molasses, rice noodles, kale, carrots, edamame, snow peas, hearts of palm, green onions, and hot water.

❷ Let sit, covered, for 3–4 minutes, until rice noodles are tender. Pour into a soup bowl and serve.

Grab and Go: Place all the ingredients, except the water, in a heat-proof container the night before. When ready to serve, fill container with 2 cups of hot water and let sit for 3–4 minutes, until noodles soften.

Roasted Butternut Squash and Spinach Salad

with Chicken, Prosciutto, and Pomegranate

SERVES 1	1500	2000	2500
For the butternut squash			
Butternut squash, cubed	1 cup (205 g)	1 cup (205 g)	1 cup (205 g)
Grapeseed oil	¼ tsp	½ tsp	½ tsp
Onion powder	½ tsp	½ tsp	½ tsp
Garlic powder	½ tsp	½ tsp	½ tsp
For the salad			
Spinach	1½ cups (45 g)	1½ cups (45 g)	1½ cups (45 g)
Chicken breast, cooked and chopped	75 g	75 g	75 g
Prosciutto	2 slices (30 g)	2 slices (30 g)	2 slices (30 g)
Red bell pepper, deseeded and sliced	¼ cup (37 g)	¼ cup (37 g)	¼ cup (37 g)
Sugar snap peas, chopped	¼ cup (25 g)	¼ cup (25 g)	¼ cup (25 g)
Pomegranate arils	¼ cup (44 g)	¼ cup (44 g)	¼ cup (44 g)
Sunflower seeds, dry roasted	¼ cup (32 g)	¼ cup (32 g)	¼ cup (32 g)
Pumpkin seeds	1 Tbsp (8 g)	1 Tbsp (8 g)	1 Tbsp (8 g)
Soft goat cheese, crumbled	1 tsp (7.5 g)	1 tsp (7.5 g)	1 tsp (7.5 g)
Balsamic Reduction (page 286)	1 tsp	1 tsp	1 tsp
Lemon wedge	1	1	1
CALORIES	515 KCAL	525 KCAL	525 KCAL

❶ Preheat the oven to 400°F. Line a baking sheet with parchment paper.
❷ Put squash, oil, onion powder, and garlic powder in a small bowl and toss to combine. Transfer to the prepared baking sheet and roast for 20–30 minutes, until fork tender.

❸ Meanwhile, in a large bowl, combine spinach, chicken, prosciutto, red peppers, sugar snap peas, pomegranate arils, sunflower seeds, pumpkin seeds, and goat cheese. When squash is ready, add to bowl and toss to combine. Drizzle balsamic reduction overtop and serve with a lemon wedge.

▽ *Cheese and Onion Crustless Quiche*

▽ *Baked Potato with Spinach Salad*

▽ *Fish Tacos with Kale Slaw and Mango Salsa*

MEAL PLAN 11

CHECKLIST*

PRODUCE
Apple (2000, 2500)
Arugula
Banana
Basil
Blackberries
Brussels sprouts
Carrots
Cherry tomatoes
Green onions
Kale
Kohlrabi
Lemon
Lime
Mango
Pineapple
Raspberries
Red bell pepper
Red cabbage
Russet potato
Shallots
Spinach

BAKERY
Corn tortillas
Whole grain bread (2500)

DELI
Sliced prosciutto

DAIRY
Cheddar cheese
Eggs
Feta cheese
Plain Greek yogurt

FROZEN
Edamame

DRY GOODS
Brown sugar (2500)
Coconut oil (2500)
Natural peanut butter
  (2500)

PREMADE
Poached Halibut (page 114)

* This list assumes that all basic ingredients (see Pantry and Freezer Staples, page 35) have been stocked.

Cheese and Onion Crustless Quiche

MAKES 6 QUICHES	1500	2000	2500
For the quiche	1 quiche	1 quiche	1 quiche
Eggs	6 large (300 g)	6 large (300 g)	6 large (300 g)
Plain Greek yogurt	3 Tbsp (53 g)	3 Tbsp (53 g)	3 Tbsp (53 g)
Cheddar cheese, shredded	½ cup (50 g)	½ cup (50 g)	½ cup (50 g)
Green onions, chopped	⅓ cup (33 g)	⅓ cup (33 g)	⅓ cup (33 g)
Prosciutto, finely chopped	4 slices (60 g)	4 slices (60 g)	4 slices (60 g)
Salt and pepper	dash each	dash each	dash each
Cooking spray			
Raspberries	1 cup (123 g)	1 cup (123 g)	1 cup (123 g)
Blackberries	½ cup (72 g)	½ cup (72 g)	½ cup (72 g)
CALORIES	232 KCAL	232 KCAL	232 KCAL

❶ Preheat the oven to 350°F. Spray a 6-cup muffin tin with cooking spray.

❷ In a medium bowl, whisk together eggs and yogurt, then fold in cheese, onions, and prosciutto. Season with a dash of salt and pepper.

❸ Pour ⅓-cup portions into the prepared muffin wells and bake for 20–25 minutes, or until center is set. Serve warm with berries.

Note: Leftover quiches will keep for up to 3 days refrigerated. Any leftovers after 3 days should be frozen.

Snacks

SERVES 1	1500	2000	2500
Vanilla, Banana, and Chocolate Smoothie 1	recipe below	recipe below	recipe below
Cinnamon-Sugar Popcorn 2	////////	////////	recipe below
Cheddar cheese, sliced	////////	20 g	////////
Apple, sliced	////////	1 (212 g)	½ (106 g)
Pistachios	⅓ cup (41 g)	////////	////////
Natural peanut butter	////////	////////	1 Tbsp
Whole grain bread	////////	////////	1 slice (24 g)

Vanilla, Banana, and Chocolate Smoothie ①

SERVES 1	1500	2000	2500
Vanilla almond milk	1¼ cups	1½ cups	1½ cups
Wheat germ	1 Tbsp	1 Tbsp	1 Tbsp
Banana	½ large (68 g)	1 large (136 g)	1 large (136 g)
Cocoa powder	1 tsp	1 tsp	1 tsp
Plain Greek yogurt	1 Tbsp	¼ cup	¼ cup
Honey	////////	1 tsp	1 tsp
CALORIES	215 KCAL	354 KCAL	354 KCAL

Put all ingredients into a blender and blend until smooth.
If the smoothie is too thick, add water (not almond milk).
If you prefer a thicker texture, add ice and blend until smooth.

Cinnamon-Sugar Popcorn ②

SERVES 1	1500	2000	2500
Air-Popped Popcorn (page 287)	////////	////////	3½ cups (28 g)
Coconut oil, melted	////////	////////	1½ tsp
Ground cinnamon	////////	////////	½ tsp
Brown sugar	////////	////////	1½ tsp
Shredded coconut, unsweetened	////////	////////	1½ tsp
CALORIES			210 KCAL

Put popcorn in a large bowl, drizzle coconut oil
overtop, and sprinkle with cinnamon, sugar, and
shredded coconut. Gently stir to combine.

Baked Potato
with Spinach Salad

SERVES 1	1500	2000	2500
For the baked potato			
Russet potato, scrubbed clean	1 (299 g)	1 (299 g)	1 (299 g)
Cherry tomatoes, halved	5 (85 g)	5 (85 g)	5 (85 g)
Sun-dried tomatoes, dry-packed	¼ cup (14 g)	¼ cup (14 g)	¼ cup (14 g)
Feta cheese, crumbled	1½ Tbsp (25 g)	1½ Tbsp (25 g)	1½ Tbsp (25 g)
Arugula	⅓ cup (7 g)	⅓ cup (7 g)	⅓ cup (7 g)
Basil leaves	5 (3 g)	5 (3 g)	5 (3 g)
Balsamic Reduction (page 286)	1½ tsp	1½ tsp	1½ tsp
For the salad			
Spinach	1½ cups (45 g)	1½ cups (45 g)	1½ cups (45 g)
Pumpkin seeds	1½ tsp	1 Tbsp	1 Tbsp
Sunflower seeds	1 Tbsp	1 Tbsp	1 Tbsp
Edamame, cooked and shelled	2½ Tbsp	¼ cup (39 g)	¼ cup (39 g)
Cherry tomatoes, halved	5 (85 g)	5 (85 g)	5 (85 g)
Flaxseeds	1 tsp	1 tsp	1 tsp
For the dressing			
Natural rice vinegar	1 tsp	1 tsp	1 tsp
Lemon juice	1 tsp	1 tsp	1 tsp
Grapeseed oil	1½ tsp	1½ tsp	1½ tsp
CALORIES	667 KCAL	719 KCAL	719 KCAL

❶ Preheat the oven to 400°F. Line a baking sheet with parchment paper.

❷ Pierce potato all over with a fork, place in microwave, and heat for 4 minutes. Flip and heat for an additional 4 minutes. Set aside to cool slightly.

❸ Place potato on the prepared baking sheet. Slice potato lengthwise, cutting halfway through potato. Use the back of a spoon to push the potato down along the opening, forming a small bowl. Top with cherry tomatoes, sun-dried tomatoes, and feta cheese. Bake for 5–10 minutes, until the cheese is golden and melted.

❹ Meanwhile, in a large bowl, combine spinach, pumpkin seeds, sunflower seeds, edamame, cherry tomatoes, and flaxseeds. In a small bowl, whisk together vinegar and lemon juice. Whisking continuously, gradually pour in oil until emulsified. Drizzle over salad and toss to combine.

❺ Transfer potato to a plate and top with arugula, basil, and balsamic reduction. Serve immediately with salad.

Fish Tacos

with Kale Slaw and Mango Salsa

SERVES 1	1500	2000	2500
For the mango salsa	2 Tbsp serving	2 Tbsp serving	2 Tbsp serving
Mango, chopped	¾ cup (132 g)	¾ cup (132 g)	¾ cup (132 g)
Pineapple, chopped	¾ cup (124 g)	¾ cup (124 g)	¾ cup (124 g)
Shallots, thinly sliced	3 Tbsp	3 Tbsp	3 Tbsp
Red bell pepper, deseeded and chopped	⅓ cup (56 g)	⅓ cup (56 g)	⅓ cup (56 g)
Lime juice	1 Tbsp	1 Tbsp	1 Tbsp
SERVES 3			
For the kale slaw	1 cup serving	1 cup serving	1 cup serving
Kale, stems removed and leaves chopped	1 cup (66 g)	1 cup (66 g)	1 cup (66 g)
Carrots, shredded	½ cup (64 g)	½ cup (64 g)	½ cup (64 g)
Kohlrabi, shredded	½ cup (68 g)	½ cup (68 g)	½ cup (68 g)
Brussels sprouts, thinly sliced	½ cup (44 g)	½ cup (44 g)	½ cup (44 g)
Red cabbage, shredded	½ cup (35 g)	½ cup (35 g)	½ cup (35 g)
SERVES 1			
For the tacos	2 tacos	2 tacos	2 tacos
Corn tortillas	2	2	2
Poached Halibut (page 114), cut in half	1	1	1
CALORIES	472 KCAL	472 KCAL	472 KCAL

❶ In a medium bowl, combine mango, pineapple, shallots, red pepper, and lime juice and mix well. (For best flavor, let marinate overnight.)
❷ When ready to serve, in a medium bowl, combine kale, carrots, kohlrabi, Brussels sprouts, and red cabbage.

❸ To assemble, place tortillas on a plate and top each with a portion of the kale slaw, halibut, and mango salsa, and serve immediately. Leftover mango salsa will keep for up to 5 days refrigerated.

▽

*Vanilla Chia Crepes
with Cream Cheese
Syrup*

▽

*White Bean
and Kale Salad*

▽

*Chicken Fingers
with Fries and
Tzatziki*

MEAL
PLAN
12

CHECKLIST*

PRODUCE
Blackberries
Blueberries (2500)
Broccoli
Carrots
Cherry tomatoes (1500, 2000)
Grapefruit (2000, 2500)
Lemon
Lime (1500, 2000)
Mint (1500, 2000)
Raspberries
Russet potatoes
Sugar snap peas

MEAT
Boneless skinless chicken breast

DAIRY
Cream cheese
Eggs
Tzatziki (page 287)

DRY GOODS
Coconut oil
Hearts of palm
Lentils, canned
Red wine vinegar
White beans, canned

PREMADE
Kale Slaw (page 130)

This list assumes that all basic ingredients (see Pantry and Freezer Staples, page 35) have been stocked.

Vanilla Chia Crepes
with Cream Cheese Syrup

MAKES ABOUT ½ CUP	1500	2000	2500
For the cream cheese syrup	2½ tsp serving	2 Tbsp serving	2½ Tbsp serving
Cream cheese, softened	¼ cup (58 g)	¼ cup (58 g)	¼ cup (58 g)
Vanilla extract	½ tsp	½ tsp	½ tsp
Pure maple syrup	1 Tbsp	1 Tbsp	1 Tbsp
Vanilla almond milk	2 Tbsp	2 Tbsp	2 Tbsp
MAKES 5			
For the crepes	2 crepes	3 crepes	3 crepes
Chia seeds	2 Tbsp	2 Tbsp	2 Tbsp
Water	6 Tbsp	6 Tbsp	6 Tbsp
Vanilla almond milk	2 cups	2 cups	2 cups
Whole grain flour	1 cup	1 cup	1 cup
Honey	3 Tbsp	3 Tbsp	3 Tbsp
Salt	¼ tsp	¼ tsp	¼ tsp
SERVES 1			
To serve			
Raspberries, puréed	½ cup (61 g)	½ cup (61 g)	1 cup (123 g)
Blackberries	½ cup (72 g)	½ cup (72 g)	½ cup (72 g)
CALORIES	467 KCAL	701 KCAL	750 KCAL

❶ Preheat the oven to 200°F. Line a baking sheet with parchment paper and place in oven.

❷ In a small bowl, whisk together cream cheese, vanilla, maple syrup, and almond milk until smooth. Set aside.

❸ In a medium bowl, combine chia seeds and water and set aside for 5 minutes, until chia seeds are gelled.

❹ In a large bowl, combine almond milk, flour, honey, and salt. Add gelled chia seeds, whisk, and set aside.

❺ Warm a large non-stick skillet over medium heat, pour ¼ cup batter into pan, and quickly tilt the skillet to spread batter in a circle. Cook for 2–3 minutes, or until crepe can be easily flipped. (The first crepe may take a bit longer to cook than the rest.) Flip crepe, cook 1 minute, then transfer to a plate. Place on the prepared baking sheet in the oven to keep warm. Repeat with remaining batter.

❻ To serve, put one crepe on a plate, fold in half, and again into quarters. Repeat with remaining crepe(s). Serve with raspberry purée, blackberries, and syrup. Leftover syrup will keep for up to 5 days refrigerated.

White Bean and Kale Salad

SERVES 1	1500	2000	2500
For the salad			
White beans, drained and rinsed	½ cup (89 g)	½ cup (89 g)	½ cup (89 g)
Lentils, drained and rinsed	¼ cup (49 g)	¼ cup (49 g)	¼ cup (49 g)
Kale Slaw (page 130)	2 cups	2 cups	2 cups
Hearts of palm, sliced	⅓ cup (49 g)	½ cup (73 g)	½ cup (73 g)
Sunflower seeds	1½ tsp	1½ tsp	1½ tsp
For the dressing			
Red wine vinegar	1 tsp	1 tsp	1½ tsp
Lemon juice	1 tsp	1 tsp	1½ tsp
Garlic powder	¼ tsp	¼ tsp	¼ tsp
Onion powder	¼ tsp	¼ tsp	¼ tsp
Grapeseed oil	1½ tsp	1½ tsp	1 Tbsp
CALORIES	323 KCAL	329 KCAL	391 KCAL

❶ In a medium bowl, combine beans, lentils, slaw, and hearts of palm and mix well. Top with sunflower seeds.

❷ In a small bowl, whisk together vinegar, lemon juice, garlic powder, and onion powder. Whisking continuously, gradually pour in oil until emulsified. Drizzle over salad and serve.

Chicken Fingers
with Fries and Tzatziki

SERVES 4		1500	2000	2500
For the fries		228 g	228 g	342 g
Water		2 cups	2 cups	2 cups
Salt		¼ tsp	¼ tsp	¼ tsp
Russet potatoes, scrubbed clean		3 large (897 g)	3 large (897 g)	3 large (897 g)
Grapeseed oil		1 Tbsp	1 Tbsp	1 Tbsp
For the chicken fingers		128 g	128 g	193 g
All-purpose flour		1 cup (125 g)	1 cup (125 g)	1 cup (125 g)
Garlic salt		2 tsp	2 tsp	2 tsp
Eggs		2 large (122 g)	2 large (122 g)	2 large (122 g)
Chicken breast, cut into 1-inch thick strips		300 g	300 g	300 g
Coconut oil		2 Tbsp	2 Tbsp	2 Tbsp
SERVES 1				
To serve				
Tzatziki (page 287)		1¼ Tbsp	1¼ Tbsp	2 Tbsp
Broccoli florets		½ cup (44 g)	½ cup (44 g)	½ cup (44 g)
Carrot sticks		½ cup (64 g)	½ cup (64 g)	½ cup (64 g)
Cherry tomatoes		5 (85 g)	5 (85 g)	////////
Sugar snap peas		1 cup (63 g)	1 cup (63 g)	1 cup (63 g)
CALORIES		640 KCAL	658 KCAL	908 KCAL

❶ In a medium bowl, combine water and salt. Cut unpeeled potatoes into ¼–½-inch-thick batons and put in a bowl of salted water, adding more water if necessary to fully cover batons. Refrigerate for at least 1 hour, but ideally 24 hours.

❷ Preheat the oven to 400°F. Line two baking sheets with parchment paper. Rub coconut oil on one of them.

❸ Drain water from potatoes and toss batons with oil. Spread batons evenly on the prepared baking sheet without coconut oil. Put fries on bottom rack of oven and bake for 10 minutes.

❹ In a large resealable plastic bag, combine flour and garlic salt and set aside.

❺ Crack eggs into a shallow bowl and whisk until combined. Dip chicken strips in eggs, put into plastic bag, seal bag, and shake to evenly coat chicken.

❻ Remove chicken strips from bag, shaking off excess flour, and place on baking sheet. Put chicken on the middle rack of the oven, bake 10 minutes, flip, and bake for another 10 minutes, until fries are golden brown and internal temperature of chicken reaches 165°F.

❼ To serve, put chicken and fries on a plate and serve with tzatziki and vegetables.

Life Made Easier: When making homemade fries, potato wedges, hash browns, etc., soaking the potatoes in salted water for at least an hour, or overnight, removes excess starchiness from the potatoes, resulting in fries that are crispy on the outside and soft on the inside.

Snacks

SERVES 1	1500	2000	2500
Coconut-Lime Mojito 2	recipe below	recipe below	////////
Vanilla almond milk	1 cup	////////	////////
Grapefruit	////////	1 large (256 g)	1 large (256 g)
Air-Popped Popcorn (page 287)	////////	3 cups (24 g)	3 cups (24 g)
Pistachios	////////	////////	¼ cup (31 g)
Blueberries	////////	////////	½ cup (72 g)
Dark chocolate	////////	15 g	10 g

Coconut-Lime Mojito ②

SERVES 1	1500	2000	2500
Mint leaves	small handful	small handful	////////
Lime juice	1 Tbsp	1 Tbsp	////////
Coconut water	1¼ cup	1¼ cup	////////
CALORIES	61 KCAL	61 KCAL	

Muddle mint leaves with lime juice in bottom of
a glass. Add ice and pour in coconut water.

MEAL PLAN 13

CHECKLIST*

PRODUCE
Baby carrots
Baby potatoes
Banana
Beet
Blueberries (2500)
Garlic
Green beans
Kohlrabi
Lemon (1500)
Lime (2000)
Mango (2000, 2500)
Mint (2000)
Orange (2500)
Pomegranate arils
Raspberries (1500, 2000)
Spinach
Sugar snap peas (2500)
Tomato
Yellow onion

MEAT
Broiler chicken, 4–5 lbs

BAKERY
Whole grain bun, low sodium

DAIRY
Butter
Cheddar cheese
Eggs
Feta cheese
Plain Greek yogurt (1500)
Vanilla Greek yogurt (2000, 2500)

DRY GOODS
Dried blueberries
Hearts of palm
Walnuts

* *This list assumes that all basic ingredients (see Pantry and Freezer Staples, page 35) have been stocked.*

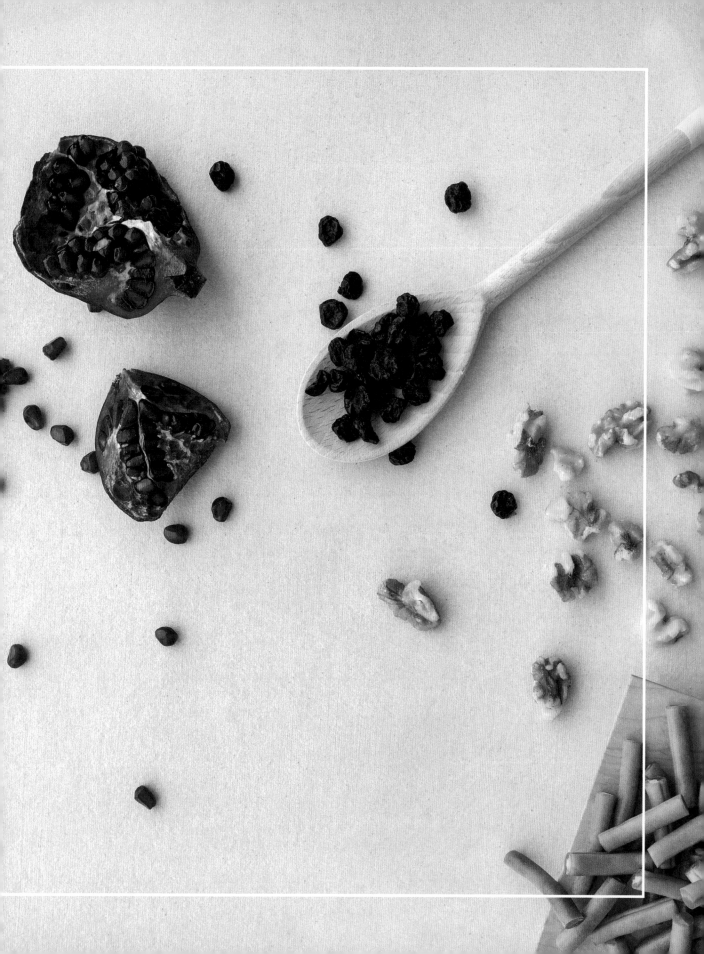

Breakfast Sandwich

SERVES 1	1500	2000	2500
Egg	1 large (50 g)	1 large (50 g)	1 large (50 g)
Egg white	////////	////////	1 large (33 g)
Whole grain bun	1 (52 g)	1 (52 g)	1 (52 g)
Mayonnaise	1½ tsp	1½ tsp	1½ tsp
Cheddar cheese, sliced	15 g	15 g	15 g
Tomato, sliced	2–3 slices (50 g)	2–3 slices (50 g)	2–3 slices (50 g)
Cooking spray			
To serve			
Raspberries	1 cup (123 g)	½ cup (61 g)	////////
Mango, sliced	////////	1 cup (165 g)	1 cup (165 g)
Blueberries	////////	////////	1 cup (145 g)
CALORIES	367 KCAL	442 KCAL	508 KCAL

❶ Spray a small microwave-safe bowl with cooking spray. Crack egg and egg white (if using) into bowl and whisk. Microwave egg for 1 minute and 20 seconds, until egg is fully cooked.

❷ To assemble sandwich, cut bun in half and evenly spread mayo on bottom bun. Top with cheddar, egg, tomato, and the top half of bun. Serve with fruit.

Snacks

SERVES 1	1500	2000	2500
Vanilla, Banana, and Chocolate Smoothie 2	recipe below	recipe below	recipe below
Coconut-Lime Mojito 3	/////////	recipe below	/////////
Sugar snap peas	/////////	/////////	1 cup (63 g)
Orange	/////////	/////////	1 (131 g)
Air-Popped Popcorn (page 287)	/////////	2 cups (16 g)	3½ cups (28 g)

Vanilla, Banana, and Chocolate Smoothie ②

SERVES 1	1500	2000	2500
Blackstrap molasses	1 Tbsp	1 Tbsp	/////////
Cocoa powder	2 tsp	2 tsp	1 Tbsp
Wheat germ	2 Tbsp	2 tsp	/////////
Banana	1 small (101 g)	1 large (136 g)	1 large (136 g)
Plain Greek yogurt	1 Tbsp	/////////	/////////
Vanilla Greek yogurt	/////////	½ cup	½ cup
Coconut water	¾ cup	/////////	/////////
Vanilla almond milk	1 cup	1½ cups	1½ cups
Honey	/////////	/////////	1 tsp
CALORIES	336 KCAL	442 KCAL	402 KCAL

Put all ingredients into a blender and blend until smooth.
If the smoothie is too thick, add water (not coconut water
or almond milk). If you prefer a thicker texture, add ice
and blend until smooth.

Coconut-Lime Mojito ③

SERVES 1	1500	2000	2500
Mint leaves	/////////	small handful	/////////
Lime juice	/////////	1½ tsp	/////////
Coconut water	/////////	1¼ cups	/////////
CALORIES		59 KCAL	

Muddle mint leaves with lime juice in bottom of
a glass. Add ice and pour in coconut water.

Green Bean, Feta, and Pomegranate Salad

SERVES 1	1500	2000	2500
For the salad			
Green beans, cut into 1-inch lengths	1 cup (110 g)	1 cup (110 g)	1½ cups (165 g)
Feta cheese, crumbled	2 tsp (10 g)	2 tsp (10 g)	1½ Tbsp (22.5 g)
Pomegranate arils	¼ cup (44 g)	¼ cup (44 g)	⅓ cup (66 g)
Dried blueberries	2 Tbsp (20 g)	2 Tbsp (20 g)	⅓ cup (53 g)
Walnuts, chopped	2 Tbsp (12 g)	2 Tbsp (12 g)	3 Tbsp (18 g)
For the dressing	1½ tsp serving	1½ tsp serving	1½ tsp serving
Balsamic vinegar	2 tsp	2 tsp	2 tsp
Honey	½ tsp	½ tsp	½ tsp
Grapeseed oil	1 Tbsp	1 Tbsp	1 Tbsp
CALORIES	277 KCAL	383 KCAL	619 KCAL

❶ In a medium bowl, combine beans, cheese, pomegranate arils, blueberries, and walnuts.
❷ In a small bowl, whisk together vinegar and honey. Whisking continuously, gradually pour in oil until emulsified. Drizzle over salad and serve.

Roast Chicken

with Baby Potatoes, Baby Carrots, and Spinach Salad

SERVES 6	1500	2000	2500
For the chicken	75 g white meat, 50 g dark meat, 335 g vegetables	75 g white meat, 75 g dark meat, 335 g vegetables	75 g white meat, 75 g dark meat, 335 g vegetables
Grapeseed oil, plus extra for brushing	3 Tbsp	3 Tbsp	3 Tbsp
Broiler chicken	1	1	1
Yellow onion	¼ large (38 g)	¼ large (38 g)	¼ large (38 g)
Butter	1 Tbsp	1 Tbsp	1 Tbsp
Baby potatoes	4 cups (508 g)	4 cups (508 g)	4 cups (508 g)
Baby carrots	4 cups (1.4 kg)	4 cups (1.4 kg)	4 cups (1.4 kg)
Garlic	2 heads	2 heads	2 heads
3 sprigs rosemary			
3 sprigs thyme			
SERVES 1			
For the salad			
Spinach	2 cups (60 g)	2 cups (60 g)	2 cups (60 g)
Beet, spiralized or shredded	¼ cup (34 g)	¼ cup (34 g)	¼ cup (34 g)
Kohlrabi, spiralized or shredded	¼ cup (34 g)	¼ cup (34 g)	¼ cup (34 g)
Hearts of palm, sliced	⅓ cup (49 g)	⅓ cup (49 g)	⅓ cup (49 g)
For the dressing			
Natural rice vinegar	1½ tsp	////////	////////
Balsamic vinegar	////////	1 tsp	2 tsp
Lemon juice	1 tsp	////////	////////
Honey	////////	¼ tsp	½ tsp
Grapeseed oil	////////	1½ tsp	1 Tbsp
CALORIES	541 KCAL	613 KCAL	745 KCAL

❶ Preheat the oven to 350°F. Pour oil in a roasting pan.

❷ Using paper towel, pat chicken dry. Check cavity of chicken for giblets and remove if there are any. Stuff onions and butter in cavity of chicken. Put chicken in a large Dutch oven, breast-side down with wings lying on top of chicken breasts. (They will burn if they are tucked under the chicken.) Scatter potatoes and carrots around chicken. Cut off top half of garlic head and brush with oil. Add to pan with rosemary and thyme. Cover pan and roast for 1 hour and 30 minutes.

❸ Remove pan from oven, flip chicken so breast side faces up, then put back in oven uncovered and cook for 15 minutes, or just long enough for skin to turn golden brown. Chicken is done when internal temperature reaches 180°F and juices run clear.

❹ Meanwhile, in a medium bowl, toss together spinach, beets, kohlrabi, and hearts of palm. In a small bowl, whisk together vinegar, lemon juice (if using), and honey (if using). Gradually pour in oil (if using), whisking continuously until emulsified. Drizzle over salad.

❺ Serve chicken with roasted vegetables and salad.

Note: Leftover chicken and vegetables will keep for 2 days refrigerated. You can use leftover chicken for meal plans that require precooked chicken, like 2, 8, 15, 16, 22, and 30. Any leftovers after 2 days should be frozen.

⏷ **Mango, Ginger, and White Chocolate Scones**

⏷ **Greek Wrap**

⏷ **Creamy Corn, Ham, and Roasted Red Pepper Chowder**

MEAL PLAN 14

CHECKLIST*

PRODUCE
Alfalfa sprouts
Apple (2500)
Baby potatoes
Banana
Blackberries (2000, 2500)
Cherry tomatoes
Collard greens, large leaves
Cucumber
Onion
Raspberries
Red bell pepper
Shallot
Spinach
Sugar snap peas (2500)
White mushrooms

MEAT
Black forest ham, low sodium

DAIRY
Butter
Buttermilk
Egg (2000, 2500)
Feta cheese
Hummus (page 287)
Milk
Parmesan cheese
Tzatziki (page 287)
Vanilla Greek yogurt
  (2000, 2500)

FROZEN
Spinach

DRY GOODS
Almond butter (2500)
Candied ginger
Couscous
Dried mango
Hearts of palm (1500, 2000)
Sugar
White chocolate

This list assumes that all basic ingredients (see Pantry and Freezer Staples, page 35) have been stocked.

Mango, Ginger, and White Chocolate Scones

MAKES 12	1500	2000	2500
For the scones	1½ scones	1½ scones	2 scones
Butter, chilled and diced	½ cup	½ cup	½ cup
Sugar	1 Tbsp	1 Tbsp	1 Tbsp
Buttermilk	1 cup + 2 Tbsp	1 cup + 2 Tbsp	1 cup + 2 Tbsp
All-purpose flour	2½ cups (312 g)	2½ cups (312 g)	2½ cups (312 g)
Baking powder	2¼ tsp	2¼ tsp	2¼ tsp
Baking soda	1¼ tsp	1¼ tsp	1¼ tsp
Flaxseeds	¼ cup	¼ cup	¼ cup
White chocolate, chopped	½ cup (85 g)	½ cup (85 g)	½ cup (85 g)
Dried mango, chopped	½ cup (68 g)	½ cup (68 g)	½ cup (68 g)
Candied ginger, chopped	¼ cup (35 g)	¼ cup (35 g)	¼ cup (35 g)
All-purpose flour, to dust			
SERVES 1			
To serve			
Raspberries	1 cup (123 g)	½ cup (61 g)	1 cup (123 g)
Blackberries	////////	½ cup (72 g)	½ cup (72 g)
Vanilla Greek yogurt	////////	½ cup (150 g)	½ cup (151 g)
Hard-boiled egg	////////	1 large (50 g)	1 large (50 g)
CALORIES	447 KCAL	627 KCAL	787 KCAL

❶ Preheat the oven to 325°F. Line a baking sheet with parchment paper.

❷ In a large bowl, combine butter, sugar, buttermilk, flour, baking powder, and baking soda. Using a stand mixer fitted with the paddle attachment, mix on medium speed until ingredients are just combined. Add flaxseeds and mix for another 5 seconds. The dough should be wet to the touch.

❸ Add chocolate, mango, and ginger to mixer and mix for 5 seconds, until combined.

❹ Transfer dough to a floured surface and gently flatten with your hand until 1-inch thick. Cut dough into 6 even squares, and then cut diagonally into triangles. Place, evenly spaced, on the prepared baking sheet. Bake for 20–25 minutes, or until golden brown on top.

❺ Serve with berries, yogurt (if using), and egg (if using).

Life Made Easier: *When adding frozen or fresh fruit to baking, lightly coat the fruit in flour before adding them to the wet ingredients. This prevents the fruit from falling to the bottom of the baked good when baking, giving the final product a professional appearance. The same can be done when adding chocolate.*

Freezer Friendly: *Put unbaked scones onto a baking sheet and freeze. Once solid, place them in an airtight container or freezer bag and store for up to 2 months. To serve, bake them according to instructions, adding another 3–4 minutes.*

Greek Wrap

SERVES 1	1500	2000	2500
Collard leaf, stem removed	1 large leaf (18 g)	1 large leaf (18 g)	1 large leaf (18 g)
Hummus (page 287)	3 Tbsp	3 Tbsp	3 Tbsp
Tzatziki (page 287)	3 Tbsp	3 Tbsp	3 Tbsp
Cooked couscous	¼ cup (39 g)	¼ cup (39 g)	¼ cup (39 g)
Cherry tomatoes, halved	5 (85 g)	5 (85 g)	5 (85 g)
Cucumber, sliced	⅓ cup (40 g)	⅓ cup (40 g)	⅓ cup (40 g)
Feta cheese, crumbled	1 Tbsp (15 g)	1 Tbsp (15 g)	1 Tbsp (15 g)
Shallot, minced	1½ tsp	1½ tsp	1½ tsp
Alfalfa sprouts, well rinsed	½ cup (17 g)	½ cup (17 g)	½ cup (17 g)
CALORIES	221 KCAL	221 KCAL	221 KCAL

Lay collard leaf flat on a large plate and evenly spread hummus and tzatziki overtop. Top with couscous, tomatoes, cucumber, feta, shallots, and alfalfa sprouts. Fold top and bottom of leaf halfway over the filling. Then fold left and right sides of leaf over, tightly sealing all the filling inside the collard wrap.

Note: If collard green leaf is too tough to handle, roll up and put in a pot of boiling water for 30 seconds. Immediately transfer to an ice water bath, and then proceed with recipe.

Creamy Corn, Ham, and Roasted Red Pepper Chowder

SERVES 8	1500	2000	2500
For the chowder	1½ cups (465 g)	1½ cups (465 g)	2¼ cups (700 g)
Corn, frozen	3 cups (492 g)	3 cups (492 g)	3 cups (492 g)
Red bell peppers, deseeded and chopped	3 (357 g)	3 (357 g)	3 (357 g)
Grapeseed oil, divided	1 Tbsp	1 Tbsp	1 Tbsp
Onion, chopped	1 large (150 g)	1 large (150 g)	1 large (150 g)
Black forest ham, cubed	2 cups (276 g)	2 cups (276 g)	2 cups (276 g)
Baby potatoes	2 cups (340 g)	2 cups (340 g)	2 cups (340 g)
All-purpose flour	2 Tbsp	2 Tbsp	2 Tbsp
Milk	8 cups	8 cups	8 cups
Parmesan cheese	3 Tbsp (19 g)	3 Tbsp (19 g)	3 Tbsp (19 g)
SERVES 1			
For the salad			
Spinach	2 cups (60 g)	1½ cups (45 g)	1½ cups (45 g)
Cherry tomatoes, halved	6 (102 g)	6 (102 g)	6 (102 g)
Sun-dried tomatoes, dry-packed	¼ cup (14 g)	¼ cup (14 g)	¼ cup (14 g)
White mushrooms, sliced	⅓ cup (23 g)	⅓ cup (23 g)	⅓ cup (23 g)
Pumpkin seeds	1½ tsp	1 Tbsp	1 Tbsp
Sunflower seeds	1½ tsp	1½ tsp	1½ tsp
For the dressing			
Balsamic vinegar	1 tsp	2 tsp	2 tsp
Honey	¼ tsp	½ tsp	½ tsp
Grapeseed oil	1½ tsp	1 Tbsp	1 Tbsp
CALORIES	536 KCAL	644 KCAL	808 KCAL

❶ Preheat the oven to 350°F. Line a baking sheet with parchment paper.

❷ In a large bowl, toss corn and peppers with 1½ tsp oil, put on prepared baking sheet, and roast for 10–15 minutes.

❸ Meanwhile, heat the remaining 1½ tsp oil in a large skillet over medium-high heat, add onions and sauté for 3–5 minutes, until translucent and fragrant.

❹ Add onions, ham, potatoes, roasted corn, and peppers into a slow cooker. Stir in flour until everything is evenly coated. Add milk and Parmesan and whisk until combined. Cook on low for 6–8 hours.

❺ When ready to serve, make a bed of spinach in a salad bowl or on a large plate. Top with cherry tomatoes, sun-dried tomatoes, mushrooms, and seeds. In a small bowl, whisk together vinegar and honey. Whisking continuously, gradually pour in oil until emulsified. Drizzle over salad.

Life Made Easier: This is a great slow-cooker recipe designed for meal planning and people on the go. If you don't have a slow cooker, simply make the recipe in a large pot and simmer for 30 minutes, or until potatoes are tender. When roasting peppers, don't be afraid to char the skins. This gives the peppers a nice smoky flavor and makes the skin easier to peel off.

Snacks

SERVES 1	1500	2000	2500
Tropical Green Smoothie	recipe below	recipe below	recipe below
Air-Popped Popcorn (page 287)	¾ cup (6 g)	2 cups (16 g)	3 cups (24 g)
Sugar snap peas	/ / / / / / /	/ / / / / / /	½ cup (32 g)
Apples with Almond Butter	/ / / / / / /	/ / / / / / /	recipe below

Tropical Green Smoothie

SERVES 1	1500	2000	2500
Spinach, frozen	⅔ cup (104 g)	½ cup (78 g)	½ cup (78 g)
Flaxseeds	1½ tsp	1½ tsp	1½ tsp
Wheat germ	1 Tbsp	1 Tbsp	/ / / / / / /
Mango, fresh or frozen	⅔ cup (110 g)	1 cup (165 g)	1 cup (165 g)
Hearts of palm	½ cup (73 g)	½ cup (73 g)	/ / / / / / /
Strawberries, fresh or frozen	½ cup (110 g)	1 cup (221 g)	1 cup (221 g)
Banana, frozen	½ large (68 g)	1 (118 g)	1 (118 g)
Coconut water	1 cup	1¼ cups	/ / / / / / /
Vanilla almond milk	/ / / / / / /	/ / / / / / /	1 cup
CALORIES	318 KCAL	430 KCAL	445 KCAL

Put all ingredients into a blender and blend until smooth.
If the smoothie is too thick, add water (not coconut water or
almond milk). If you prefer a thicker texture, add ice and
blend until smooth.

Apples with Almond Butter

SERVES 1	1500	2000	2500
Ground cinnamon	/ / / / / / /	/ / / / / / /	½ tsp
Apple, sliced	/ / / / / / /	/ / / / / / /	1 large (212 g)
Almond butter	/ / / / / / /	/ / / / / / /	1½ tsp
CALORIES			162 KCAL

In a small bowl, mix together cinnamon and
apple slices. Serve with almond butter.

▽
**Butternut Squash
Pancakes**

▽
**Mango BBQ Chicken
Pizza**

▽
**Stuffed Squash with
Tahini Sauce**

MEAL PLAN 15

CHECKLIST*

PRODUCE
Acorn squash
Avocado (2500)
Blueberries (2500)
Cantaloupe
Cherry tomatoes
Garlic
Green onions
Lemon
Mango
Orange (2500)
Raspberries (1500)
Red bell pepper
Red onion
Spinach
Sugar snap peas (2000, 2500)

BAKERY
8-inch whole wheat tortilla

MEAT
Cooked boneless skinless
   chicken breast
Mild Italian turkey sausage

DAIRY
Egg
Mozzarella cheese
Plain Greek yogurt
Vanilla Greek yogurt (2500)

FROZEN
Butternut squash

DRY GOODS
Barbecue sauce
Extra-virgin olive oil
Tahini
Tomato purée, no salt
   (1500, 2000)
Vegetable broth
Walnuts
White vinegar

* This list assumes that all basic ingredients (see Pantry and Freezer Staples, page 35) have been stocked.

Butternut Squash Pancakes

MAKES 12 PANCAKES	1500	2000	2500
For the pancakes	4 pancakes	4 pancakes	4 pancakes
Chia seeds	1 Tbsp	1 Tbsp	1 Tbsp
Water	3 Tbsp	3 Tbsp	3 Tbsp
Butternut squash, frozen	3 cups (720 g)	3 cups (720 g)	3 cups (720 g)
Plain Greek yogurt	⅓ cup	⅓ cup	⅓ cup
Coconut water	⅓ cup	⅓ cup	⅓ cup
Whole grain flour	1 cup (120 g)	1 cup (120 g)	1 cup (120 g)
Flaxseeds	⅓ cup (40 g)	⅓ cup (40 g)	⅓ cup (40 g)
Wheat germ	3 Tbsp	3 Tbsp	3 Tbsp
Onion powder	1 tsp	1 tsp	1 tsp
Garlic powder	1 tsp	1 tsp	1 tsp
Mozzarella cheese, shredded	⅓ cup (37 g)	⅓ cup (37 g)	⅓ cup (37 g)
Green onions, chopped	½ cup (50 g)	½ cup (50 g)	½ cup (50 g)
Cooking spray			
SERVES 1			
For the topping			
Tomato purée	⅓ cup (83 g)	⅓ cup (83 g)	////////
White vinegar	1 Tbsp	1 Tbsp	1 Tbsp
Egg	1 small (38 g)	1 large (50 g)	1 large (50 g)
CALORIES	510 KCAL	572 KCAL	495 KCAL

❶ Preheat the oven to 200°F.

❷ In a small bowl, mix together chia seeds and water and set aside to gel.

❸ Put squash in a large microwave-safe bowl and heat for 2–3 minutes in the microwave. Mash until smooth. Add the gelled chia seeds, yogurt, and coconut water and mix well.

❹ In a medium bowl, mix together flour, flaxseeds, wheat germ, onion powder, and garlic powder. Add flour mixture to squash mixture and stir until just combined. Fold in cheese and onions.

❺ Heat a large skillet over medium-high heat and spray with cooking spray. Ladle ¼ cup batter into the skillet and cook 2–3 minutes, until edges of pancake start to dry and slightly turn golden brown. Flip and cook another 1–2 minutes, or until edges look dry and no longer glisten.

Place pancake on an ovenproof plate and keep warm in the oven. Repeat for remaining batter.

❻ Bring a large pot of water to a boil. When water begins to simmer, mix in vinegar. When the water reaches a boil, gently stir water in a circular motion to create a little whirlpool. While whirlpool is spinning, crack egg into the pot. Leave egg to cook for 3–5 minutes. Remove with a slotted spoon. Serve with tomato purée (if using) and poached egg.

Mix It Up: This batter also makes delicious waffles. To make, preheat a waffle iron and spray with cooking spray. Add a third of the batter (about 1½ cups) to the iron and cook one waffle per serving for all three calorie diets.

Snacks

SERVES 1	1500	2000	2500
Hot Chocolate 6	recipe below	recipe below	recipe below
Cantaloupe, chopped	½ cup (80 g)	1 cup (160 g)	1 cup (160 g)
Raspberries	½ cup (61 g)	////////	////////
Mango, chopped	////////	¾ cup (124 g)	½ cup (82 g)
Blueberries	////////	////////	½ cup (72 g)
Vanilla Greek yogurt	////////	////////	½ cup (151 g)
Coconut water	1 cup	////////	////////
Sugar snap peas	////////	1 cup (63 g)	1 cup (63 g)
Orange	////////	////////	1 large (184 g)
Air-Popped Popcorn (page 287)	////////	////////	3 cups (24 g)

Hot Chocolate ⑥

SERVES 1	1500	2000	2500
Vanilla almond milk	1 cup	1½ cups	1½ cups
Cocoa powder	2 tsp	1 Tbsp	2 tsp
Honey	////////	1 tsp	1½ tsp
CALORIES	101 KCAL	170 KCAL	177 KCAL

In a microwave-safe mug, mix together milk, cocoa
powder, and honey (if using). Warm for 2 minutes.
Stir and warm for an additional minute.

Mango BBQ Chicken Pizza

SERVES 1	1500	2000	2500
For the pizza	½ pizza	1 pizza	1 pizza
Whole wheat tortilla	1 (48 g)	1 (48 g)	1 (48 g)
Barbecue sauce	1 Tbsp	1 Tbsp	1 Tbsp
Mango, cubed	⅓ cup (55 g)	⅓ cup (55 g)	⅓ cup (55 g)
Cooked chicken breast, cubed	⅓ cup (47 g)	⅓ cup (47 g)	⅓ cup (47 g)
Mozzarella cheese, shredded	3½ Tbsp (25 g)	3½ Tbsp (25 g)	3½ Tbsp (25 g)
Flat-leaf parsley, to garnish			
For the salad			
Spinach	2¼ cups (67 g)	1½ cups (45 g)	1½ cups (45 g)
Cherry tomatoes, halved	6 (102 g)	6 (102 g)	6 (102 g)
Avocado, sliced	////////	////////	⅓ (67 g)
Walnuts, chopped	1 Tbsp (6 g)	1 Tbsp (6 g)	1 Tbsp (6 g)
Flaxseeds	¼ tsp	¼ tsp	¼ tsp
Sunflower seeds	1 Tbsp	1½ tsp	////////
For the dressing			
Natural rice vinegar	1 Tbsp	////////	////////
Balsamic vinegar	////////	1 tsp	1 tsp
Honey	////////	¼ tsp	¼ tsp
Grapeseed oil	////////	1½ tsp	1½ tsp
CALORIES	298 KCAL	509 KCAL	593 KCAL

❶ Preheat the oven to 325°F. Line a baking sheet with parchment paper.
❷ Put tortilla on baking sheet and spread barbecue sauce evenly overtop. Top with mango, chicken, and mozzarella and bake for 5–7 minutes, until cheese is melted and bubbling.

❸ Meanwhile, make a bed of spinach in a salad bowl or on a large plate. Top with tomatoes, avocado (if using), walnuts, flaxseeds, and sunflower seeds (if using). In a small bowl, whisk together vinegar and honey (if using). Whisking continuously, gradually pour in oil (if using) until emulsified. Drizzle over salad.

Stuffed Squash
with Tahini Sauce

MAKES ABOUT ⅔ CUP	1500	2000	2500
For the tahini sauce	2½ tsp serving	1 Tbsp serving	2 Tbsp serving
Roasted Garlic (page 287)	2 heads	2 heads	2 heads
Tahini	½ cup	½ cup	½ cup
Water	⅓ cup	⅓ cup	⅓ cup
Lemon juice	2 Tbsp	2 Tbsp	2 Tbsp
Cooking spray			
SERVES 2			
For the squash	½ squash	½ squash	½ squash
Acorn squash, halved, seeds and stringy bits removed	1 (410 g)	1 (410 g)	1 (410 g)
Extra-virgin olive oil	1½ tsp	1½ tsp	1½ tsp
Onion powder	½ tsp	½ tsp	½ tsp
Black pepper	¼ tsp	¼ tsp	¼ tsp
Quinoa	¼ cup	¼ cup	¼ cup
Vegetable broth	½ cup	½ cup	½ cup
Mild Italian turkey sausage, casing removed, crumbled	100 g	100 g	100 g
Red bell pepper, deseeded and chopped	¼ cup (37 g)	¼ cup (37 g)	¼ cup (37 g)
Red onion, minced	¼ cup (40 g)	¼ cup (40 g)	¼ cup (40 g)
Spinach, chopped	2 cups (60 g)	2 cups (60 g)	2 cups (60 g)
Mozzarella cheese, shredded	2 Tbsp (14 g)	2 Tbsp (14 g)	2 Tbsp (14 g)
CALORIES	541 KCAL	613 KCAL	745 KCAL

❶ Preheat the oven to 400°F. Line a baking sheet with parchment paper.

❷ Trim a small portion off the top and bottom of squash and then cut in half. Brush each cut half with oil, then season with onion powder and pepper. Bake for 30 minutes, until fork tender.

❸ Meanwhile, prepare the quinoa. Put quinoa and broth into a medium saucepan and bring to a boil, uncovered, over high heat. Reduce heat to a simmer, cover, and cook for 15–20 minutes, until all the liquid is absorbed and quinoa is fluffy.

❹ Place sausage in a skillet and cook on medium-high heat for 12–15 minutes, until fully cooked. Transfer to a mixing bowl and set aside.

❺ In the same skillet, add peppers and onions and sauté for 3–5 minutes, until softened.

❻ Add spinach and cook for another 30 seconds. Remove from heat.

❼ Add quinoa and vegetables to the bowl with the cooked sausage and stir to combine. Spoon mixture into each squash. Top with shredded mozzarella and broil for 1–2 minutes, until cheese turns golden and begins to bubble.

❽ To make tahini sauce, remove garlic cloves by pinching the end to squeeze out cloves and put them all in a food processor or blender. (Alternatively, use a fork to remove the cloves.) Add the tahini, water, and lemon juice and blend until smooth. Serve squash with tahini sauce.

▽
Chocolate Chia Pudding with Strawberry Sauce

▽
Spinach and Egg Salad

▽
Chicken Noodle Soup

MEAL PLAN 16

CHECKLIST*

PRODUCE
Avocado
Banana
Blueberries (2500)
Broccoli (2000)
Carrots
Celery
Cremini mushrooms
Cucumber (2000)
Dill
Orange (1500)
Orange juice (2500)
Shallot
Spinach
Strawberries (1500)
Watermelon (2000, 2500)

DELI
Sliced prosciutto

MEAT
Cooked boneless skinless
  chicken thighs and breast

DAIRY
Cheddar cheese
Egg
Hummus (page 287) (2000)
Parmesan cheese
Vanilla Greek yogurt

FROZEN
Pineapple

DRY GOODS
Cacao nibs
Chocolate almond milk
Multigrain rotini noodles
Shallot Dressing (page 70)

This list assumes that all basic ingredients (see Pantry and Freezer Staples, page 35) have been stocked.

Chocolate Chia Pudding
with Strawberry Sauce

SERVES 3		1500	2000	2500
For the pudding		1 serving	1 serving	1 serving
Chocolate almond milk		2 cups	2 cups	2 cups
Dark chocolate, roughly chopped		30 g	30 g	30 g
Chia seeds		¼ cup	¼ cup	¼ cup
Vanilla Greek yogurt		½ cup	½ cup	½ cup
Cacao nibs, plus extra to garnish		2 Tbsp	2 Tbsp	2 Tbsp
Cocoa powder		1 Tbsp	1 Tbsp	1 Tbsp
Strawberries, frozen		2¼ cups (500 g)	2¼ cups (500 g)	2¼ cups (500 g)
Honey		1½ tsp	1½ tsp	1½ tsp
CALORIES		356 KCAL	356 KCAL	356 KCAL

❶ In a small saucepan, bring almond milk to a gentle simmer over medium-low heat. Add chocolate and stir until melted. Set aside to cool.

❷ Pour the chocolate mixture into a large bowl and add chia seeds, yogurt, cacao nibs, and cocoa powder. Cover and refrigerate for at least 3 hours or overnight, until set.

❸ When ready to serve, in a medium saucepan, warm strawberries and honey over medium-low heat for 5–7 minutes, until strawberries are defrosted and liquid comes to a gentle simmer.

❹ Using a potato masher or an immersion blender, roughly mash the strawberries until chunky.

❺ Pour the chia seed mixture into three bowls and top with the strawberry sauce. Serve immediately or put back in the fridge to grab for a quick breakfast on the go. Leftovers will keep for up to a week refrigerated.

Spinach and Egg Salad

SERVES 1	1500	2000	2500
Spinach	3 cups (90 g)	3 cups (90 g)	3 cups (90 g)
Shallot, thinly sliced	1 Tbsp	1 Tbsp	1 Tbsp
Cremini mushrooms, sliced	½ cup (108 g)	½ cup (108 g)	½ cup (108 g)
Cheddar cheese, shredded	2 Tbsp (10 g)	3 Tbsp (15 g)	3 Tbsp (15 g)
Pumpkin seeds	4 tsp	1½ Tbsp	2 Tbsp
Sun-dried tomatoes, dry-packed, chopped	¼ cup (14 g)	////////	////////
Hard-boiled egg, sliced	1 small (38 g)	1 large (50 g)	1 large (50 g)
Avocado, sliced	¼ (50 g)	½ (101 g)	½ (101 g)
Prosciutto	1 slice (15 g)	2 slices (30 g)	2 slices (30 g)
Shallot Dressing (page 70)	1½ Tbsp	1½ Tbsp	1½ Tbsp
CALORIES	466 KCAL	589 KCAL	613 KCAL

❶ In a large bowl, combine spinach, shallot, mushrooms, cheddar, pumpkin seeds, sun-dried tomatoes (if using), egg, and avocado.

❷ Warm a small skillet over medium heat. Add prosciutto and cook for 30 seconds on one side, flip, and cook for another 30 seconds to a minute, until prosciutto is crispy and golden brown. Crumble over salad.

❸ Drizzle dressing over salad and serve.

Note: *For a lighter, summery version of the salad, do not fry the prosciutto; slice it into strips instead.*

Chicken Noodle Soup

SERVES 4	1500	2000	2500
For the soup	1 serving	1 serving	1½ servings
Chicken Stock (page 287)	6 cups	6 cups	6 cups
Carrots, chopped	2 large (144 g)	2 large (144 g)	2 large (144 g)
Celery stalk, chopped	1 (64 g)	1 (64 g)	1 (64 g)
Cooked chicken thighs, chopped	½ cup (70 g)	½ cup (70 g)	½ cup (70 g)
Cooked chicken breast, chopped	½ cup (70 g)	½ cup (70 g)	½ cup (70 g)
Multigrain rotini noodles, cooked	1½ cups (140 g)	1½ cups (140 g)	1½ cups (140 g)
Fresh dill, to garnish (optional)	4 Tbsp	4 Tbsp	4 Tbsp
SERVES 1			
Parmesan cheese	////////	1 tsp	1½ tsp
CALORIES	383 KCAL	388 KCAL	603 KCAL

❶ Add stock, carrots, and celery to a stockpot and bring to a boil over high heat, then reduce heat to medium-low and simmer for 15–20 minutes, until carrots and celery are tender. Add chicken and noodles and cook for another 2–3 minutes, until warmed through.

❷ Ladle soup into a bowl, sprinkle dill and Parmesan (if using) overtop, and serve. Leftovers will keep for up to 2 days refrigerated. Any leftovers after 2 days can be frozen.

Snacks

SERVES 1	1500	2000	2500
Morning Smoothie	recipe below	recipe below	recipe below
Orange	½ small (66 g)	/ / / / / / /	/ / / / / / /
Strawberries	6 (72 g)	/ / / / / / /	/ / / / / / /
Broccoli florets	/ / / / / / /	1 cup (88 g)	/ / / / / / /
Cucumber	/ / / / / / /	½ cup (59 g)	/ / / / / / /
Hummus (page 287)	/ / / / / / /	2 Tbsp	/ / / / / / /
Watermelon, chopped	/ / / / / / /	1½ cup (228 g)	1 cup (152 g)
Blueberries	/ / / / / / /	/ / / / / / /	1 cup (145 g)
Air-Popped Popcorn (page 287)	/ / / / / / /	2 cups (16 g)	3 cups (24 g)
Dark chocolate	/ / / / / / /	/ / / / / / /	30 g

Morning Smoothie

SERVES 1	1500	2000	2500
Pineapple, frozen	½ cup (77 g)	1 cup (155 g)	1 cup (155 g)
Mango, frozen	⅔ cup (110 g)	1 cup (165 g)	1 cup (165 g)
Banana, frozen	1 large (136 g)	1 large (136 g)	1 large (136 g)
Wheat germ	1 Tbsp	/ / / / / / /	/ / / / / / /
Vanilla almond milk	½ cup	½ cup	/ / / / / / /
Coconut water	¾ cup	1 cup	/ / / / / / /
Vanilla Greek yogurt	/ / / / / / /	⅓ cup	½ cup
Orange juice	/ / / / / / /	/ / / / / / /	1 cup
CALORIES	337 KCAL	470 KCAL	528 KCAL

Put all ingredients into a blender and blend until smooth.
If the smoothie is too thick, add water (not almond milk,
coconut water, or orange juice). If you prefer a thicker texture,
add ice and blend until smooth.

▽   ▽   ▽

Britt's Brussels   *Turkey Crepe Sandwich*   *Sole en Papillote with Roasted Vegetables*

MEAL PLAN 17

CHECKLIST*

PRODUCE
Alfalfa sprouts
Asparagus
Baby potatoes
Blueberries (2500)
Brussels sprouts
Carrots
Cherry tomatoes
Cucumber
Garlic
Grapes
Green onion
Lemon
Mango
Pineapple (2500)
Raspberries (1500)
Red bell pepper
Spinach
Sugar snap peas
Yellow bell pepper
Zucchini

DELI
Sliced prosciutto
Sliced turkey breast

BAKERY
Whole grain bread, low sodium

FISH
Sole

DAIRY
Boursin® Garlic & Fine Herbs
Butter
Cheddar cheese
Eggs
Milk
Parmesan cheese
Vanilla Greek yogurt (2500)

DRY GOODS
Flaxseed meal
Granola (page 287) (2500)
Whole grain mustard

   * This list assumes that all basic ingredients (see Pantry and Freezer Staples, page 35) have been stocked.

Britt's Brussels

SERVES 1	1500	2000	2500
Brussels sprouts, trimmed, leaves separated	2 cups (176 g)	2 cups (176 g)	2 cups (176 g)
Butter	1½ tsp	1½ tsp	1½ tsp
Garlic, thinly sliced	2 cloves	2 cloves	2 cloves
Whole grain bread	1 slice (29 g)	1 slice (29 g)	1 slice (29 g)
Boursin® Garlic & Fine Herbs	½ tsp	1½ tsp	1½ tsp
Egg, sunny-side up	1 large (50 g)	1 large (50 g)	1 large (50 g)
Pumpkin seeds	1 Tbsp	1 tsp	1 tsp
Mango	⅓ cup (55 g)	1 cup (165 g)	1 cup (165 g)
CALORIES	384 KCAL	444 KCAL	552 KCAL

❶ Wash and dry Brussels sprout leaves. Set aside.
❷ Melt butter in a large skillet over medium heat. Add garlic and sauté for 1 minute. Add Brussels sprout leaves and cook for 10–15 minutes, until leaves crisp.
❸ Toast bread and spread Boursin® overtop. Top with Brussels sprouts, egg, and pumpkin seeds, and serve with mango. You will soon discover why my sister's go-to breakfast is now one of my favorites!

Note: Instead of a sunny-side up egg, you can make this recipe with a poached or fried egg.

Turkey Crepe Sandwich

SERVES 4		1500	2000	2500
For the crepes		1 crepe	1 crepe	1 crepe
All-purpose flour		½ cup (62 g)	½ cup (62 g)	½ cup (62 g)
Salt		¼ tsp	¼ tsp	¼ tsp
Milk		¾ cup	¾ cup	¾ cup
Egg whites		2 large (66 g)	2 large (66 g)	2 large (66 g)
Egg		1 large (50 g)	1 large (50 g)	1 large (50 g)
Flaxseed meal		1 Tbsp	1 Tbsp	1 Tbsp
SERVES 1				
For the sandwich				
Prosciutto		1 slice (15 g)	1 slice (15 g)	1 slice (15 g)
Mayonnaise		2 tsp	1 Tbsp	1 Tbsp
Whole grain mustard		1½ tsp	1½ tsp	1½ tsp
Cheddar cheese, sliced		15 g	20 g	25 g
Turkey breast, sliced		50 g	60 g	75 g
Cucumber, sliced		⅓ cup (40 g)	⅓ cup (40 g)	⅓ cup (40 g)
Cherry tomatoes, halved		5 (85 g)	5 (85 g)	5 (85 g)
Spinach		¾ cup (22 g)	½ cup (15 g)	½ cup (15 g)
Alfalfa sprouts, well rinsed		1 cup (33 g)	1 cup (33 g)	1 cup (33 g)
Flaxseeds		1½ tsp	1½ tsp	2 tsp
CALORIES		392 KCAL	444 KCAL	665 KCAL

❶ In a medium bowl, mix together flour, salt, milk, eggs, and flaxseed meal. Stir until well combined.

❷ Heat a non-stick skillet over medium-low heat, ladle in a quarter of the batter, and tilt skillet to evenly spread the batter. Cook for 1 minute and then carefully flip. Cook for another minute. Place crepe on plate and repeat until all the batter has been used up.

❸ Warm skillet over medium-high heat. Add prosciutto and cook for 30 seconds on one side, flip, and cook another 30 seconds to 1 minute, until crispy and golden brown. Remove from heat and set aside.

❹ Spread mayonnaise and mustard on a quarter of a crepe. Top with cheese, turkey, prosciutto, cucumber, tomatoes, spinach, sprouts, and flaxseeds. Carefully fold the crepe in half and then into a quarter and serve.

Note: Leftover crepes can be used in Lemon-Ricotta Crepes, page 182.

Grab and Go: Recipe can be made the night before and refrigerated. Store cucumbers and tomatoes in a separate resealable container and add them to sandwich just before serving to avoid crepe becoming soggy.

Snacks

SERVES 1	1500	2000	2500
Yogurt Parfait 2	/////////	/////////	recipe below
Vanilla-Cinnamon Steamer 1	recipe below	recipe below	recipe below
Grapes	1 cup (154 g)	1½ cups (231 g)	1½ cups (231 g)
Air-Popped Popcorn (page 287)	/////////	2 cups (16 g)	2 cups (16 g)
Sugar snap peas	1¼ cups (79 g)	1 cup (63 g)	1 cup (63 g)
Pistachios	/////////	¼ cup (31 g)	⅓ cup (41 g)
Pineapple, chopped	/////////	/////////	1 cup (155 g)
Dark chocolate	/////////	/////////	15 g
Raspberries	½ cup (61 g)	/////////	/////////

Yogurt Parfait ②

SERVES 1	1500	2000	2500
Vanilla Greek yogurt	/////////	/////////	⅓ cup
Blueberries	/////////	/////////	½ cup (72 g)
Granola (page 287)	/////////	/////////	1½ Tbsp
CALORIES			202 KCAL

Put yogurt in a small glass and top with
blueberries and granola.

Vanilla-Cinnamon Steamer ①

SERVES 1	1500	2000	2500
Vanilla almond milk	1½ cups	1½ cups	1½ cups
Vanilla extract	¼ tsp	½ tsp	½ tsp
Ground cinnamon	¼ tsp	½ tsp	½ tsp
Honey	/////////	½ tsp	1 tsp
CALORIES	141 KCAL	157 KCAL	167 KCAL

Put all ingredients into a microwave-safe mug
and mix well. Cover and microwave on high for
2 minutes. Stir and microwave for another minute.

Sole en Papillote
with Roasted Vegetables

SERVES 1	1500	2000	2500
For the roasted vegetables			
Asparagus spears	8 (128 g)	8 (128 g)	8 (128 g)
Zucchini, chopped	1 cup (113 g)	1 cup (113 g)	1 cup (113 g)
Baby potatoes, whole	1½ cups (190 g)	1½ cups (190 g)	1½ cups (190 g)
Carrots, chopped	2 small (110 g)	2 small (110 g)	2 small (110 g)
Garlic, finely chopped	2 tsp	2 tsp	2 tsp
Rosemary, chopped	½ tsp	½ tsp	½ tsp
Grapeseed oil	1 tsp	2 tsp	2 tsp
Parmesan cheese, shredded	1½ tsp	1 Tbsp	1 Tbsp
Lemon juice	1 tsp	1 tsp	1 tsp
For the fish			
Sole fillet, deboned and skinned	1 (90 g)	1 (90 g)	1 (90 g)
Red bell pepper, deseeded and cut into strips	½ (60 g)	½ (60 g)	½ (60 g)
Yellow bell pepper, deseeded and cut into strips	½ large (93 g)	½ large (93 g)	½ large (93 g)
Green onion, cut into strips	1 large (25 g)	1 large (25 g)	1 large (25 g)
Garlic, finely chopped	1 clove	1 clove	1 clove
Butter	½ tsp	½ tsp	½ tsp
CALORIES	496 KCAL	529 KCAL	529 KCAL

❶ Preheat the oven to 400°F. Line a baking sheet with parchment paper.

❷ In a large bowl, combine asparagus, zucchini, potatoes, carrots, garlic, rosemary, and oil and mix well. Place vegetables on the prepared baking sheet and sprinkle Parmesan overtop. Roast the vegetables for 20–25 minutes, until they are fork tender. Sprinkle lemon juice over vegetables, cover with tinfoil to keep warm, and set aside.

❸ Reduce oven to 350°F.

❹ To make a parchment paper pouch for the fish, cut a piece of parchment to arm's length. Fold in half widthwise, then fold each side over about an inch, leaving the top of the pocket open.

❺ Gently place fish in the pouch and add peppers, onions, garlic, and butter. Fold top of pouch closed, place on a baking sheet, and bake for 10–15 minutes, or until fish is opaque, white, and flaky. (Safe internal temperature for fish is 158°F.)

❻ Serve fish with the roasted vegetables.

Note: Be careful when opening pouch as a lot of steam will be released.

Healthy Choices: Grapeseed oil is high in polyunsaturated fats (the good kind!), including omega-6. It also has a higher smoke point, which means you can use it for high-temperature cooking methods, such as frying.

MEAL PLAN 18

CHECKLIST*

PRODUCE
Alfalfa sprouts
Baby potatoes
Banana
Blackberries (1500)
Blueberries (2000, 2500)
Broccoli
Brussels sprouts
Cantaloupe
Carrots
Granny Smith apple
Lemon
Onion
Orange (2500)
Raspberries (1500, 2000)
Spinach
Strawberries (2000, 2500)
Sugar snap peas (2000, 2500)

BAKERY
Whole grain bread

MEAT
Bacon
Pork tenderloin

DAIRY
Butter
Egg
Hummus (page 287)
  (2000, 2500)
Milk
Ricotta cheese, part skim

DRY GOODS
Walnuts (1500, 2000)

PREMADE
Crepes (page 176)

This list assumes that all basic ingredients (see Pantry and Freezer Staples, page 35) have been stocked.

Lemon-Ricotta Crepe

SERVES 1	1500	2000	2500
Crepe(s) (page 176)	1	2	2
MAKES ABOUT ½ CUP			
For the filling	3 Tbsp serving	¼ cup serving	6 Tbsp serving
Ricotta cheese	½ cup (123 g)	½ cup (123 g)	½ cup (123 g)
Honey	1½ tsp	1½ tsp	1½ tsp
Lemon juice	1½ tsp	1½ tsp	1½ tsp
SERVES 1			
To serve			
Raspberries	1 cup (123 g)	½ cup (61 g)	////////
Blackberries	1 cup (144 g)	////////	////////
Strawberries, sliced	////////	½ cup (83 g)	½ cup (83 g)
Blueberries	////////	½ cup (72 g)	½ cup (72 g)
Walnuts, chopped	1½ Tbsp	1½ Tbsp	////////
Pure maple syrup	½ tsp	1 Tbsp	1 Tbsp
CALORIES	388 KCAL	546 KCAL	503 KCAL

❶ In a small bowl, whisk together ricotta, honey, and lemon juice. Set aside.

❷ Warm crepe in skillet over medium-low heat for 30 seconds on each side. Transfer crepe to a plate. Repeat for remaining crepe (if using).

❸ Spoon filling down the center(s) of crepe(s). Gently roll up crepe(s) and serve with fruit, walnuts (if using), and syrup.

Snacks

SERVES 1	1500	2000	2500
Chocolate-Vanilla Smoothie	recipe below	recipe below	recipe below
Orange	/ / / / / / / /	/ / / / / / / /	1 (131 g)
Air-Popped Popcorn (page 287)	1½ cups (12 g)	2 cups (16 g)	2 cups (16 g)
Broccoli florets	½ cup (44 g)	/ / / / / / / /	/ / / / / / / /
Cantaloupe, chopped	/ / / / / / / /	1 cup (160 g)	1 cup (160 g)
Dark chocolate	/ / / / / / / /	15 g	20 g
Pistachios	/ / / / / / / /	/ / / / / / / /	¼ cup (31 g)

Chocolate-Vanilla Smoothie

SERVES 1	1500	2000	2500
Blackstrap molasses	1 Tbsp + 1 tsp	/ / / / / / / /	/ / / / / / / /
Wheat germ	1 Tbsp	1 Tbsp	1 Tbsp
Cocoa powder	2 tsp	2 tsp	2 tsp
Banana	½ small (51 g)	1 (118 g)	1 large (136 g)
Ice	1 cup	1 cup	1 cup
Vanilla almond milk	1⅓ cups	1½ cups	1½ cups
Honey	/ / / / / / / /	/ / / / / / / /	1½ tsp
CALORIES	264 KCAL	276 KCAL	367 KCAL

Put all ingredients into a blender and blend until smooth.
If the smoothie is too thick, add water (not almond milk). If you
prefer a thicker texture, add more ice and blend until smooth.

Spicy Egg Salad on a Chia-Flax Bagel

MAKES 6	1500	2000	2500
For the bagel	1 bagel	1 bagel	1 bagel
Chia seeds	1 Tbsp	1 Tbsp	1 Tbsp
Water	3 Tbsp	3 Tbsp	3 Tbsp
Sunflower seeds	½ tsp	½ tsp	½ tsp
Pumpkin seeds	1 Tbsp	1 Tbsp	1 Tbsp
Whole grain flour	1 cup (120 g)	1 cup (120 g)	1 cup (120 g)
Baking powder	½ tsp	½ tsp	½ tsp
Baking soda	½ tsp	½ tsp	½ tsp
Flaxseeds	3 Tbsp	3 Tbsp	3 Tbsp
Honey	1 Tbsp	1 Tbsp	1 Tbsp
Milk	½ cup	½ cup	½ cup
Butter, melted	2 Tbsp	2 Tbsp	2 Tbsp
Cooking spray			
SERVES 1			
For the egg salad			
Egg, hard-boiled and chopped	1 large (50 g)	1 large (50 g)	1 large (50 g)
Mayonnaise	1½ tsp	1½ tsp	1½ tsp
Sriracha	¼ tsp	¼ tsp	¼ tsp
For the topping			
Spinach	¼ cup (8 g)	¼ cup (8 g)	¼ cup (8 g)
Alfalfa sprouts, well rinsed	½ cup (17 g)	½ cup (17 g)	½ cup (17 g)
To serve			
Cantaloupe, chopped	1 cup (160 g)	////////	////////
Broccoli florets	////////	½ cup (44 g)	½ cup (44 g)
Sugar snap peas	////////	1 cup (63 g)	1 cup (63 g)
Hummus (page 287)	////////	2 Tbsp	2 Tbsp
CALORIES	341 KCAL	382 KCAL	380 KCAL

❶ Preheat the oven to 350°F.

❷ Mix together chia seeds and water in a small bowl and set aside to gel.

❸ Spray a 6-cavity donut pan with cooking spray and evenly distribute sunflower seeds and pumpkin seeds into each ring. Set aside.

❹ In a large measuring cup, combine flour, baking powder, baking soda, and flaxseeds.

❺ In a separate small bowl, whisk together honey, milk, and butter. Add gelled chia seeds and stir. Add the wet ingredients to the dry ingredients and stir until just combined. (Do not overmix or the bagels will be very dense.) Divide batter evenly among donut rings and bake for 12–15 minutes, until lightly golden. Set aside to cool.

❻ Meanwhile, in a small bowl, gently mix together egg, mayonnaise, and Sriracha.

❼ To assemble sandwich, slice bagel in half, evenly spread egg salad filling over one half, and top with spinach, alfalfa sprouts, and the other half of the bagel.

❽ Serve with cantaloupe (if using) or vegetables and hummus (if using).

Note: You can freeze the extra bagels in an airtight container or resealable freezer bag for up to 2 months.

Grab and Go: Make bagels and egg salad the night before and assemble in the morning.

Healthy Choices: While a store-bought bagel—typically made from white flour—counts for a minimum of four grain portions, these smaller bagels are made with whole grain flour and numerous seeds, which boost their nutrient density.

Stuffed Pork Roast

SERVES 5	1500	2000	2500
For the pork	256 g pork	256 g pork	384 g pork
Pork tenderloin	2 lbs	2 lbs	2 lbs
Onion, finely chopped	¼ large (38 g)	¼ large (38 g)	¼ large (38 g)
Granny Smith apple, cored and diced	1 large (206 g)	1 large (206 g)	1 large (206 g)
Whole grain bread, cubed	1 slice (26 g)	1 slice (26 g)	1 slice (26 g)
Ricotta cheese	¼ cup (62 g)	¼ cup (62 g)	¼ cup (62 g)
Bacon, cooked and crumbled	1½ tsp	1½ tsp	1½ tsp
Butter	1 Tbsp	1 Tbsp	1 Tbsp
Rosemary	1 Tbsp	1 Tbsp	1 Tbsp
Thyme	1½ Tbsp	1½ Tbsp	1½ Tbsp
Grapeseed oil, divided	3 Tbsp	3 Tbsp	3 Tbsp
For the Brussels sprouts	1 cup (88 g)	1 cup (88 g)	1 cup (88 g)
Brussels sprouts, whole	5 cups (440 g)	5 cups (440 g)	5 cups (440 g)
For the carrots	⅓ cup (43 g)	½ cup (64 g)	½ cup (64 g)
Carrots, chopped	1⅔ cups (212 g)	1⅔ cups (212 g)	1⅔ cups (212 g)
For the potatoes	⅓ cup (125 g)	¾ cup (173 g)	¾ cup (173 g)
Baby potatoes	3¾ cups (865 g)	3¾ cups (865 g)	3¾ cups (865 g)
CALORIES	532 KCAL	585 KCAL	765 KCAL

❶ Place tenderloin on cutting board. Using a sharp knife, butterfly the tenderloin. Firmly place your hand flat on top of the tenderloin. Hold your knife so that it's parallel to the cutting board and carefully cut the side of the tenderloin lengthwise, cutting about halfway through (you don't want to cut it in half), until you are about a ½ inch from the end. Open the tenderloin so it lays flat.

❷ In a medium bowl, mix together onions, apples, bread, ricotta, bacon, butter, herbs, and 2 Tbsp oil. Spread filling over the meat, then roll up the tenderloin lengthwise. Use butcher twine to tie the stuffed roast together.

❸ Heat a skillet over medium-high heat. Rub the outside of the pork with remaining 1 Tbsp oil, put in skillet, and cook each side of the roast for 2–3 minutes, until browned.

❹ Place the stuffed roast into a slow cooker, add the Brussels sprouts, carrots, and potatoes (while keeping them separate from each other, so they can easily be portioned out later) and 1 cup of water, and cook on low for 8–10 hours.

❺ To serve, cut tenderloin into 5 even portions, remove butcher twine, and place on plate. Serve with Brussels sprouts, carrots, and potatoes on the side.

▽

Prosciutto Cup

▽

Quinoa Taco Bowl

▽

Spaghetti Squash Bowl with Sun-Dried Tomatoes, Mozzarella, and Pesto

MEAL PLAN 19

CHECKLIST*

PRODUCE
Banana (2000, 2500)
Beets
Blueberries
Carrots
Collard greens
Green onions
Kohlrabi
Raspberries (1500, 2000)
Spaghetti squash
Spinach
Strawberries (2500)
Watermelon

DELI
Sliced prosciutto

BAKERY
Whole grain bread (2500)

DAIRY
Cheddar cheese
Cottage cheese, dry curd
Eggs
Mozzarella cheese
Plain Greek yogurt
Ricotta cheese, part skim
Vanilla Greek yogurt
  (2000, 2500)

FROZEN
Papaya (2000, 2500)
Pineapple (2000, 2500)

DRY GOODS
Basil Pesto (page 286)
Coconut milk beverage
  (2000, 2500)
Natural peanut butter
  (2500)
Salsa
Tomato purée

* This list assumes that all basic ingredients (see Pantry and Freezer Staples, page 35) have been stocked.

Prosciutto Cup

MAKES 1	1500	2000	2500
Prosciutto	2 slices (30 g)	2 slices (30 g)	2 slices (30 g)
Tomato purée	⅓ cup	⅓ cup	⅓ cup
Egg	1 large (50 g)	1 large (50 g)	1 large (50 g)
Egg white	1 large (33 g)	1 large (33 g)	1 large (33 g)
Plain Greek yogurt	1 Tbsp	1 Tbsp	1 Tbsp
Cottage cheese	2 Tbsp (18 g)	2 Tbsp (18 g)	2 Tbsp (18 g)
Sun-dried tomatoes, dry-packed, chopped	2 Tbsp (7 g)	2 Tbsp (7 g)	2 Tbsp (7 g)
Collard greens, stems removed, leaves roughly chopped	⅓ cup (12 g)	⅓ cup (12 g)	⅓ cup (12 g)
SERVES 1			
To serve			
Blueberries	½ cup (72 g)	½ cup (72 g)	1 cup (145 g)
Raspberries	⅓ cup (41 g)	½ cup (61 g)	////////
Strawberries	////////	////////	1 cup (166 g)
Whole grain bread	////////	////////	1 slice (29 g)
Natural peanut butter	////////	////////	1½ tsp
CALORIES	293 KCAL	304 KCAL	496 KCAL

❶ Preheat the oven to 350°F.

❷ Overlap prosciutto in a small ovenproof dish to make a small prosciutto bowl. Pour tomato purée into the prosciutto bowl.

❸ In a separate small bowl, whisk together eggs, yogurt, cottage cheese, sun-dried tomatoes, and collard greens. Pour egg mixture over tomato purée and bake for 25–30 minutes, or until eggs have set and are cooked through. Serve with fruit and toast and peanut butter (if using).

Snacks

SERVES 1	1500	2000	2500
Tropical Smoothie 2	////////	recipe below	recipe below
Hot Chocolate 7	recipe below	////////	////////
Watermelon, chopped	½ cup (76 g)	1 cup (152 g)	1 cup (152 g)
Air-Popped Popcorn (page 287)	1½ cups (12 g)	////////	3 cups (24 g)
Pistachios	////////	¼ cup (31 g)	¼ cup (31 g)
Cheddar cheese, sliced	////////	////////	15 g
Dried apricots	////////	////////	¼ cup (63 g)
Dark chocolate	////////	////////	15 g

Tropical Smoothie ②

SERVES 1	1500	2000	2500
Papaya, fresh or frozen	////////	⅓ cup (47 g)	½ cup (70 g)
Pineapple, fresh or frozen	////////	⅓ cup (52 g)	½ cup (77 g)
Mango, fresh or frozen	////////	⅓ cup (55 g)	½ cup (82 g)
Banana	////////	1 large (136 g)	1 large (136 g)
Vanilla Greek yogurt	////////	⅓ cup	⅓ cup
Coconut milk beverage	////////	1 cup	1 cup
Coconut water	////////	1 cup	////////
CALORIES		359 KCAL	354 KCAL

Put all ingredients into a blender and blend until smooth.
If the smoothie is too thick, add water (not coconut milk
beverage or coconut water). If you prefer a thicker texture,
add ice and blend until smooth.

Hot Chocolate ⑦

SERVES 1	1500	2000	2500
Vanilla almond milk	1 cup	////////	////////
Cocoa powder	1 tsp	////////	////////
CALORIES	95 KCAL		

Mix together milk and cocoa in a microwave-safe
mug. Cover and microwave on high for 2 minutes,
stir, and heat for another minute.

Quinoa Taco Bowl

SERVES 1	1500	2000	2500
Cooked Quinoa (page 286)	1 cup (139 g)	1 cup (139 g)	1 cup (139 g)
Black beans, drained and rinsed	½ cup (86 g)	½ cup (86 g)	½ cup (86 g)
Corn, defrosted	½ cup (82 g)	½ cup (82 g)	½ cup (82 g)
Green onions, chopped	¼ cup (25 g)	¼ cup (25 g)	¼ cup (25 g)
Salsa	¼ cup (66 g)	¼ cup (66 g)	¼ cup (66 g)
Cheddar cheese, shredded	2 Tbsp (10 g)	2 Tbsp (10 g)	2 Tbsp (10 g)
CALORIES	412 KCAL	412 KCAL	412 KCAL

In a medium bowl, combine quinoa, beans, corn, and green onions. Top with salsa and cheddar and serve.

Grab and Go: Prepare the night before or in the morning, store in a resealable container, and enjoy at lunch.

Spaghetti Squash Bowl

with Sun-Dried Tomatoes, Mozzarella, and Pesto

SERVES 1	1500	2000	2500
For the squash bowl			
Spaghetti squash, halved lengthwise, seeds removed	½ (310 g)	½ (310 g)	½ (310 g)
Ricotta cheese	⅓ cup (82 g)	⅓ cup (82 g)	⅓ cup (82 g)
Basil Pesto (page 286)	2 tsp	2 tsp	2 tsp
Tomato purée	1 cup (250 g)	1 cup (250 g)	1 cup (250 g)
Sun-dried tomatoes, dry-packed, chopped	⅓ cup (18 g)	⅓ cup (18 g)	⅓ cup (18 g)
Mozzarella cheese, shredded	¼ cup (28 g)	¼ cup (28 g)	¼ cup (28 g)
For the salad			
Spinach	1½ cups (45 g)	1½ cups (45 g)	1½ cups (45 g)
Carrots, shredded	¼ cup (32 g)	¼ cup (32 g)	½ cup (64 g)
Beet, shredded	2 Tbsp	2 Tbsp	2 Tbsp
Kohlrabi, shredded	2 Tbsp	2 Tbsp	2 Tbsp
Flaxseeds	2 tsp	2 tsp	2 tsp
Sunflower seeds	1 Tbsp	1 Tbsp	1 Tbsp
For the dressing			
Balsamic vinegar	2 tsp	2 tsp	2 tsp
Honey	½ tsp	½ tsp	½ tsp
Grapeseed oil	1 Tbsp	1 Tbsp	1 Tbsp
CALORIES	699 KCAL	699 KCAL	712 KCAL

❶ Preheat the oven to 400°F. Line a baking sheet with parchment paper.

❷ Place squash, cut-side down, on the prepared baking sheet and bake 30–45 minutes, until fork tender. When cool enough to handle, use fork to separate squash into "spaghetti."

❸ Meanwhile, combine ricotta and pesto in a small bowl and stir. Top spaghetti squash with tomato purée and ricotta mixture, and scatter sun-dried tomatoes and mozzarella overtop.

❹ Bake for another 20–30 minutes, until sauce starts to bubble. Broil for a minute, until cheese is golden brown and bubbling.

❺ Meanwhile, make a bed of spinach in a salad bowl or on a large plate. Top with carrots, beets, kohlrabi, flaxseeds, and sunflower seeds. In a small bowl, whisk together vinegar and honey. Whisking continuously, gradually pour in oil until emulsified. Drizzle over salad.

❻ Serve squash bowl with salad.

▽
*Creamy Berry
Farina Cereal*

▽
*Asian Lettuce
Wraps*

▽
*Turkey Sausage and
Zucchini Pizza Loaf
with Spinach Salad*

MEAL PLAN
20

CHECKLIST*

PRODUCE
Butter lettuce
Cantaloupe
Carrots
Carrot juice
Cremini mushrooms
Cucumber
Garlic
Ginger
Grapes (2500)
Green onions
Mango
Onion
Orange juice
Portobello mushrooms
Raspberries
Spinach
Sugar snap peas (1500)
Zucchini

BAKERY
Whole grain loaf

MEAT
Ground chicken
Turkey sausage

DAIRY
Egg (2500)
Mozzarella cheese

FROZEN
Blackberries (2000, 2500)
Blueberries
Edamame (1500, 2000)
Raspberries (1500, 2000)

DRY GOODS
Carbonated water
Maple sugar
Ponzu sauce
Red wine vinegar
Roasted peanuts
Water chestnuts
Wheat farina

This list assumes that all basic ingredients (see Pantry and Freezer Staples, page 35) have been stocked.

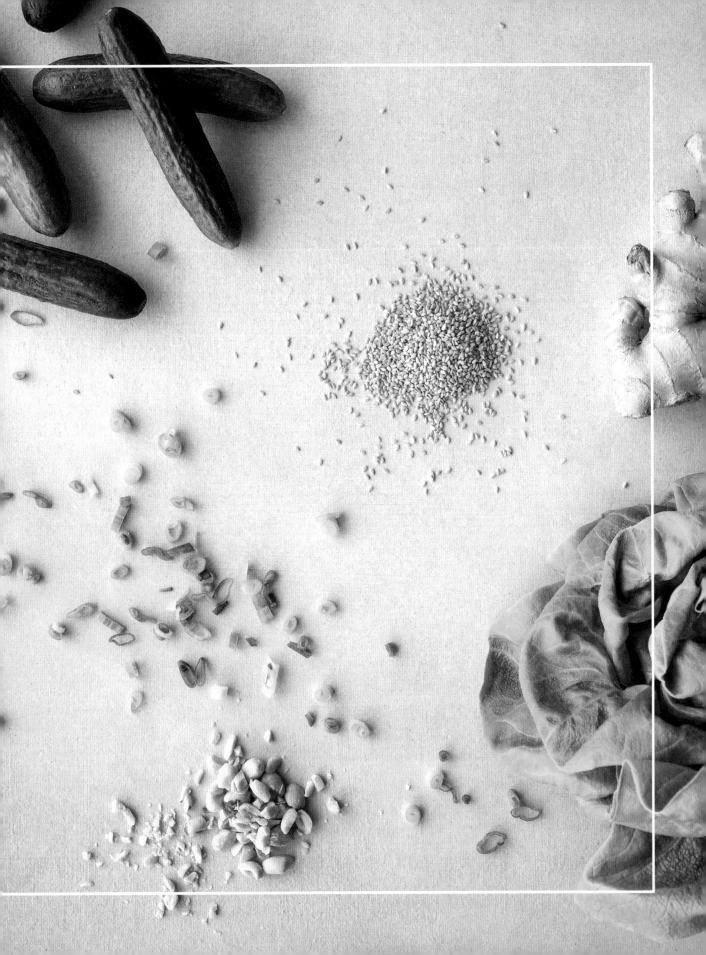

Creamy Berry Farina Cereal

SERVES 1	1500	2000	2500
Vanilla almond milk	1 cup	1 cup	1 cup
Wheat farina	¼ cup (44 g)	¼ cup (44 g)	¼ cup (44 g)
Strawberries, frozen	½ cup (110 g)	½ cup (110 g)	¾ cup (166 g)
Blueberries, frozen	½ cup (77 g)	½ cup (77 g)	¾ cup (116 g)
Raspberries, frozen	¼ cup (31 g)	¼ cup (31 g)	////////
Blackberries, frozen	////////	¼ cup (38 g)	¼ cup (38 g)
Water	2 Tbsp	2 Tbsp	2 Tbsp
Honey	////////	1 tsp	1 Tbsp
Maple sugar	½ tsp	1 Tbsp	1 Tbsp + 1 tsp
To serve			
Vanilla almond milk	////////	¼ cup	////////
Hard-boiled egg	////////	////////	1 large (50 g)
CALORIES	414 KCAL	450 KCAL	575 KCAL

❶ In a medium saucepan, bring almond milk to a boil over medium-high heat. Add wheat farina, reduce heat to medium-low, and stir for 3 minutes, until mixture thickens.

❷ In a separate medium saucepan, combine berries, water, and honey (if using) and simmer over medium heat for 5–7 minutes, until berries break down.

❸ Put wheat farina in a bowl, top with warm berries, and scatter maple sugar overtop. Serve with more almond milk (if using) and egg (if using).

Snacks

SERVES 1	1500	2000	2500
Chia and Fruit Fizz	recipe below	recipe below	recipe below
Cantaloupe, chopped	1 cup (160 g)	1 cup (160 g)	1¼ cup (200 g)
Sugar snap peas	1 cup (63 g)	////////	////////
Air-Popped Popcorn (page 287)	////////	2 cups (16 g)	3 cups (24 g)
Pistachios	////////	////////	⅓ cup (41 g)
Grapes	////////	////////	1½ cups (231 g)

Chia and Fruit Fizz

SERVES 1	1500	2000	2500
Coconut water	½ cup + ⅓ cup	½ cup	½ cup
Chia seeds	1½ Tbsp	1½ Tbsp	1½ Tbsp
Raspberries	¼ cup (31 g)	¼ cup (31 g)	¼ cup (31 g)
Mango	¼ cup (41 g)	⅓ cup (55 g)	½ cup (82 g)
Orange juice	¼ cup	½ cup	½ cup
Carbonated water	½ cup	½ cup	½ cup
Carrot juice	¼ cup	¼ cup	¼ cup
CALORIES	210 KCAL	232 KCAL	250 KCAL

❶ Pour ½ cup coconut water into a small resealable container, stir in chia seeds, and place in refrigerator overnight, to let chia seeds gel.
❷ When ready to serve, put raspberries in a small bowl and lightly mash.

❸ Put mango into a blender and blend. Pour mango purée into a glass, spoon in raspberries, add chia seed mixture, ⅓ cup coconut water (if using), orange juice, carbonated water, and carrot juice, and lightly stir to combine. Serve cold.

Asian Lettuce Wraps

MAKES 6		1500	2000	2500
For the wraps		2 wraps	2 wraps	2 wraps
Blackstrap molasses		3 Tbsp	3 Tbsp	3 Tbsp
Low-sodium soy sauce		3 Tbsp	3 Tbsp	3 Tbsp
Ponzu sauce		1 Tbsp	1 Tbsp	1 Tbsp
Garlic, smashed		2 cloves	2 cloves	2 cloves
Ginger, grated		2 tsp	2 tsp	2 tsp
Ground chicken		450 g	450 g	450 g
Water chestnuts, sliced		½ cup (70 g)	½ cup (70 g)	½ cup (70 g)
Butter lettuce leaves, whole		6 large	6 large	6 large
Carrots, diced		½ cup (64 g)	½ cup (64 g)	½ cup (64 g)
Cucumber, diced		½ cup (59 g)	½ cup (59 g)	½ cup (59 g)
Green onions, sliced		⅓ cup (33 g)	⅓ cup (33 g)	⅓ cup (33 g)
Roasted peanuts, chopped		1½ Tbsp	1½ Tbsp	1½ Tbsp
Sesame seeds, toasted		1 Tbsp	1 Tbsp	1 Tbsp
Cooking spray				
SERVES 1				
Edamame		¼ cup (39 g)	⅓ cup (52 g)	////////
CALORIES		399 KCAL	414 KCAL	351 KCAL

❶ In a small bowl, combine molasses, soy sauce, and ponzu sauce and mix well. Set aside.

❷ Spray a large skillet with cooking spray and warm over medium heat. Add garlic and ginger and cook for 1–2 minutes, until fragrant. Add chicken and cook for 5–8 minutes, until fully cooked. Pour in the molasses mixture, add water chestnuts, and cook for another 2–3 minutes, until sauce has heated through.

❸ Put lettuce leaves on a plate and divide chicken mixture, carrots, cucumber, water chestnuts, and green onions evenly among leaves. Sprinkle peanuts and sesame seeds overtop. Serve with edamame (if using).

Grab and Go: Prepare chicken mixture the night before, cool, and store in a resealable container in the refrigerator. In a separate resealable container, store butter lettuce leaves along with carrots, cucumber, green onions, edamame (if using), peanuts (omit if you work in a peanut-free environment), and sesame seeds. When ready to serve, warm chicken mixture for 45 seconds to 1 minute in the microwave. Evenly distribute chicken mixture between two lettuce leaves and top with vegetables, nuts, and seeds.

Turkey Sausage and Zucchini Pizza Loaf

with Spinach Salad

MAKES 10 SLICES	1500	2000	2500
For the pizza loaf	1 slice	2 slices	2 slices
Onion, sliced	½ large (75 g)	½ large (75 g)	½ large (75 g)
Turkey sausage, casing removed, crumbled	2 (182 g)	2 (182 g)	2 (182 g)
Zucchini, sliced	1 large (323 g)	1 large (323 g)	1 large (323 g)
Cremini mushrooms, sliced	1 cup (72 g)	1 cup (72 g)	1 cup (72 g)
Whole grain loaf	500 g	500 g	500 g
Tomato paste, low sodium	1 can (6 oz)	1 can (6 oz)	1 can (6 oz)
Mozzarella cheese, shredded	2 cups (224 g)	2 cups (224 g)	2 cups (224 g)
Cooking spray			
SERVES 1			
For the spinach salad			
Portobello mushrooms, sliced thick	⅓ cup (40 g)	⅓ cup (40 g)	⅓ cup (40 g)
Spinach	2½ cups (75 g)	2 cups (60 g)	1½ cups (45 g)
Sun-dried tomatoes, dry-packed	⅓ cup (18 g)	¼ cup (14 g)	¼ cup (14 g)
Sunflower seeds	2 tsp	1 Tbsp	1 Tbsp
For the dressing	1 Tbsp serving	1½ Tbsp serving	1½ Tbsp serving
Red wine vinegar	1½ Tbsp	1½ Tbsp	1½ Tbsp
Honey	1½ tsp	1½ tsp	1½ tsp
Garlic powder	¼ tsp	¼ tsp	¼ tsp
Safflower oil	2 Tbsp	2 Tbsp	2 Tbsp
CALORIES	**462 KCAL**	**774 KCAL**	**770 KCAL**

❶ Spray a large skillet with cooking spray and warm over medium-high heat. Add onions and sausage and cook for 7 minutes, until onions are fragrant and sausage is nearly cooked through. Add the zucchini and cremini mushrooms and cook for another 2–3 minutes.

❷ Turn oven to broil. Line a baking sheet with parchment paper. Cut loaf in half lengthwise and place on the prepared baking sheet. Spread tomato paste on the cut sides and top with sausage mixture. Scatter mozzarella overtop and broil for 3–5 minutes, until golden brown.

❸ Meanwhile, spray a cast-iron grill pan or skillet with cooking spray and warm over medium-high heat. Add portobello mushrooms and grill or sauté for 2–3 minutes, until tender.

❹ Make a bed of spinach in a salad bowl or on a large plate. Top with mushrooms, sun-dried tomatoes, and sunflower seeds. In a small bowl, whisk together vinegar, honey, and garlic powder. Whisking continuously, gradually pour in oil until emulsified. Drizzle over salad.

❺ Serve pizza loaf with salad.

Note: *Leftovers can be refrigerated for up to 3 days. Wrap slices individually in plastic wrap and then store in a resealable plastic bag and grab as you need, even for a quick lunch. Any leftovers after 3 days can be frozen. Reheat a whole frozen loaf in the oven for 15–18 minutes at 400°F, until heated through.*

▽
Soft-Boiled Egg and Soldiers

▽
Tuna Quinoa Bake

▽
Watermelon, Goat Cheese, and Beet Salad

MEAL PLAN 21

CHECKLIST*

PRODUCE
Arugula
Banana
Beets
Blueberries (2500)
Brussels sprouts (1500)
Cantaloupe
Cherry tomatoes (1500)
Cucumber (2000, 2500)
Garlic
Lemon (1500)
Mango (2000, 2500)
Orange
Parsley
Raspberries (1500, 2000)
Red leaf lettuce (1500)
Spinach
Strawberries
Sugar snap peas
Watermelon

MEAT
Cooked boneless skinless
    chicken breast

BAKERY
Whole grain bread

DAIRY
Butter
Egg
Kefir
Provolone cheese
Soft goat cheese
Tzatziki (page 287) (2000,
    2500)
Vanilla Greek yogurt (2500)

DRY GOODS
Canned white tuna,
    unsalted, packed in water
Tomato purée
Walnuts

* This list assumes that all basic ingredients (see Pantry and Freezer Staples, page 35) have been stocked.

Soft-Boiled Egg and Soldiers

SERVES 1	1500	2000	2500
Egg	1 large (50 g)	1 large (50 g)	1 large (50 g)
Whole grain bread	1 slice (24 g)	1 slice (24 g)	2 slices (48 g)
Butter	½ tsp	½ tsp	1½ tsp
To serve			
Cantaloupe, chopped	1 cup (160 g)	½ cup (80 g)	½ cup (80 g)
Raspberries	1 cup (123 g)	½ cup (61 g)	////////
Mango, sliced	////////	½ cup (82 g)	1 cup (165 g)
Blueberries	////////	////////	1 cup (145 g)
CALORIES	278 KCAL	271 KCAL	478 KCAL

❶ Place egg in a saucepan. Fill with water until about 1 inch over egg and bring to a boil. Cook for 4 minutes, then transfer egg to a small bowl of cold water.

❷ Using a sharp knife, carefully slice top off egg, exposing the runny yolk. Toast and butter bread. Cut toast into long strips or "soldiers."

❸ Serve with fruit.

Tuna Quinoa Bake

SERVES 2-3	1500	2000	2500
For the bake	296-g portion	296-g portion	296-g portion
Garlic	2 cloves	2 cloves	2 cloves
Grapeseed oil	½ tsp	½ tsp	½ tsp
White tuna, drained	1 can (172 g)	1 can (172 g)	1 can (172 g)
Cooked Quinoa (page 286)	2 cups (277 g)	2 cups (277 g)	2 cups (277 g)
Sun-dried tomatoes, dry-packed, chopped	⅓ cup (18 g)	⅓ cup (18 g)	⅓ cup (18 g)
Tomato purée	1 cup (250 g)	1 cup (250 g)	¾ cup (188 g)
Kefir	¼ cup	¼ cup	¼ cup
Parsley, chopped	¼ cup	¼ cup	¼ cup
Provolone cheese, shredded	75 g	75 g	75 g
Cooking spray			
SERVES 1			
Red leaf lettuce, shredded	2 cups (56 g)	////////	////////
Brussels sprouts, shredded	5 (95 g)	////////	////////
Cherry tomatoes, halved	5 (85 g)	////////	////////
Lemon juice	1 Tbsp	////////	////////
Sugar snap peas	////////	1 cup (63 g)	1 cup (63 g)
Cucumber	////////	½ cup (59 g)	½ cup (59 g)
Tzatziki (page 287)	////////	1½ Tbsp	1½ Tbsp
CALORIES	439 KCAL	603 KCAL	572 KCAL

❶ Preheat the oven to 375°F and spray an 8-inch square baking dish with cooking spray.

❷ In a large bowl, combine garlic, oil, tuna, quinoa, sun-dried tomatoes, tomato purée, kefir, and parsley. Stir until well combined and then spread mixture in prepared baking dish. Top with provolone and bake for 15–20 minutes, until warmed through and cheese has melted. Increase heat to broil and cook for 1–2 minutes, until cheese has browned.

❸ For the 1500 meal plan, make a bed of red leaf lettuce on a large plate. Top with shredded Brussels sprouts, cherry tomatoes, and lemon juice and serve with tuna bake. For 2000 and 2500 meal plans, serve tuna bake with vegetables and tzatziki on the side.

Note: To reheat, turn toaster oven to 350°F, cover a portion with tinfoil and bake for 5–7 minutes, until heated through. Alternatively, place in microwave uncovered and warm for 1–2 minutes.

Snacks

SERVES 1	1500	2000	2500
Vanilla-Cinnamon Smoothie	recipe below	recipe below	recipe below
Strawberries	¾ cup (124 g)	⅓ cup (60 g)	½ cup (84 g)
Sugar snap peas	1 cup (63 g)	////////	////////
Orange	1 small (96 g)	1 large (184 g)	1 large (184 g)
Pistachios	////////	////////	¼ cup (31 g)
Air-Popped Popcorn (page 287)	////////	////////	3 cups (24 g)
Buttered Popcorn	recipe below	recipe below	////////
Dark chocolate	////////	10 g	////////
Watermelon, chopped	////////	////////	1 cup (152 g)

Vanilla-Cinnamon Smoothie

SERVES 1	1500	2000	2500
Banana, frozen	½ large (68 g)	1 large (136 g)	1 large (136 g)
Blackstrap molasses	1 Tbsp	1½ tsp	////////
Wheat germ	1½ tsp	1 Tbsp	////////
Ground cinnamon	½ tsp	½ tsp	½ tsp
Vanilla extract	½ tsp	½ tsp	½ tsp
Vanilla almond milk	1½ cups	1½ cups	1½ cups
Vanilla Greek yogurt	////////	////////	½ cup
CALORIES	267 KCAL	317 KCAL	377 KCAL

Put all ingredients into a blender and blend until smooth.
If the smoothie is too thick, add water (not almond milk).
If you prefer a thicker texture, add ice and blend until smooth.

Buttered Popcorn

SERVES 1	1500	2000	2500
Air-Popped Popcorn (page 287)	2 cups (16 g)	2½ cups (20 g)	////////
Butter, melted	½ tsp	½ tsp	////////
Salt	⅛ tsp	⅛ tsp	////////
CALORIES	79 KCAL	94 KCAL	

Put popcorn in a large bowl, drizzle butter overtop,
sprinkle with salt, and gently stir to combine.

Watermelon, Goat Cheese, and Beet Salad

SERVES 1	1500	2000	2500
For the salad			
Beets, cubed	1½ (123 g)	1½ (123 g)	1½ (123 g)
Spinach	2 cups (60 g)	2 cups (60 g)	2 cups (60 g)
Arugula	1 cup (20 g)	1 cup (20 g)	1 cup (20 g)
Watermelon, cubed	½ cup (76 g)	½ cup (76 g)	½ cup (76 g)
Soft goat cheese, crumbled	20 g	25 g	30 g
Walnuts, toasted and chopped	2 Tbsp (12 g)	¼ cup (25 g)	¼ cup (25 g)
Chicken breast, cooked and chopped	75 g	75 g	125 g
Cooking spray			
For the dressing	1 Tbsp serving	1½ Tbsp serving	1½ Tbsp serving
Balsamic vinegar	1 tsp	1 tsp	1 tsp
Honey	1 tsp	1 tsp	1 tsp
Garlic powder	¼ tsp	¼ tsp	¼ tsp
Onion powder	¼ tsp	¼ tsp	¼ tsp
Safflower oil	1½ tsp	1½ tsp	1½ tsp
CALORIES	440 KCAL	557 KCAL	665 KCAL

❶ Preheat the oven to 400°F. Line a baking sheet with parchment paper.
❷ Spread beets on the prepared baking sheet, spray with cooking spray, and bake for 10-20 minutes, until fork tender.
❸ Meanwhile, mix spinach and arugula in a large bowl. Top with beets, watermelon, goat cheese, walnuts, and chicken.

❹ In a small bowl, whisk together vinegar, honey, garlic powder, and onion powder. Whisking continuously, gradually pour in oil until emulsified. Drizzle over salad and serve.

▽

Banana Parfait

▽

Chicken-Gruyère Crepe with Shiitake-Truffle Sauce

▽

Poached Halibut with Baked Quinoa and Collard Greens

MEAL PLAN 22

CHECKLIST*

PRODUCE
Banana
Blueberries
Cantaloupe (2000, 2500)
Cherry tomatoes
Collard greens
Garlic
Mango (2500)
Raspberries
Shallot
Shiitake mushrooms
Spinach

MEAT AND FISH
Cooked boneless skinless
  chicken breast
Halibut

DAIRY
Butter
Gruyère cheese
Mozzarella cheese
Vanilla Greek yogurt

DRY GOODS
Cacao nibs
Chocolate hazelnut spread
Coconut oil (2500)
Granola (page 287)
Hearts of palm (1500, 2500)
Low-sodium tomato sauce,
  canned
Sugar (2500)
Worcestershire sauce

PREMADE
Crepes (page 176)

This list assumes that all basic ingredients (see Pantry and Freezer Staples, page 35) have been stocked.

Banana Parfait

SERVES 1	1500	2000	2500
Vanilla Greek yogurt	⅓ cup	½ cup	½ cup
Flaxseeds	1½ tsp	1¼ tsp	1 tsp
Banana, sliced	1 (118 g)	1 large (136 g)	1 large (136 g)
Blueberries	½ cup (72 g)	½ cup (72 g)	1 cup (144 g)
Raspberries	½ + ⅓ cup (103 g)	½ cup (61 g)	½ cup (61 g)
Chocolate hazelnut spread	1½ tsp	1 Tbsp	1 Tbsp
Vanilla almond milk	1½ tsp	1 Tbsp	1 Tbsp
Wheat germ	////////	1½ Tbsp	////////
Cacao nibs	1½ tsp	1½ tsp	1½ tsp
Shredded coconut, unsweetened	1 Tbsp	1 Tbsp	1 Tbsp
Granola (page 287)	1 Tbsp	1½ Tbsp	1½ Tbsp
CALORIES	482 KCAL	630 KCAL	628 KCAL

❶ Put yogurt in a glass and top with flaxseeds, banana, blueberries, and raspberries.
❷ In a small bowl, whisk together chocolate hazelnut spread, almond milk, and wheat germ (if using), and add to parfait. Top with cacao nibs, shredded coconut, and granola.

Chicken-Gruyère Crepe
with Shiitake-Truffle Sauce

SERVES 1	1500	2000	2500
For the filling			
Grapeseed oil	½ tsp	½ tsp	½ tsp
Shiitake mushrooms	¾ cup (109 g)	¾ cup (109 g)	¾ cup (109 g)
Worcestershire sauce	1 Tbsp	1 Tbsp	1 Tbsp
Balsamic vinegar	¾ tsp	¾ tsp	¾ tsp
Honey	¾ tsp	¾ tsp	¾ tsp
Cornstarch	⅛ tsp	⅛ tsp	⅛ tsp
Truffle oil	⅛ tsp	⅛ tsp	⅛ tsp
Crepe (page 176)	1 crepe	1 crepe	1 crepe
Gruyère cheese, shredded	15 g	15 g	15 g
Cooked chicken breast, chopped	38 g	38 g	38 g
For the salad			
Spinach	2 cups (60 g)	1½ cups (45 g)	2 cups (60 g)
Cherry tomatoes, halved	6 (102 g)	5 (85 g)	5 (85 g)
Hearts of palm, sliced	⅓ cup (49 g)	////////	¼ cup (36 g)
Sunflower seeds	1½ tsp	1 Tbsp	1½ tsp
For the dressing	1½ tsp serving	1 Tbsp serving	1 Tbsp serving
Balsamic vinegar	2 tsp	2 tsp	2 tsp
Honey	½ tsp	½ tsp	½ tsp
Grapeseed oil	1 Tbsp	1 Tbsp	1 Tbsp
CALORIES	461 KCAL	499 KCAL	489 KCAL

❶ Heat oil in a skillet over medium heat. Add mushrooms and cook for 2–3 minutes, until they are reduced and tender.

❷ In a small bowl, combine Worcestershire sauce, vinegar, honey, and cornstarch. Add mixture to mushrooms and cook for 1–2 minutes, until sauce has just thickened. Add truffle oil, stir, and remove skillet from heat.

❸ Put crepe on a plate. Place cheese on half of crepe, top with chicken and truffle-mushroom sauce, and fold in half. Put crepe in skillet and warm for 1 minute, until cheese has melted.

❹ Make a bed of spinach in a salad bowl or on a large plate. Top with tomatoes, hearts of palm (if using), and sunflower seeds. In a small bowl, whisk together vinegar and honey. Whisking continuously, gradually pour in oil until emulsified. Drizzle over salad.

❺ Serve crepe with salad.

Grab and Go: Make filling the night before and store in a microwave-safe resealable container in the refrigerator. Store crepe and cheese in another resealable container in the refrigerator. Make salad and dressing and store in separate resealable containers in the refrigerator. To serve, warm filling in microwave for 45 seconds to 1 minute. Warm crepe on its own, on a microwave-safe plate, for 15 seconds. Sprinkle cheese evenly over half the crepe and top with filling. Toss salad with dressing and enjoy.

Snacks

SERVES 1	1500	2000	2500
Vanilla Wheat Germ Smoothie	recipe below	////////	////////
Cantaloupe, chopped	////////	1 cup (160 g)	1 cup (160 g)
Mango, chopped	////////	////////	1 cup (165 g)
Cinnamon-Vanilla Milk	////////	recipe below	recipe below
Cinnamon-Sugar Popcorn 3	////////	////////	recipe below

Vanilla Wheat Germ Smoothie

SERVES 1	1500	2000	2500
Banana	½ (59 g)	////////	////////
Wheat germ	2 Tbsp	////////	////////
Blackstrap molasses	1 Tbsp	////////	////////
Cocoa powder	2 tsp	////////	////////
Vanilla almond milk	½ cup	////////	////////
Coconut water	1 cup	////////	////////
CALORIES	251 KCAL		

Put all ingredients into a blender and blend until smooth.
If the smoothie is too thick, add water (not almond milk or
coconut water). If you prefer a thicker texture, add ice and
blend until smooth.

Cinnamon-Vanilla Milk

SERVES 1	1500	2000	2500
Blackstrap molasses	////////	1 Tbsp	////////
Vanilla extract	////////	½ tsp	½ tsp
Ground cinnamon	////////	½ tsp	½ tsp
Vanilla almond milk	////////	1½ cups	1½ cups
CALORIES		194 KCAL	146 KCAL

Combine ingredients in a microwave-safe mug.
Cover and microwave on high for 2 minutes.
Stir and heat for another minute.

Cinnamon-Sugar Popcorn ③

SERVES 1	1500	2000	2500
Air-Popped Popcorn (page 287)	////////	////////	3 cups (24 g)
Coconut oil, melted	////////	////////	1 tsp
Ground cinnamon	////////	////////	½ tsp
Sugar	////////	////////	1½ tsp
CALORIES			159 KCAL

Put popcorn in a large bowl, drizzle coconut oil
overtop, sprinkle with cinnamon and sugar, and
gently stir to combine.

Poached Halibut

with Baked Quinoa and Collard Greens

SERVES 4	1500	2000	2500
For the baked quinoa	⅔ cup quinoa	1 cup quinoa	1⅓ cups quinoa
Water	1 cup	1 cup	1 cup
Quinoa, uncooked	½ cup (69 g)	½ cup (69 g)	½ cup (69 g)
Tomato sauce	1 cup	1 cup	1 cup
Mozzarella cheese, shredded	½ cup (56 g)	½ cup (56 g)	½ cup (56 g)
For the fish	75 g	112 g	150 g
Butter	2 Tbsp	2 Tbsp	2 Tbsp
Halibut fillet, skin on	1 (300 g)	1 (300 g)	1 (300 g)
Chopped herbs (optional, see Note below)			
SERVES 1			
For the collard greens			
Grapeseed oil	1 tsp	1½ tsp	1 tsp
Garlic, minced	2 cloves	2 cloves	2 cloves
Shallot, minced	3 Tbsp	3 Tbsp	3 Tbsp
Collard greens, stems removed, leaves chopped	2½ cups (90 g)	2½ cups (90 g)	2 cups (72 g)
CALORIES	368 KCAL	524 KCAL	634 KCAL

❶ Bring water to a boil in a large saucepan over medium-high heat. Add quinoa and stir. Reduce heat to low, cover, and simmer for 15–20 minutes, until water is absorbed and quinoa is fluffy.

❷ Preheat the oven to broil. Mix quinoa with tomato sauce and pour into an 8-inch square baking dish, or divide evenly between 4 ramekins. Top with mozzarella and broil for 2–3 minutes, until cheese turns golden brown and begins to bubble. Cover with foil to keep warm and set aside.

❸ Reduce oven heat to 350°F.

❹ Melt butter in a small ovenproof skillet over medium-low heat. Add fillet, skin-side down, and using a spoon, baste fish with butter for 2 minutes.

❺ Put skillet in the oven and bake for 10–12 minutes, or until fish is opaque, flaky, and cooked through. (Safe internal temperature for fish is 158°F.)

❻ Meanwhile, make the collard greens. Heat oil in a large skillet over medium-high heat. Add garlic and shallots and cook for 1 minute, until fragrant. Add collards and sauté for 3–5 minutes, until fork tender.

❼ To serve, spoon butter over fish and then plate (discarding extra butter) along with baked quinoa and collard greens.

Note: You can flavor the butter with dried or fresh herbs. Also, using clarified butter to poach fish prevents milk solids from burning. To clarify butter, melt butter in a saucepan over medium heat, skim the white milk solids from the top and discard. The remaining golden liquid is the clarified butter.

Note: Fish will keep for up to 2 days refrigerated. To reheat, warm in a 300°F oven for 3–5 minutes in a cast-iron pan or on a parchment-lined baking sheet. Leftover quinoa will keep for up to a week refrigerated.

▽

**Sweet Potato
Breakfast Stack**

▽

**Lentil Taco
Lettuce Wraps**

▽

**Slow-Cooked
Chicken Pot Pie**

MEAL PLAN 23

CHECKLIST*

PRODUCE
Avocado
Blueberries (2500)
Brussels sprouts
Butter lettuce
Carrots
Celery
Cherry tomatoes
Kiwi (1500)
Mango
Onion
Potatoes
Raspberries (1500)
Spinach
Sweet potato
Watermelon (2000, 2500)

DELI
Sliced prosciutto

MEAT
Boneless skinless chicken
 breast

DAIRY
Boursin® Garlic & Fine Herbs
Butter
Egg
Sour cream
Vanilla Greek yogurt (2500)

FROZEN
Edamame (1500)
Phyllo dough

DRY GOODS
Hearts of palm (1500)
Lentils
No-salt tomato purée,
 canned
Pumpkin purée, canned
Red wine vinegar
Salsa
White vinegar

This list assumes that all basic ingredients (see Pantry and Freezer Staples, page 35) have been stocked.

Sweet Potato Breakfast Stack

MAKES 1	1500	2000	2500
Sweet potato, skin on, washed, cut into ½-inch-thick rounds	2 rounds (50 g)	2 rounds (50 g)	2 rounds (50 g)
White vinegar	1 Tbsp	1 Tbsp	1 Tbsp
Egg	1 large (50 g)	1 large (50 g)	1 large (50 g)
Prosciutto	1 slice (15 g)	1 slice (15 g)	1 slice (15 g)
Boursin® Garlic & Fine Herbs	1 Tbsp	1 Tbsp	1½ Tbsp
Spinach	¼ cup (8 g)	¼ cup (8 g)	¼ cup (8 g)
Sun-dried tomatoes, dry-packed, chopped	2 Tbsp (7 g)	2 Tbsp (7 g)	2 Tbsp (7 g)
Tomato purée	¼ cup (63 g)	¼ cup (63 g)	¼ cup (63 g)
Mango, sliced	¾ cup (124 g)	½ cup (82 g)	1 cup (165 g)
CALORIES	332 KCAL	305 KCAL	359 KCAL

❶ Preheat the oven to 400°F. Line a baking sheet with parchment paper.

❷ Place sweet potato rounds on the prepared baking sheet and bake for 15–20 minutes, or until golden and fork tender.

❸ Bring a large pot of water to a boil. When water begins to simmer, mix in vinegar. When the water reaches a boil, gently stir water in a circular motion to create a little whirlpool. While whirlpool is spinning, crack egg into the pot. Leave egg to cook for 3–5 minutes. Remove with a slotted spoon and set aside.

❹ Heat a small skillet over medium heat, add prosciutto, and cook for 30 seconds on one side. Flip and cook for another 30 seconds to a minute, until prosciutto is crispy and golden brown. Crumble and set aside.

❺ Spread Boursin® over each potato round. Top one round with crumbled prosciutto, spinach, sun-dried tomatoes, the second round, and the poached egg.

❻ Warm tomato purée over medium heat, or in a covered microwave-safe container, for 30–45 seconds.

❼ Pour tomato purée over stack and serve with mango.

Lentil Taco Lettuce Wraps

MAKES 3	1500	2000	2500
For the tacos	2 wraps	3 wraps	3 wraps
Taco Seasoning (page 286)	2 Tbsp	2 Tbsp	2 Tbsp
Water	¼ cup	¼ cup	¼ cup
Lentils, drained and rinsed	6 Tbsp (74 g)	6 Tbsp (74 g)	6 Tbsp (74 g)
Black beans, drained and rinsed	3 Tbsp (32 g)	3 Tbsp (32 g)	3 Tbsp (32 g)
Corn, frozen	3 Tbsp (30 g)	3 Tbsp (30 g)	3 Tbsp (30 g)
Butter lettuce leaves, whole	3 leaves	3 leaves	3 leaves
Cherry tomatoes, halved	6 (102 g)	6 (102 g)	6 (102 g)
Avocado, pitted, sliced	⅓ (67 g)	⅓ (67 g)	⅓ (67 g)
Salsa	1½ Tbsp	1½ Tbsp	1½ Tbsp
Sour cream	1 Tbsp	1 Tbsp	1 Tbsp
Cooking spray			
CALORIES	273 KCAL	399 KCAL	399 KCAL

❶ In a small bowl, mix taco seasoning with water.

❷ Warm a skillet over medium heat and spray with cooking spray. Add lentils, beans, corn, and taco seasoning mixture and cook for 3–5 minutes, until water has evaporated. Remove from heat.

❸ Evenly distribute mixture between the lettuce leaves. Top with cherry tomatoes, avocado, salsa, and sour cream. Serve immediately.

Leftovers: To reheat, warm lentil mixture in the microwave for 45 seconds to 1 minute. Assemble lettuce wraps by topping with lentil mixture, tomatoes, avocado, salsa, and sour cream.

Snacks

SERVES 1	1500	2000	2500
Pumpkin-Cinnamon Smoothie	recipe below	recipe below	recipe below
Kiwi	1 (91 g)	/ / / / / / / /	/ / / / / / / /
Watermelon, chopped	/ / / / / / / /	1½ cups (228 g)	1½ cups (228 g)
Pistachios	/ / / / / / / /	/ / / / / / / /	¼ cup (31 g)
Dark chocolate	/ / / / / / / /	10 g	15 g
Air-Popped Popcorn (page 287)	/ / / / / / / /	1½ cups (12 g)	2 cups (16 g)
Raspberries	½ cup (61 g)	/ / / / / / / /	/ / / / / / / /
Blueberries	/ / / / / / / /	/ / / / / / / /	¾ cup (109 g)

Pumpkin-Cinnamon Smoothie

SERVES 1	1500	2000	2500
Pumpkin purée	¼ cup (61 g)	¼ cup (61 g)	¼ cup (61 g)
Honey	1 tsp	1 tsp	1 Tbsp
Ground cinnamon	1 tsp	1 tsp	1 tsp
Wheat germ	1 Tbsp + 1 tsp	1 Tbsp	/ / / / / / / /
Vanilla almond milk	1½ cups	1½ cups	1½ cups
Vanilla Greek yogurt	/ / / / / / / /	/ / / / / / / /	½ cup
CALORIES	219 KCAL	211 KCAL	306 KCAL

Put all ingredients into a blender and blend until smooth.
If the smoothie is too thick, add water (not almond milk).
If you prefer a thicker texture, add ice and blend until smooth.

Slow-Cooked Chicken Pot Pie

SERVES 8	1500	2000	2500
For the chicken pot pie	1 pie	2 pies	2 pies
Butter, divided	2 Tbsp + 1 tsp	2 Tbsp + 1 tsp	2 Tbsp + 1 tsp
Onion, chopped	1 large (150 g)	1 large (150 g)	1 large (150 g)
Carrots, chopped	3 large (216 g)	3 large (216 g)	3 large (216 g)
Celery stalk, chopped	1 large (64 g)	1 large (64 g)	1 large (64 g)
Potatoes, skin on, diced	4 (1476 g)	4 (1476 g)	4 (1476 g)
Chicken breast, diced	2½ cups (350 g)	2½ cups (350 g)	2½ cups (350 g)
All-purpose flour	2 Tbsp	2 Tbsp	2 Tbsp
Chicken Stock (page 287)	6 cups	6 cups	6 cups
Thyme	1 Tbsp	1 Tbsp	1 Tbsp
Phyllo dough (16.5-inch × 12-inch sheets)	8	8	8
SERVES 1			
For the salad			
Spinach	1½ cups (45 g)	1½ cups (45 g)	1½ cups (45 g)
Brussels sprouts, raw and thinly shaved	3 (57 g)	3 (57 g)	3 (57 g)
Hearts of palm	⅓ cup (49 g)	////////	////////
Edamame	¼ cup (39 g)	////////	////////
Cherry tomatoes, halved	////////	////////	5 (85 g)
Sunflower seeds	2 tsp	1 Tbsp	1 Tbsp
Flaxseeds	2 tsp	2 tsp	2 tsp
For the dressing	1 Tbsp serving	1 Tbsp serving	1 Tbsp serving
Red wine vinegar	1½ Tbsp	1½ Tbsp	1½ Tbsp
Honey	1½ tsp	1½ tsp	1½ tsp
Garlic powder	¼ tsp	¼ tsp	¼ tsp
Safflower oil	2 Tbsp	2 Tbsp	2 Tbsp
CALORIES	628 KCAL	905 KCAL	920 KCAL

❶ To make pot pie filling, melt 1 Tbsp butter in a large skillet over medium-high heat. Add onions and sauté for 5–7 minutes, until translucent. Add carrots, celery, and potatoes, lower heat to medium, and sauté for another 15 minutes, until golden brown.

❷ Add chicken and flour and stir until everything is well coated. Transfer contents to a slow cooker. Stir in chicken stock and thyme, then cover and cook on low for 6–8 hours, or on high for 4 hours.

❸ To make pot pie, preheat the oven to 350°F.

❹ Portion out equal amounts of chicken filling into 8 ovenproof ramekins and set aside. Melt remaining butter in microwave. Working quickly, unroll phyllo pastry and remove a single sheet.

(Keep remaining sheets covered with a damp tea towel to prevent them from drying out.) Brush butter over the top of the phyllo pastry sheet. Fold pastry sheet in half and brush the top with butter again. Repeat two more times, then place pastry over a ramekin and prick with a fork. Repeat with the remaining phyllo and ramekins and then bake for 10–15 minutes, until golden and crispy.

❺ Meanwhile, make a bed of spinach in a salad bowl or on a large plate. Top with Brussels sprouts, hearts of palm (if using), edamame (if using), cherry tomatoes (if using), sunflower seeds, and flaxseeds. In a small bowl, whisk together vinegar, honey, and garlic powder. Whisking continuously, gradually pour in oil until emulsified. Drizzle over salad and serve with pot pie(s).

▽

*Tropical Dollar
Pancakes with
Mango Syrup*

▽

*Not-Your-Average
Cobb Salad*

▽

Vegetable Bake

MEAL PLAN

24

CHECKLIST*

PRODUCE
Acorn squash
Avocado
Banana
Basil
Blueberries
Broccoli
Cherry tomatoes
Chives
Eggplant
Garlic
Onion
Portobello mushroom
Spinach
Strawberries (2000, 2500)
Watermelon
Zucchini

DELI
Sliced prosciutto

DAIRY
Butter
Cheddar cheese
Eggs
Milk
Parmesan cheese
Plain Greek yogurt

DRY GOODS
Canned diced tomatoes, low
   sodium
Dried peaches (2000, 2500)
Quick oats
Red wine vinegar
Sugar

This list assumes that all basic ingredients (see Pantry and Freezer Staples, page 35) have been stocked.

Tropical Dollar Pancakes
with Mango Syrup

MAKES 12		1500	2000	2500
For the pancakes		6 pancakes	6 pancakes	12 pancakes
Egg		1 large (50 g)	1 large (50 g)	1 large (50 g)
Plain Greek yogurt		⅓ cup + 2 Tbsp	⅓ cup + 2 Tbsp	⅓ cup + 2 Tbsp
Banana		1 large (118 g)	1 large (118 g)	1 large (118 g)
Quick oats		¼ cup (24 g)	¼ cup (24 g)	¼ cup (24 g)
Cooked Quinoa (page 286)		¼ cup (35 g)	¼ cup (35 g)	¼ cup (35 g)
Sugar		1¼ tsp	1¼ tsp	1¼ tsp
Shredded coconut, unsweetened, divided		2 Tbsp	2 Tbsp	2 Tbsp
Baking powder		¼ tsp	¼ tsp	¼ tsp
SERVES 1				
For the mango syrup		⅔ cup serving	⅔ cup serving	1¼ cup serving
Mango, fresh or frozen, cubed		1 cup (165 g)	1 cup (165 g)	1 cup (165 g)
Water		¼ cup	¼ cup	¼ cup
Honey		1 tsp	1 tsp	1 tsp
CALORIES		309 KCAL	309 KCAL	618 KCAL

❶ Preheat the oven to 200°F. Line a baking sheet with parchment paper.

❷ Place egg, yogurt, banana, oats, quinoa, sugar, 1½ Tbsp coconut, and baking powder in a blender and blend until smooth.

❸ Heat a non-stick skillet over medium-low heat. Pour batter onto the pan in 2-Tbsp portions and cook for 2–3 minutes, until bubbles form on the surface and the sides are cooked. Flip and cook pancakes for another 1–2 minutes. Place on prepared baking sheet to keep warm. Repeat with remaining batter.

❹ Meanwhile, combine mango, water, and honey in a small saucepan and simmer over medium heat for 3–5 minutes, until fruit starts to break down. Remove from heat and use an immersion blender to roughly blend into a chunky syrup. Serve over pancakes and sprinkle remaining 1½ tsp coconut overtop.

Not-Your-Average Cobb Salad

SERVES 1	1500	2000	2500
For the salad			
Prosciutto	2 slices (30 g)	2 slices (30 g)	2 slices (30 g)
Spinach	2½ cups (75 g)	3 cups (90 g)	3 cups (90 g)
Blueberries	½ cup (72 g)	½ cup (72 g)	½ cup (72 g)
Cherry tomatoes, halved	7 (119 g)	7 (119 g)	7 (119 g)
Avocado, diced	¼ (50 g)	½ (101 g)	½ (101 g)
Cheddar cheese, shredded	3 Tbsp (15 g)	3 Tbsp (15 g)	3 Tbsp (15 g)
Sun-dried tomatoes, dry-packed, chopped	⅓ cup (18 g)	¼ cup (14 g)	¼ cup (14 g)
Egg, hard-boiled and sliced	1 small (38 g)	1 large (50 g)	1 large (50 g)
Chives, chopped	1 Tbsp	1 Tbsp	1 Tbsp
Flaxseeds	2 tsp	2 tsp	2 tsp
Sunflower seeds	2 tsp	////////	////////
For the dressing	1 Tbsp + 1 tsp serving	2 Tbsp + ¼ tsp serving	2 Tbsp + ¼ tsp serving
Red wine vinegar	1½ Tbsp	1½ Tbsp	1½ Tbsp
Honey	1½ tsp	1½ tsp	1½ tsp
Garlic powder	¼ tsp	¼ tsp	¼ tsp
Safflower oil	2 Tbsp	2 Tbsp	2 Tbsp
CALORIES	552 KCAL	649 KCAL	649 KCAL

❶ Warm a skillet over medium-low heat. Add prosciutto to the skillet and cook for 30 seconds, flip, and cook for another 30 seconds to a minute, until prosciutto is crispy and golden brown. Remove from heat and set aside.

❷ Make a bed of spinach in a salad bowl or on a large plate. Top with blueberries, cherry tomatoes, avocado, cheddar, sun-dried tomatoes, egg, prosciutto, chives, flaxseeds, and sunflower seeds (if using).

❸ In a small bowl, whisk together vinegar, honey, and garlic powder. Whisking continuously, gradually pour in oil until emulsified. Drizzle over salad.

Vegetable Bake

SERVES 3	1500	2000	2500
For the bake	1 serving	1 serving	1½ servings
Eggplant, sliced lengthwise into strips	1 large (548 g)	1 large (548 g)	1 large (548 g)
Zucchini, sliced lengthwise into strips	2 (646 g)	2 (646 g)	2 (646 g)
Acorn squash, peeled, seeds removed, sliced lengthwise into strips	1 large (646 g)	1 large (646 g)	1 large (646 g)
For the marinara sauce			
Onion, chopped	1 (105 g)	1 (105 g)	1 (105 g)
Garlic, chopped	3 cloves	3 cloves	3 cloves
Canned diced tomatoes	5¼ cups	5¼ cups	5¼ cups
Tomato paste	3 Tbsp	3 Tbsp	3 Tbsp
Fresh basil leaves	10	10	10
Cooking spray			
For the cheese sauce			
Butter	1 Tbsp	1 Tbsp	1 Tbsp
Garlic, chopped	1 clove	1 clove	1 clove
All-purpose flour	1 Tbsp	1 Tbsp	1 Tbsp
Milk	3 cups	3 cups	3 cups
Parmesan cheese, shredded	¼ cup (20 g)	¼ cup (20 g)	¼ cup (20 g)
Cheddar cheese, shredded	⅓ cup (38 g)	⅓ cup (38 g)	⅓ cup (38 g)
Nutritional yeast	2 Tbsp + 2 tsp	2 Tbsp + 2 tsp	2 Tbsp + 2 tsp
SERVES 1			
For the broccoli and mushrooms			
Broccoli florets	2 cups (176 g)	2 cups (176 g)	2 cups (176 g)
Butter	½ tsp	½ tsp	½ tsp
Onion powder	½ tsp	½ tsp	½ tsp
Garlic powder	½ tsp	½ tsp	½ tsp
Portobello mushroom	1 cup (121 g)	1 cup (121 g)	1 cup (121 g)
Balsamic Reduction (page 286)	1 tsp	1 tsp	1 tsp
CALORIES	433 KCAL	433 KCAL	596 KCAL

❶ To make the marinara sauce, heat a large saucepan over medium-high heat and spray with cooking spray. Add onions and garlic and cook for 5–7 minutes, until onions are translucent and fragrant.

❷ Add the diced tomatoes and tomato paste and stir. Reduce heat to low and simmer for 10–15 minutes, until sauce has thickened. Stir in basil and set aside.

❸ To make the cheese sauce, melt butter in a large saucepan over medium heat. Add garlic and sauté for 2–3 minutes, until fragrant. Add flour, reduce to low heat, and stir for 1–2 minutes (this removes the raw taste from the flour). Slowly add 1 cup milk to the pan, stirring continuously until smooth. Repeat until all the milk has been used. Stir in Parmesan, cheddar, and yeast and remove from heat. (Milk burns easily, so watch carefully and stir continuously.)

❹ To make the bake, preheat the oven to 350°F and spray a loaf pan with cooking spray.

❺ Pour a bit of the marinara sauce on the bottom of the loaf pan. Lay eggplant strips side by side to cover. Spoon marinara sauce overtop. Lay zucchini strips side by side to cover and then repeat with squash strips. Spoon cheese sauce overtop. Repeat layers until all ingredients have been used up. (About 2–3 times.)

❻ Cover dish with foil and bake 45–60 minutes, until sauce is bubbling and squash is fork tender. Uncover and bake for another 10 minutes, until cheese sauce is browned. Tent with foil to keep warm and let rest for 15–20 minutes.

❼ Meanwhile, bring 1–2 inches of water to a boil in a medium saucepan. Add broccoli, cover, and steam for 3–5 minutes, until broccoli is al dente (do not overcook). Drain and mix in butter, onion powder, and garlic powder.

❽ Heat a cast-iron grill over medium-high heat. Add mushrooms and grill for 2–3 minutes, flip, and cook for another 2–3 minutes. Brush with balsamic reduction.

❾ Serve bake with broccoli and mushrooms.

Snacks

SERVES 1	1500	2000	2500
Vanilla-Cinnamon Milk	recipe below	////////	////////
Vanilla-Cinnamon Smoothie	////////	recipe below	recipe below
Dried peaches	////////	½ cup (129 g)	⅓ cup (86 g)
Watermelon, chopped	1 cup (152 g)	1½ cups (228 g)	2 cups (304 g)
Dark chocolate	////////	12.5 g	20 g
Air-Popped Popcorn (page 287)	////////	2 cups (16 g)	2 cups (16 g)
Strawberries	////////	7 (84 g)	5 (60 g)

Vanilla-Cinnamon Milk/Smoothie

SERVES 1	1500	2000	2500
Vanilla almond milk	1½ cups	1½ cups	1½ cups
Blackstrap molasses	1 Tbsp	////////	////////
Ground cinnamon	½ tsp	½ tsp	½ tsp
Vanilla extract	½ tsp	½ tsp	½ tsp
Plain Greek yogurt	////////	½ cup	½ cup
Honey	////////	1½ tsp	1½ tsp
CALORIES	194 KCAL	267 KCAL	267 KCAL

To make milk (for 1500), put all ingredients in a microwave-safe mug and mix well. Cover and microwave on high for 2 minutes, stir and microwave for 1 minute more.

To make smoothie (for 2000 and 2500), put all ingredients into a blender and blend until smooth. If the smoothie is too thick, add water (not almond milk). If you prefer a thicker texture, add ice and blend until smooth.

▽
Breakfast Pizza

▽
*Grilled Squash
Salad*

▽
*Pork Schnitzel with
Asparagus and
Shiitake-Truffle Pilaf*

MEAL PLAN 25

CHECKLIST*

PRODUCE
Asparagus
Basil
Blueberries (2500)
Cantaloupe (1500, 2000)
Eggplant
Garlic
Grapes (2500)
Lemon
Mango
Raspberries (1500, 2000)
Shiitake mushrooms
Spinach
Sugar snap peas (1500, 2000)
Yellow bell pepper
Yellow squash
Zucchini

BAKERY
8-inch whole wheat tortilla

DELI
Extra-lean deli ham, sliced

MEAT
Pork loin chops, boneless

DAIRY
Bocconcini
Eggs
Soft goat cheese

DRY GOODS
Carbonated water
Coconut oil
Mango nectar
Maple sugar
Panko crumbs
Sun-dried tomato pesto
Vegetable oil
Whole grain mustard

This list assumes that all basic ingredients (see Pantry and Freezer Staples, page 35) have been stocked.

Breakfast Pizza

SERVES 1	1500	2000	2500
Whole wheat tortilla	1 (48 g)	1 (48 g)	1 (48 g)
Sun-dried tomato pesto	1½ Tbsp	1½ Tbsp	1½ Tbsp
Egg	1 large (50 g)	1 large (50 g)	1 large (50 g)
Egg white	1 large (33 g)	1 large (33 g)	1 large (33 g)
Sun-dried tomatoes, dry-packed, chopped	⅓ cup (18 g)	⅓ cup (18 g)	⅓ cup (18 g)
Extra-lean deli ham, chopped	1 slice (28 g)	1 slice (28 g)	1 slice (28 g)
Soft goat cheese	1 Tbsp + 1 tsp (20 g)	1 Tbsp + 1 tsp (20 g)	1 Tbsp + 1 tsp (20 g)
Basil, chopped	¼ cup (11 g)	¼ cup (11 g)	¼ cup (11 g)
Mango, chopped, to serve	½ cup (82 g)	1 cup (165 g)	1 cup (165 g)
Blueberries, to serve	////////	////////	1 cup (145 g)
CALORIES	464 KCAL	528 KCAL	578 KCAL

❶ Preheat the oven to broil. Line a baking sheet with parchment paper.

❷ Evenly spread pesto over tortilla and place on the prepared baking sheet.

❸ Warm a small non-stick skillet over medium-low heat. In a small bowl, whisk together egg and egg white, pour into skillet, and scramble for 2–3 minutes, until nearly cooked. Spread eggs on top of pesto. Top with sun-dried tomatoes, ham, and goat cheese.

❹ Place pizza under the broiler and cook for 2–4 minutes, until eggs finish cooking and goat cheese turns golden. Remove from oven, transfer to a plate, and top with basil. Serve with mango and blueberries (if using).

Snacks

SERVES 1	1500	2000	2500
Tropical Fizzy Chia Drink	recipe below	recipe below	recipe below
Vanilla Almond Milk with Maple Sugar	recipe below	recipe below	recipe below
Cinnamon-Sugar Popcorn 4	////////	recipe below	recipe below
Cantaloupe, chopped	¾ cup (120 g)	1 cup (160 g)	////////
Raspberries	⅓ cup (41 g)	½ cup (61 g)	////////
Grapes	////////	////////	1½ cups (231 g)
Sugar snap peas	1 cup (63 g)	1 cup (63 g)	////////
Pistachios	////////	////////	¼ cup (31 g)
Dried apricots	⅓ cup (83 g)	////////	////////

Tropical Fizzy Chia Drink

SERVES 1	1500	2000	2500
Coconut water	½ cup	½ cup	½ cup
Chia seeds	1½ Tbsp	1½ Tbsp	1½ Tbsp
Mango nectar	¼ cup	¼ cup	¼ cup
Carbonated water	1 cup	1 cup	1 cup
CALORIES	165 KCAL	165 KCAL	165 KCAL

Pour coconut water into a small resealable container and stir
in chia seeds. Place in refrigerator overnight, to let chia seeds gel.
When ready to enjoy, stir all ingredients together in a glass.

Vanilla Almond Milk with Maple Sugar

SERVES 1	1500	2000	2500
Vanilla almond milk	1¼ cups	1½ cups	1½ cups
Maple sugar	1½ tsp	2 tsp	2 tsp
CALORIES	130 KCAL	158 KCAL	158 KCAL

In a microwave-safe mug, combine almond milk with sugar and mix
well. Microwave on high for 2 minutes, stir, and heat for another
minute on high.

Cinnamon-Sugar Popcorn ④

SERVES 1	1500	2000	2500
Air-Popped Popcorn (page 287)	////////	2½ cups (20 g)	3 cups (24 g)
Coconut oil, melted	////////	1½ tsp	1 tsp
Ground cinnamon	////////	¼ tsp	¼ tsp
Sugar	////////	1½ tsp	2 tsp
CALORIES		161 KCAL	165 KCAL

Put popcorn in a large bowl, drizzle coconut oil overtop, sprinkle
with cinnamon and sugar, and gently stir to combine.

Grilled Squash Salad

SERVES 1	1500	2000	2500
For the salad			
Zucchini, cut into ¼-inch-thick slices	½ cup (56 g)	½ cup (56 g)	½ cup (56 g)
Yellow squash, cut into ¼-inch-thick slices	½ cup (56 g)	½ cup (56 g)	½ cup (56 g)
Eggplant, cut into ¼-inch-thick slices	¼ cup (137 g)	¼ cup (137 g)	¼ cup (137 g)
Yellow bell pepper, deseeded and chopped	⅓ large (62 g)	⅓ large (62 g)	⅓ large (62 g)
Grapeseed oil	1½ tsp	1½ tsp	1½ tsp
Garlic, finely chopped	1 clove	1 clove	1 clove
Onion powder	½ tsp	½ tsp	½ tsp
Spinach	2½ cups (75 g)	2 cups (60 g)	2 cups (60 g)
Bocconcini, halved	4 balls (38 g)	6 balls (50 g)	6 balls (50 g)
For the dressing	1½ tsp serving	1 Tbsp serving	1 Tbsp serving
Balsamic vinegar	2 Tbsp	2 Tbsp	2 Tbsp
Honey	2 tsp	2 tsp	2 tsp
Whole grain mustard	1 tsp	1 tsp	1 tsp
Grapeseed oil	¼ cup	¼ cup	¼ cup
CALORIES	291 KCAL	358 KCAL	358 KCAL

❶ Heat a cast-iron grill or skillet over medium-high heat. In a large bowl, combine zucchini, squash, eggplant, yellow pepper, oil, garlic, and onion powder and mix until vegetables are evenly coated. Grill vegetables for 2–3 minutes, until golden. Flip and grill for another 2–3 minutes, until fork tender and golden.

❷ In a small bowl, whisk together vinegar, honey, and mustard. Whisking continuously, gradually pour in oil until emulsified.

❸ To serve, make a bed of spinach in a salad bowl or on a large plate. Top with grilled vegetables and bocconcini and drizzle dressing overtop.

Grab and Go: Prepare the grilled vegetables the night before and place in a resealable microwave-safe container. In a separate container, place spinach and bocconcini. Store dressing in a small resealable container. Place all in refrigerator overnight. When ready to serve, heat vegetable mixture in the microwave for 1–2 minutes and place on a bed of spinach. Drizzle with dressing and serve. Salad can also be served cold.

Pork Schnitzel

with Asparagus and Shiitake-Truffle Pilaf

SERVES 2–4	1500	2000	2500
For the schnitzel	134 g schnitzel	178 g schnitzel	268 g schnitzel
Pork loin chops	4 (360 g)	4 (360 g)	4 (360 g)
Egg whites	3 large (99 g)	3 large (99 g)	3 large (99 g)
Panko crumbs	½ cup (27 g)	½ cup (27 g)	½ cup (27 g)
Almond flour	½ cup (32 g)	½ cup (32 g)	½ cup (32 g)
Vegetable oil	2 Tbsp	2 Tbsp	2 Tbsp
Lemon wedge	1	1	1
SERVES 4			
For the asparagus	1 serving	1 serving	1 serving
Asparagus spears, ends trimmed	40 (640 g)	40 (640 g)	40 (640 g)
Lemon juice	4 tsp	4 tsp	4 tsp
Cooking spray			
For the rice pilaf	1 serving	1 serving	1 serving
Shiitake mushrooms	1⅓ cups (192 g)	1⅓ cups (192 g)	2 cups (288 g)
Cooked Wild Rice (page 286)	2 cups (328 g)	4 cups (656 g)	4 cups (656 g)
Truffle oil	¼ tsp	¼ tsp	¼ tsp
CALORIES	394 KCAL	556 KCAL	729 KCAL

❶ Preheat the oven to 350°F. Line two baking sheets with parchment paper.

❷ Place one pork chop between two pieces of parchment paper. Using a mallet, pound the pork chop to a ¼-inch thickness. Place meat on a plate and set aside. Repeat with the remaining pork chops.

❸ Put egg whites in a shallow bowl and whisk. Put panko and almond flour in another shallow bowl and mix. Dip each pork chop in the egg whites, then into the panko mixture, and place on one of the prepared baking sheets.

❹ Warm oil in a large cast-iron skillet over medium-high heat. Add pork chops, working in batches if necessary to avoid overcrowding, and sear for 1–2 minutes, until browned. Flip and sear for another 1–2 minutes. Transfer pork back to baking sheet, place on the middle rack of the oven and bake for 15–20 minutes, until golden and reaches an internal temperature of 160°F.

❺ Meanwhile, place asparagus on the other prepared baking sheet and spray with cooking spray. Place on top rack of oven and roast for 5–7 minutes, until tender.

❻ While asparagus is roasting, make the rice pilaf. Heat a cast-iron grill or skillet over medium-high heat. Add mushrooms and cook for 2–3 minutes on each side, until golden brown and fork tender. In a medium bowl, combine the wild rice, mushrooms, and truffle oil and mix well.

❼ Serve pork chop(s) with asparagus, wild rice pilaf, and lemon wedge. Drizzle lemon juice over the asparagus and serve.

Healthy Choices: *Using cast-iron cookware is a great way to boost your iron intake. As food cooks, it absorbs iron from the cookware (especially acidic ingredients like tomatoes).*

MEAL PLAN 26

CHECKLIST*

PRODUCE
Acorn squash
Arugula
Banana (2000, 2500)
Basil
Blueberries
Carrots
Garlic
Grapes (2500)
Lemon
Parsley
Portobello mushroom
Raspberries (1500, 2000)
Shallot
Strawberries (2000, 2500)
Sugar snap peas
Tomato

BAKERY
Whole grain bun

MEAT
Boneless skinless
  chicken breast

DAIRY
Eggs
Provolone cheese
Vanilla Greek yogurt
  (2000, 2500)

FROZEN
Papaya (2000, 2500)

DRY GOODS
Almond milk
Chia Drink Base
  (page 286)
Icing sugar
Instant coffee
White beans, canned

* *This list assumes that all basic ingredients (see Pantry and Freezer Staples, page 35) have been stocked.*

Pop-up Pancakes

MAKES 12		1500	2000	2500
For the pancakes		3 pancakes	4 pancakes	4 pancakes
Eggs		4 large (200 g)	4 large (200 g)	4 large (200 g)
Egg whites		½ cup (121 g)	½ cup (121 g)	½ cup (121 g)
Almond milk		1 cup	1 cup	1 cup
Vanilla extract		1 tsp	1 tsp	1 tsp
Almond flour		½ cup (32 g)	½ cup (32 g)	½ cup (32 g)
All-purpose flour		½ cup (62 g)	½ cup (62 g)	½ cup (62 g)
Wheat germ		¼ cup (29 g)	¼ cup (29 g)	¼ cup (29 g)
Salt		¼ tsp	¼ tsp	¼ tsp
Cooking spray				
SERVES 1				
To serve				
Blueberries		½ cup (72 g)	½ cup (72 g)	½ cup (72 g)
Raspberries		¼ cup (31 g)	½ cup (61 g)	////////
Strawberries		////////	½ cup (83 g)	⅔ cup (111 g)
Icing sugar		1½ tsp	1 Tbsp	1 Tbsp
Lemon juice		2 tsp	1½ tsp	1 Tbsp
CALORIES		288 KCAL	415 KCAL	394 KCAL

❶ Preheat the oven to 350°F. Spray a 12-cup muffin tin with cooking spray.

❷ In a large bowl, combine eggs, egg whites, milk, and vanilla and mix well. In a separate large bowl, mix together almond flour, flour, wheat germ, and salt. Add dry ingredients to wet ingredients and gently fold together until just combined. Do not overmix.

❸ Divide batter evenly among the prepared muffin wells. Bake for 20–25 minutes, until pancakes have popped up and a toothpick inserted comes out clean.

❹ Top pancakes with berries, icing sugar, and lemon juice.

Snacks

SERVES 1	1500	2000	2500
Mochachia 1	recipe below	recipe below	recipe below
Tropical Smoothie 3	////////	recipe below	recipe below
Coconut water	1¼ cups	////////	////////
Carrots, chopped	½ cup (64 g)	½ cup (64 g)	½ cup (64 g)
Sugar snap peas	1 cup (63 g)	1 cup (63 g)	1 cup (63 g)
Pistachios	////////	////////	⅓ cup (41 g)
Grapes	////////	////////	½ cup (77 g)

Mochachia ①

SERVES 1	1500	2000	2500
Vanilla almond milk	1 cup	1 cup	1 cup
Instant coffee	1 tsp	1 tsp	1 tsp
Cocoa powder	2 tsp	2 tsp	2 tsp
Blackstrap molasses	1½ tsp	////////	////////
Honey	½ tsp	½ tsp	½ tsp
Wheat germ	1½ tsp	////////	////////
Chia Drink Base (page 286)	1 serving	1 serving	1 serving
CALORIES	250 KCAL	213 KCAL	213 KCAL

Put almond milk, instant coffee, cocoa powder, molasses (if using),
honey, and wheat germ (if using) into a large cup and mix well.
Stir in chia drink base and serve over ice, if desired.

Tropical Smoothie ③

SERVES 1	1500	2000	2500
Coconut water	////////	1½ cups	1½ cups
Mango, frozen	////////	1 cup (165 g)	1 cup (165 g)
Banana, frozen	////////	1 small (101 g)	1 large (136 g)
Papaya, frozen	////////	⅓ cup (47 g)	½ cup (70 g)
Vanilla Greek yogurt	////////	¼ cup	⅓ cup
CALORIES		339 KCAL	397 KCAL

Put all ingredients into a blender and blend until smooth.
If the smoothie is too thick, add water (not coconut water).
If you prefer a thicker texture, add ice and blend until smooth.

Portobello Mushroom Sandwich

SERVES 1	1500	2000	2500
Portobello mushroom cap, stem and gills removed	1 (85 g)	1 (85 g)	1 (85 g)
Balsamic vinegar	1 tsp	1 tsp	1 tsp
Mayonnaise	1½ tsp	1½ tsp	1½ tsp
Garlic powder	dash	dash	dash
Lemon juice	⅛ tsp	⅛ tsp	⅛ tsp
Grapeseed oil	½ tsp	½ tsp	½ tsp
Garlic, finely chopped	1 small clove	1 small clove	1 small clove
Provolone cheese	15 g	20 g	20 g
Whole grain bun, lightly toasted	1 (64 g)	1 (64 g)	1 (64 g)
Balsamic Reduction (page 286)	1 tsp	1 tsp	1 tsp
Arugula	1 cup (20 g)	1 cup (20 g)	1 cup (20 g)
Tomato, sliced	2 slices (41 g)	2 slices (41 g)	2 slices (41 g)
CALORIES	312 KCAL	347 KCAL	347 KCAL

❶ Put mushroom cap in a small bowl or resealable bag, drizzle with balsamic vinegar, and set aside for 5 minutes to marinate.

❷ In a separate small bowl, combine mayonnaise, garlic powder, and lemon juice, and set aside.

❸ Heat oil in a non-stick grill pan or skillet over medium-high heat, add garlic, and sauté for 1 minute, until fragrant. Add mushroom and cook for 3–5 minutes, until mushroom has grill marks. Flip and cook for another 3–5 minutes, until fork tender. Top with provolone cheese, cover, and cook for another 1–2 minutes, until cheese has melted.

❹ Evenly spread mayonnaise on toasted bun, top with mushroom, balsamic reduction, arugula, tomato, and other half of bun. Serve.

Grab and Go: The night before, prepare garlic mayonnaise and spread on bun. Cover in plastic wrap. Place arugula and cheese in a resealable container. Place tomato slices and balsamic reduction in another resealable container. Make a parchment paper pouch to fit the mushroom, similar to the method provided on page 178 for the sole. Place in a resealable plastic bag or container. Place all in refrigerator overnight. At lunch, remove mushroom from resealable plastic bag, but leave in parchment paper pouch. Warm mushroom in microwave for 3 minutes on high, or until warm and slightly tender. While mushroom is cooking, prepare sandwich by topping bun with arugula, tomatoes, and cheese. When mushroom is done, place on sandwich over cheese so it melts and enjoy.

Chimichurri Chicken
with Beans and Squash

SERVES 4	1500	2000	2500
For the beans and squash	1 serving	1 serving	1 serving
Acorn squash, halved and sliced (skin optional)	4 cups (820 g)	4 cups (820 g)	4 cups (820 g)
White beans, drained and rinsed	2⅔ cups (476 g)	2⅔ cups (476 g)	2⅔ cups (476 g)
Cooking spray			
SERVES 4–6			
For the chimichurri sauce	2½ Tbsp serving	3 Tbsp serving	¼ cup serving
Natural rice vinegar	½ cup	½ cup	½ cup
Garlic	3 cloves	3 cloves	3 cloves
Shallot, diced	1 Tbsp	1 Tbsp	1 Tbsp
Lemon zest	1 Tbsp	1 Tbsp	1 Tbsp
Lemon juice	1 Tbsp	1 Tbsp	1 Tbsp
Sriracha	1 tsp	1 tsp	1 tsp
Oregano, dried	½ tsp	½ tsp	½ tsp
Paprika	¼ tsp	¼ tsp	¼ tsp
Salt	⅛ tsp	⅛ tsp	⅛ tsp
Grapeseed oil	¾ cup	¾ cup	¾ cup
Parsley	½ cup (30 g)	½ cup (30 g)	½ cup (30 g)
Basil	1 cup (44 g)	1 cup (44 g)	1 cup (44 g)
For the chicken	100 g chicken	100 g chicken	150 g chicken
Chicken breast	600 g	600 g	600 g
CALORIES	605 KCAL	629 KCAL	808 KCAL

❶ For the chimichurri sauce, add vinegar, garlic, shallot, lemon zest and juice, Sriracha, oregano, paprika, and salt to a blender or food processor and blend until smooth. Slowly add oil to mixture and continue to blend. Add parsley and basil and pulse to gently chop herbs. Transfer half the sauce to a bowl or container and refrigerate.

❷ Pour other half of sauce into a large resealable bag. Add chicken and marinate overnight in the refrigerator.

❸ Preheat the oven to 400°F. Line a baking sheet with parchment paper.

❹ Place squash on prepared baking sheet, spray with cooking spray, and bake for 25 minutes, until golden and fork tender. Add the beans to the baking sheet and cook for 3 minutes, until beans are warmed through. Set aside.

❺ Preheat barbecue or cast-iron grill pan to medium-high heat. Add chicken (discarding extra marinade) and cook for 3–5 minutes, flip, and cook for another 3–5 minutes, until cooked through and juices run clear. (Safe internal temperature for chicken is 165°F.)

❻ Place squash and beans on a plate, top with chicken, and drizzle extra sauce (from refrigerated half, not chicken marinade) overtop.

Note: Leftover chicken can be used for the Chicken Chimichurri Melt on day 27, page 256. Leftover chicken will keep for up to 2 days refrigerated. Any leftovers after 2 days should be frozen.

▽
Sweet Potato
Frittata

▽
Chicken
Chimichurri Melt

▽
Bison Taco
Salad

MEAL PLAN 27

CHECKLIST*

PRODUCE
Apple (2500)
Avocado (2000, 2500)
Banana (1500, 2000)
Blackberries (1500, 2000)
Blueberries (2500)
Broccoli
Cantaloupe (1500)
Cherry tomatoes
Grapes
Lime (2500)
Mango (2500)
Onion
Raspberries (1500, 2000)
Spinach
Strawberries (2500)
Sugar snap peas
Sweet potato
Tomato

BAKERY
Whole grain loaf

MEAT
Bacon
Ground bison
  (or extra-lean ground beef)

DAIRY
Cheddar cheese
Cottage cheese, dry curd
Eggs
Plain Greek yogurt (2000)
Provolone cheese
Vanilla Greek yogurt (2500)

FROZEN
Papaya (2000)

DRY GOODS
Ranch Dressing (page 288)
Salsa

PREMADE
Chimichurri Chicken (page 250)
Chimichurri Sauce (page 250)

This list assumes that all basic ingredients (see Pantry and Freezer Staples, page 35) have been stocked.

Sweet Potato Frittata

SERVES 6	1500	2000	2500
For the frittata	1 slice	1 slice	1 slice
Broccoli, chopped	1 cup (88 g)	1 cup (88 g)	1 cup (88 g)
Bacon, chopped	3 slices (68 g)	3 slices (68 g)	3 slices (68 g)
Onion, chopped	½ (80 g)	½ (80 g)	½ (80 g)
Eggs	8 large (400 g)	8 large (400 g)	8 large (400 g)
Cottage cheese, dry curd, plus extra to garnish	¾ cup (109 g)	¾ cup (109 g)	¾ cup (109 g)
Sun-dried tomatoes, dry-packed, chopped	½ cup (27 g)	¾ cup (41 g)	¾ cup (41 g)
Sweet potato, shredded	2½ cups (375 g)	2½ cups (375 g)	2½ cups (375 g)
Cooking spray			
CALORIES	256 KCAL	262 KCAL	262 KCAL

❶ Preheat the oven to 350°F.

❷ Heat an ovenproof cast-iron skillet over medium-high heat and spray with cooking spray. Add broccoli, bacon, and onions and sauté for 5–7 minutes, until bacon is golden brown and broccoli and onions are fork tender. Transfer mixture to a plate and set aside.

❸ Whisk eggs in a large bowl and stir in cottage cheese and sun-dried tomatoes. Place sweet potato evenly on the bottom of the skillet and pour egg mixture overtop. Sprinkle broccoli mixture overtop and bake for 35–40 minutes, until frittata is firm and golden. Divide into 6 portions and serve.

Chicken Chimichurri Melt

SERVES 1	1500	2000	2500
Chimichurri Sauce (page 250)	1 Tbsp	1 Tbsp	1 Tbsp
Whole grain loaf	1 slice (32 g)	1 slice (32 g)	1 slice (32 g)
Avocado, sliced	////////	¼ (50 g)	½ (101 g)
Tomato, sliced	⅓ cup (60 g)	⅓ cup (60 g)	½ cup (90 g)
Cooked Chimichurri Chicken (page 250)	75 g	75 g	75 g
Provolone cheese	15 g	20 g	20 g
Sriracha	¼ tsp	¼ tsp	¼ tsp
To serve			
Grapes	1 cup (154 g)	////////	////////
Sugar snap peas	////////	1 cup (63 g)	1 cup (63 g)
Cherry tomatoes	////////	////////	6 (102 g)
CALORIES	458 KCAL	476 KCAL	580 KCAL

❶ Preheat the oven to broil.

❷ Spread chimichurri sauce over piece of bread. Top with avocado (if using), tomato, chicken, and provolone. Place open-faced sandwich on a baking sheet and broil on the bottom rack for 3–5 minutes, or until cheese is golden and bubbling. Drizzle with Sriracha and serve with grapes (if using), sugar snap peas (if using), and cherry tomatoes (if using).

Grab and Go: The night before, spread Sriracha on bread, top with cheese, and wrap with plastic wrap. Place chimichurri sauce in a resealable plastic container. Place avocado, tomato, and chicken in another separate container. Store all in refrigerator overnight. At work, assemble sandwich and warm in toaster oven for 5–7 minutes, until cheese is golden and bubbling. Serve. (If you only have access to a microwave, prepare sandwich the night before, including broiling. Let cool, then wrap in parchment paper and then tinfoil. At lunch, remove from tinfoil and warm parchment-wrapped sandwich in the microwave for 1–2 minutes, until heated through.)

Bison Taco Salad

SERVES 1	1500	2000	2500
Ground bison	75 g	75 g	75 g
Taco Seasoning (page 286)	1 tsp	1 tsp	1 tsp
Spinach	3 cups (90 g)	3 cups (90 g)	3 cups (90 g)
Cooked Quinoa (page 286)	½ cup (93 g)	½ cup (93 g)	½ cup (93 g)
Cherry tomatoes, halved	8 (136 g)	8 (136 g)	8 (136 g)
Black beans, drained and rinsed	⅓ cup (57 g)	⅓ cup (57 g)	⅓ cup (57 g)
Corn, frozen	⅓ cup (55 g)	⅓ cup (55 g)	⅓ cup (55 g)
Cheddar cheese, shredded	////////	2 Tbsp (10 g)	2 Tbsp (10 g)
Salsa	¼ cup	¼ cup	⅓ cup
Ranch Dressing (page 288)	1½ tsp	1 Tbsp	1 Tbsp
CALORIES	474 KCAL	549 KCAL	555 KCAL

❶ Heat a large skillet over medium-high heat. Add ground bison and cook for 5–10 minutes, until cooked through.

❷ Mix taco seasoning with ¼ cup water in a small bowl. Add to skillet, stir, and cook for 3–5 minutes, until water has evaporated.

❸ Make a bed of spinach in a salad bowl or on a large plate. Top with quinoa, tomatoes, beans, corn, bison, cheddar, salsa, and ranch dressing.

Snacks

SERVES 1	1500	2000	2500
Vanilla-Cinnamon Steamer 2	////////	recipe below	recipe below
Banana-Flax Smoothie	recipe page 259	recipe page 259	////////
Apple, sliced	////////	////////	1 cup (70 g)
Sugar snap peas	1¼ cups (79 g)	////////	////////
Cantaloupe, chopped	1 cup (160 g)	////////	////////
Grapes	////////	1 cup (154 g)	1½ cups (231 g)
Pistachios	////////	////////	¼ cup (31 g)
Raspberries	¾ cup (92 g)	½ cup (61 g)	////////
Blackberries	⅔ cup (96 g)	½ cup (72 g)	////////
Spicy Lime Popcorn	////////	////////	recipe page 259
Yogurt Parfait 3	////////	////////	recipe page 259

Vanilla-Cinnamon Steamer ②

SERVES 1	1500	2000	2500
Vanilla almond milk	////////	1¼ cups	1½ cups
Ground cinnamon	////////	¼ tsp	¼ tsp
Honey	////////	½ tsp	1 tsp
CALORIES		126 KCAL	159 KCAL

Put all ingredients into a microwave-safe mug and mix well. Cover and microwave on high for 1 minute. Stir and microwave for another minute.

Banana-Flax Smoothie

SERVES 1	1500	2000	2500
Banana	½ large (68 g)	1 large (136 g)	////////
Cocoa powder	2 tsp	////////	////////
Flaxseeds	2 tsp	1½ tsp	////////
Vanilla almond milk	1¼ cups	////////	////////
Mango, frozen	////////	1 cup (165 g)	////////
Papaya, frozen	////////	½ cup (70 g)	////////
Plain Greek yogurt	////////	⅓ cup	////////
Coconut water	////////	1¼ cups	////////
Honey	////////	½ tsp	////////
CALORIES	217 KCAL	411 KCAL	

Put all ingredients into a blender and blend until smooth.
If the smoothie is too thick, add water (not almond milk or
coconut water). If you prefer a thicker texture, add ice and
blend until smooth.

Spicy Lime Popcorn

SERVES 1	1500	2000	2500
Paprika	////////	////////	⅛ tsp
Garlic powder	////////	////////	⅛ tsp
Air-Popped Popcorn (page 287)	////////	////////	3 cups (24 g)
Lime juice	////////	////////	sprinkle
CALORIES			95 KCAL

Mix together paprika and garlic powder in a small bowl.
Put popcorn in a large bowl. Sprinkle lime juice and spice
mixture overtop and gently stir to combine.

Yogurt Parfait ③

SERVES 1	1500	2000	2500
Vanilla Greek yogurt	////////	////////	1 cup
Mango	////////	////////	¾ cup (124 g)
Strawberries	////////	////////	½ cup (83 g)
Blueberries	////////	////////	½ cup (72 g)
Flaxseeds	////////	////////	1½ tsp
CALORIES			369 KCAL

Put yogurt in a medium bowl. Layer fruit overtop and
sprinkle with flaxseeds.

▽
*Apple Pie Chia
Pudding*

▽
*Spicy Hawaiian
Pizza*

▽
*Turkey Sausage
Soup in an Acorn
Squash Bowl*

MEAL PLAN 28

CHECKLIST*

PRODUCE
Acorn squash
Apples
Beet
Blackberries (1500)
Blueberries
Broccoli
Brussels sprouts
Carrots
Cherry tomatoes (1500)
Cremini mushrooms
Garlic
Green beans
Kale
Mango (2000, 2500)
Onion
Orange (1500)
Pineapple
Rutabaga
Spinach
Sugar snap peas
Watermelon (2000)

DELI
Sliced prosciutto

BAKERY
8-inch whole wheat
  tortilla

MEAT
Turkey sausage

DAIRY
Cheddar cheese
Mozzarella cheese
Tzatziki (page 287)
Vanilla Greek yogurt

DRY GOODS
Applesauce,
  unsweetened
Coconut oil
Granola (page 287)
Hearts of palm
  (1500)
Vegetable broth

* *This list assumes that all basic ingredients (see Pantry and Freezer Staples, page 35) have been stocked.*

Apple Pie Chia Pudding

SERVES 3	1500	2000	2500
For the pudding	1 pudding	1 pudding	1½ puddings
Almond milk, original or vanilla	1 cup	1 cup	1 cup
Vanilla Greek yogurt	¼ cup	¼ cup	¼ cup
Honey	1½ tsp	1½ tsp	1½ tsp
Applesauce	½ cup	½ cup	½ cup
Ground cinnamon, divided	1 tsp	1 tsp	1 tsp
Vanilla extract	1 tsp	1 tsp	1 tsp
Chia seeds	3 Tbsp	3 Tbsp	3 Tbsp
Coconut oil	1 Tbsp	1 Tbsp	1 Tbsp
Apples, cored, peeled, and chopped	2 (340 g)	2 (340 g)	2 (340 g)
Pure maple syrup	1 Tbsp	1 Tbsp	1 Tbsp
Wheat germ	1 Tbsp	////////	////////
Granola (page 287)	1 Tbsp	2 Tbsp	4 Tbsp
SERVES 1			
Blueberries	½ cup (72 g)	½ cup (72 g)	1 cup (145 g)
Mango	////////	1 cup (165 g)	////////
CALORIES	377 KCAL	517 KCAL	694 KCAL

❶ In a medium bowl, combine almond milk, yogurt, honey, applesauce, ½ tsp cinnamon, vanilla, and chia seeds. Cover and refrigerate for at least 3 hours or overnight, to let chia seeds gel.

❷ Melt coconut oil in a skillet over medium-high heat. Add apples and cook for 2–3 minutes, until apples begin to soften and become fragrant. Add remaining ½ tsp cinnamon and maple syrup and cook for another 2–3 minutes, or until the syrup begins to caramelize and thickens. Remove from heat and set aside.

❸ Remove the chia pudding from the fridge, give it a good stir, and divide between 3 mason jars. Right before serving, top with apples, wheat germ (if using), and granola. Serve with blueberries and mango (if using).

Note: Leftovers will keep for up to a week refrigerated.

Spicy Hawaiian Pizza

SERVES 1	1500	2000	2500
Whole wheat tortilla	1 (48 g)	1 (48 g)	1 (48 g)
Tomato paste	2½ Tbsp	2½ Tbsp	2½ Tbsp
Mozzarella cheese, shredded	¼ cup (30 g)	¼ cup (30 g)	¼ cup (30 g)
Cheddar cheese, shredded	1 Tbsp (5 g)	1 Tbsp (5 g)	1 Tbsp (5 g)
Prosciutto, chopped	1½ slices (23 g)	1½ slices (23 g)	1½ slices (23 g)
Pineapple, chopped	¼ cup (39 g)	¼ cup (39 g)	¼ cup (39 g)
Sriracha	1 tsp	1 tsp	1 tsp
Microgreens, to garnish (optional)			
To serve			
Broccoli florets	1 cup (88 g)	1 cup (88 g)	1 cup (88 g)
Carrot sticks	½ cup (64 g)	½ cup (64 g)	½ cup (64 g)
Cremini mushrooms	½ cup (108 g)	½ cup (108 g)	½ cup (108 g)
Tzatziki (page 287)	1½ Tbsp	3 Tbsp	1½ Tbsp
CALORIES	448 KCAL	461 KCAL	448 KCAL

❶ Preheat the oven to broil. Line a baking sheet with parchment paper.

❷ Place tortilla on prepared baking sheet and spread tomato paste overtop. Top with mozzarella, cheddar, prosciutto, and pineapple and bake for 3–5 minutes, until cheese is golden and bubbling. Drizzle Sriracha overtop, top with microgreens (if using), and serve with vegetables and tzatziki.

Turkey Sausage Soup in an Acorn Squash Bowl

SERVES 4	1500	2000	2500
For the soup	1 serving	1 serving	1 serving
Turkey sausage, casing removed, crumbled	2 (182 g)	2 (182 g)	2 (182 g)
Grapeseed oil, divided	1 Tbsp + 2 tsp	1 Tbsp + 2 tsp	1 Tbsp + 2 tsp
Onion, chopped	1 (110 g)	1 (110 g)	1 (110 g)
Garlic, finely chopped	2 cloves	2 cloves	2 cloves
Tomato paste	½ can (3 oz)	½ can (3 oz)	½ can (3 oz)
Vegetable broth	4 cups	4 cups	4 cups
Rutabaga, cubed	¼ (193 g)	¼ (193 g)	¼ (193 g)
Carrots, chopped	2 (108 g)	2 (108 g)	2 (108 g)
Acorn squash, cut in half, deseeded and stringy bits removed	2	2	2
Salt and pepper	dash each	dash each	dash each
Quinoa, uncooked	6 Tbsp (64 g)	6 Tbsp (64 g)	6 Tbsp (64 g)
Kale, stems removed and leaves chopped	2 leaves (67 g)	2 leaves (67 g)	2 leaves (67 g)
Green beans, chopped	½ cup (103 g)	½ cup (103 g)	½ cup (103 g)
SERVES 1			
For the salad			
Spinach	2 cups (60 g)	2 cups (60 g)	2 cups (60 g)
Brussels sprouts, thinly shaved	5 (95 g)	5 (95 g)	5 (95 g)
Beet, peeled, raw and shredded or spiralized	¼ cup (34 g)	¼ cup (34 g)	¼ cup (34 g)
Hearts of palm, sliced	¼ cup (36 g)	////////	////////
Pumpkin seeds	1 Tbsp	1½ tsp	1 Tbsp
Sunflower seeds	1 Tbsp	1½ tsp	1 Tbsp
For the dressing	1 Tbsp serving	1 Tbsp serving	1 Tbsp serving
Balsamic vinegar	1 tsp	1 tsp	1 tsp
Honey	½ tsp	½ tsp	½ tsp
Grapeseed oil	1 Tbsp	1 Tbsp	1 Tbsp
CALORIES	659 KCAL	585 KCAL	602 KCAL

❶ Preheat the oven to 375°F.

❷ Heat a large Dutch oven over medium-high heat, add sausage, and cook for 7–10 minutes, until cooked through. Spoon into a bowl and set aside.

❸ Return Dutch oven to medium-high heat and add 1 Tbsp oil. Add onions and garlic and sauté for 5–7 minutes, until onions are translucent. Add tomato paste and stir for another minute. Pour in vegetable broth, add rutabaga, carrots, and turkey, and bring to a boil. Reduce to a simmer, cover, and cook for 30–45 minutes, until rutabaga is tender.

❹ Meanwhile, line a baking sheet with parchment paper. Cut a small portion off the top and bottom of both squash to ensure bowl sits flat. (Don't cut too deep or your bowl will leak. Cut just enough so it sits flat.) Cut both squash in half, making two bowls each, and remove seeds. Place squash on prepared baking sheet, bowl side up, brush with 2 tsp oil, and season with salt and pepper. Bake for 20–25 minutes, or until the squash is tender.

❺ Add quinoa to soup, cover, and simmer for 15–20 minutes, until quinoa is cooked. Remove Dutch oven from heat and stir in kale and green beans.

❻ Make a bed of spinach in a salad bowl. Top with Brussels sprouts, beets, hearts of palm (if using), pumpkin seeds, and sunflower seeds. In a small bowl, whisk together vinegar and honey. Whisking continuously, gradually pour in oil until emulsified. Drizzle over salad.

❼ Ladle soup into squash bowl and serve with salad.

Snacks

SERVES 1	1500	2000	2500
Sugar snap peas	1 cup (63 g)	1 cup (63 g)	1 cup (63 g)
Orange	1 small (96 g)	////////	////////
Blackberries	¼ cup (36 g)	////////	////////
Pistachios	////////	¼ cup (31 g)	¼ cup (31 g)
Cheddar cheese, sliced	////////	15 g	15 g
Cherry tomatoes	4 (68 g)	////////	////////
Watermelon, chopped	////////	2 cups (304 g)	////////
Air-Popped Popcorn (page 287)	////////	2½ cups (20 g)	3 cups (24 g)
Dark chocolate	////////	////////	15 g
Yogurt Parfait 4	////////	////////	recipe below

Yogurt Parfait ④

SERVES 1	1500	2000	2500
Vanilla Greek yogurt	////////	////////	¾ cup
Mango, cubed	////////	////////	1 cup (165 g)
Raspberries	////////	////////	½ cup (61 g)
CALORIES			305 KCAL

Put yogurt in a small glass and top with fruit.

▽

Breakfast Burrito

▽

*Roasted Balsamic
Tomato Bowl*

▽

*Spicy Maple Salmon
with Grilled Vegetables
and Wild Rice*

MEAL PLAN

29

CHECKLIST*

PRODUCE
Arugula
Asparagus
Avocado (2500)
Banana (2000, 2500)
Basil
Blackberries (1500)
Blueberries (2500)
Cantaloupe (1500, 2000)
Carrots
Garlic
Grapes (2500)
Napa cabbage
Shiitake mushrooms
Snow peas
Spinach
Sugar snap peas (2000)
Tomatoes

BAKERY
8-inch whole wheat tortilla

FISH
Salmon

DAIRY
Cheddar cheese
Eggs
Plain Greek yogurt (2000,
    2500)
Soft goat cheese

FROZEN
Pineapple (2500)
Raspberries (1500, 2000)

DRY GOODS
Brown sugar
Salsa

This list assumes that all basic ingredients (see Pantry and Freezer Staples, page 35) have been stocked.

Breakfast Burrito

SERVES 1	1500	2000	2500
Egg	1 small (38 g)	1 large (50 g)	1 large (50 g)
Egg white	1 large (33 g)	1 large (33 g)	1 large (33 g)
Black beans, drained and rinsed	⅓ cup (57 g)	⅓ cup (57 g)	⅓ cup (57 g)
Whole wheat tortilla	1 (48 g)	1 (48 g)	1 (48 g)
Cheddar cheese, shredded	2 Tbsp (10 g)	2 Tbsp (10 g)	3 Tbsp (15 g)
Avocado, sliced	////////	////////	½ (101 g)
Salsa	¼ cup	¼ cup	¼ cup
Spinach	1½ cups (45 g)	1½ cups (45 g)	1½ cups (45 g)
Cooking spray			
CALORIES	346 KCAL	362 KCAL	543 KCAL

❶ Spray a small non-stick skillet with cooking spray and warm over medium heat.

❷ In a small bowl, whisk together egg and egg whites. Gently stir in black beans.

❸ Add egg mixture to the pan and slowly scramble the eggs for 2–3 minutes, scraping around the outside of the pan in a circle and pulling to the center until eggs are cooked through.

❹ Put tortilla on a plate and top with eggs, cheddar, avocado (if using), salsa, and spinach. Fold over the ends of the tortilla and roll. Serve.

Snacks

SERVES 1	1500	2000	2500
Tropical Mango Smoothie	recipe below	recipe below	recipe below
Vanilla-Almond Steamer	recipe below	recipe below	recipe below
Cantaloupe, chopped	1 cup (160 g)	1 cup (160 g)	////////
Blackberries	⅓ cup (48 g)	////////	////////
Sugar snap peas	////////	1 cup (63 g)	////////
Grapes	////////	////////	½ cup (77 g)
Blueberries	////////	////////	1 cup (145 g)
Dark chocolate	////////	20 g	20 g
Air-Popped Popcorn (page 287)	////////	1½ cups (12 g)	////////

Tropical Mango Smoothie

SERVES 1	1500	2000	2500
Mango, fresh or frozen	⅓ cup (55 g)	1 cup (165 g)	1 cup (165 g)
Raspberries, fresh or frozen	1 cup (123 g)	1 cup (123 g)	////////
Banana	////////	½ (59 g)	1 large (136 g)
Pineapple, fresh or frozen	////////	////////	½ cup (77 g)
Wheat germ	1½ Tbsp	1 Tbsp	////////
Coconut water	1¼ cups	1¼ cups	1 cup
Honey	////////	1 tsp	1 tsp
Plain Greek yogurt	////////	¼ cup	⅓ cup
CALORIES	197 KCAL	374 KCAL	393 KCAL

Put all ingredients into a blender and blend until smooth.
If the smoothie is too thick, add water (not coconut water).
If you prefer a thicker texture, add ice and blend until smooth.

Vanilla-Almond Steamer

SERVES 1	1500	2000	2500
Vanilla almond milk	1½ cups	1½ cups	1½ cups
Blackstrap molasses	1 Tbsp	////////	////////
Cocoa powder	2 tsp	////////	////////
Honey	½ tsp	////////	1 tsp
Ground cinnamon	////////	¼ tsp	¼ tsp
CALORIES	204 KCAL	258 KCAL	159 KCAL

Put all ingredients into a microwave-safe mug
and mix well. Cover and microwave on high for
1 minute. Stir and microwave for another minute.

Roasted Balsamic Tomato Bowl

SERVES 2	1500	2000	2500
For the tomato bowl	1 serving	1 serving	1 serving
Assorted tomatoes	248 g	248 g	248 g
Balsamic vinegar	1 Tbsp	1 Tbsp	1 Tbsp
Grapeseed oil	2 Tbsp	2 Tbsp	2 Tbsp
Cooked Quinoa (page 286)	1 cup (138 g)	2 cups (277 g)	2 cups (277 g)
Basil, fresh	1 cup (44 g)	1 cup (44 g)	1 cup (44 g)
Arugula	1 cup (20 g)	1 cup (20 g)	1 cup (20 g)
Soft goat cheese, crumbled	1 Tbsp + 1 tsp (20 g)	2 Tbsp + 2 tsp (40 g)	2 Tbsp + 2 tsp (40 g)
Balsamic Reduction (page 286)	1 tsp	1 Tbsp	1 Tbsp
CALORIES	277 KCAL	407 KCAL	407 KCAL

❶ Preheat the oven to 400°F. Line a baking sheet with parchment paper.

❷ In a medium bowl, toss tomatoes with balsamic vinegar and grapeseed oil until coated. Place on the prepared baking sheet and roast for 30–45 minutes, until tomatoes reduce and vinegar caramelizes.

❸ To serve, put quinoa in a bowl and top with basil, arugula, goat cheese, and roasted tomatoes. Drizzle with balsamic reduction.

Grab and Go: This bowl is delicious cold, but if you would prefer to enjoy it warm, store everything but the basil, arugula, and goat cheese in a microwave-safe container. Warm in microwave for 1–2 minutes, then top mix with greens and cheese.

Spicy Maple Salmon
with Grilled Vegetables and Wild Rice

SERVES 4–6	1500	2000	2500
For the salmon	153 g salmon	153 g salmon	230 g salmon
Salmon fillet, deboned (skin on or off)	750 g	750 g	750 g
Pure maple syrup	2 Tbsp	2 Tbsp	2 Tbsp
Brown sugar, packed	2 Tbsp	2 Tbsp	2 Tbsp
Honey	1 Tbsp	1 Tbsp	1 Tbsp
Natural rice vinegar	¼ cup	¼ cup	¼ cup
Low-sodium soy sauce	1 Tbsp	1 Tbsp	1 Tbsp
Garlic, minced	½ tsp	½ tsp	½ tsp
Sriracha	½ tsp	½ tsp	½ tsp
SERVES 4			
For the vegetables	213 g vegetables	213 g vegetables	213 g vegetables
Grapeseed oil	1 Tbsp	1 Tbsp	1 Tbsp
Garlic, chopped	2 tsp	2 tsp	2 tsp
Carrots	4 small (127 g)	4 small (127 g)	4 small (127 g)
Napa cabbage, leaves	146 g	146 g	146 g
Asparagus	16 (268 g)	16 (268 g)	16 (268 g)
Shiitake mushrooms, halved	¾ cup (109 g)	¾ cup (109 g)	¾ cup (109 g)
Snow peas	1½ cups (147 g)	1½ cups (147 g)	1½ cups (147 g)
Natural rice vinegar	1 Tbsp	1 Tbsp	1 Tbsp
Sesame oil	1½ tsp	1½ tsp	1½ tsp
Soy sauce	1 tsp	1 tsp	1 tsp
Sesame seeds, toasted	1 Tbsp	1 Tbsp	1 Tbsp
SERVES 1			
To serve			
Cooked Wild Rice (page 286)	⅓ cup (55 g)	½ cup (82 g)	1 cup (164 g)
CALORIES	485 KCAL	512 KCAL	749 KCAL

❶ Preheat the oven to 425°F. Line a baking sheet with parchment paper.

❷ Place salmon on the prepared baking sheet and bake for 8–12 minutes, until opaque and easily flakes with a fork. (Depending on the thickness of your salmon, the cook time will vary. It takes 4–6 minutes for each ½-inch thickness.)

❸ Meanwhile, combine maple syrup, sugar, honey, vinegar, soy sauce, garlic, and Sriracha in a small saucepan over medium-high heat and boil for 15–20 minutes, until glaze reduces and thickens.

❹ Remove salmon from oven and turn oven to broil. Brush salmon with maple glaze and broil for 2–3 minutes, until sticky and caramelized.

(Keep a close eye to make sure the sugars in the glaze do not burn.)

❺ Heat oil in a cast-iron grill pan over medium-high heat. Add garlic and sauté for 1 minute, until golden and fragrant. Grill carrots, asparagus, and cabbage for 2–3 minutes on each side, long enough to get grill marks.

❻ Add mushrooms and snow peas and sauté for another 4–6 minutes, until mushrooms just begin to soften. Remove vegetables from heat and toss with vinegar, sesame oil, and soy sauce. Top with sesame seeds.

❼ Serve salmon with grilled vegetables and wild rice.

▽
*Mulberry Puffed
Quinoa Cereal*

▽
BBQ Chicken Salad

▽
*Slow-Cooked
Bison Stew*

MEAL PLAN

30

CHECKLIST*

PRODUCE
Arugula
Avocado (2000, 2500)
Baby potatoes
Blueberries (2000, 2500)
Cantaloupe (1500)
Carrots
Cherry tomatoes
Grapes (2000, 2500)
Mango
Onion
Spinach
Sugar snap peas (1500)
White mushrooms (1500)

MEAT
Bacon
Bison stewing meat
Cooked boneless skinless
  chicken breast

DAIRY
Butter
Cheddar cheese
Vanilla Greek yogurt (2500)

FROZEN
Peas

DRY GOODS
Barbecue sauce
Bran buds with psyllium
Chia Drink Base (page 286)
Coconut oil
Dried goji berries
Dried mulberries
Instant coffee
Puffed quinoa
Quick oats
Ranch Dressing (page 288)
Vegetable broth
Wheat bran

* This list assumes that all basic ingredients (see Pantry and Freezer Staples, page 35) have been stocked.

Mulberry Puffed Quinoa Cereal

SERVES 12	1500	2000	2500
For the cereal	⅔ cup (62 g)	¾ cup (72 g)	¾ cup (72 g)
Quick oats	2 cups (189 g)	2 cups (189 g)	2 cups (189 g)
Wheat bran	¼ cup (15 g)	¼ cup (15 g)	¼ cup (15 g)
Flaxseeds	¼ cup (39 g)	¼ cup (39 g)	¼ cup (39 g)
Bran buds with psyllium	2 cups (168 g)	2 cups (168 g)	2 cups (168 g)
Coconut oil, melted	⅓ cup	⅓ cup	⅓ cup
Honey, divided	6 Tbsp	6 Tbsp	6 Tbsp
Water	½ cup	½ cup	½ cup
Puffed quinoa	6 cups (336 g)	6 cups (336 g)	6 cups (336 g)
Shredded coconut, unsweetened	½ cup (37 g)	½ cup (37 g)	½ cup (37 g)
Dried mulberries	1½ cups (180 g)	1½ cups (180 g)	1½ cups (180 g)
Dried goji berries	½ cup (48 g)	½ cup (48 g)	½ cup (48 g)
Sunflower seeds	½ cup (64 g)	½ cup (64 g)	½ cup (64 g)
Pumpkin seeds	½ cup (113 g)	½ cup (113 g)	½ cup (113 g)
Almond milk	1 cup	1 cup	1 cup
SERVES 1			
Mango	1 cup (165 g)	1 cup (165 g)	1 cup (165 g)
Blueberries	////////	½ cup (72 g)	////////
CALORIES	456 KCAL	549 KCAL	507 KCAL

❶ Preheat the oven to 325°F. Line two baking sheets with parchment paper.

❷ In a large bowl, combine oats, bran, flaxseeds, bran buds, coconut oil, and 2 Tbsp honey and mix together. Scatter on one of the prepared baking sheets, gently pressing down to flatten, and bake for 20 minutes.

❸ Meanwhile combine water and remaining ¼ cup honey in a small saucepan over medium-high heat, stir, and bring to a boil. Reduce heat to medium-low and simmer for 15–20 minutes, until sauce has thickened.

❹ When oat mixture is done baking, remove from oven and set aside. Reduce oven temperature to 250°F.

❺ Put puffed quinoa in a large bowl and pour honey syrup overtop. Gently stir to combine. Transfer the quinoa to second prepared baking sheet and bake for 15 minutes.

❻ In a large bowl, combine the oat mixture, puffed quinoa, coconut, dried berries, and seeds.

❼ To serve, pour cereal into a bowl, add milk, and enjoy with fruit. Store extra cereal in a dry sealed container at room temperature for up to 5 months.

Note: Psyllium fiber helps to lower your LDL cholesterol, the type of cholesterol linked to heart disease. Plus, it helps you feel fuller longer!

BBQ Chicken Salad

SERVES 1	1500	2000	2500
Corn, frozen	⅓ cup (55 g)	⅓ cup (55 g)	⅓ cup (55 g)
Grapeseed oil	½ tsp	½ tsp	½ tsp
Salt	dash	dash	dash
Spinach	2 cups (60 g)	2 cups (60 g)	2 cups (60 g)
Arugula	1 cup (20 g)	1 cup (20 g)	1 cup (20 g)
Cherry tomatoes, halved	8 (136 g)	8 (136 g)	8 (136 g)
Black beans, drained and rinsed	⅓ cup (57 g)	⅓ cup (57 g)	⅓ cup (57 g)
Sun-dried tomatoes, dry-packed, chopped	⅓ cup (18 g)	¼ cup (14 g)	¼ cup (14 g)
Avocado, pitted and sliced	////////	¼ (50 g)	⅓ (67 g)
Cooked chicken breast, chopped	60 g	60 g	75 g
Cheddar cheese, shredded	2 Tbsp (10 g)	2 Tbsp (10 g)	¼ cup (20 g)
Barbecue sauce	1½ tsp	1 Tbsp	1 Tbsp
Ranch Dressing (page 288)	1½ Tbsp	1½ Tbsp	1½ Tbsp
CALORIES	485 KCAL	574 KCAL	664 KCAL

❶ Preheat the oven to 400°F. Line a baking sheet with parchment paper.

❷ In a small bowl, mix together corn, oil, and salt. Spread evenly on the prepared baking sheet and roast for 15–20 minutes, until corn turns golden.

❸ To serve, make a bed of spinach and arugula in a salad bowl or on a large plate. Top with roasted corn, tomatoes, beans, sun-dried tomatoes, avocado (if using), chicken, cheddar, barbecue sauce, and ranch dressing.

Grab and Go: Prepare night before or in the morning. Place all ingredients in a resealable container, except for barbecue sauce and ranch dressing. Place barbecue sauce and ranch dressing in separate resealable containers. When ready to enjoy, mix in barbecue sauce and ranch dressing.

Slow-Cooked Bison Stew

SERVES 4–6	1500	2000	2500
For the stew	334 g stew	501 g stew	501 g stew
Butter	2 Tbsp	2 Tbsp	2 Tbsp
Bison stewing meat	500 g	500 g	500 g
Onion, diced	1 large (150 g)	1 large (150 g)	1 large (150 g)
Bacon, chopped	3 slices (114 g)	3 slices (114 g)	3 slices (114 g)
Tomato paste	1 can (6 oz)	1 can (6 oz)	1 can (6 oz)
All-purpose flour	1½ Tbsp	1½ Tbsp	1½ Tbsp
Vegetable broth	1½ cups	1½ cups	1½ cups
Carrots, chopped	3 large (216 g)	3 large (216 g)	3 large (216 g)
Baby potatoes, skin on	2 cups (300 g)	2 cups (300 g)	2 cups (300 g)
Peas, frozen	1 cup (160 g)	1 cup (160 g)	1 cup (160 g)
CALORIES	333 KCAL	499 KCAL	666 KCAL

❶ Melt butter in a large non-stick skillet warmed to medium-high heat. Add bison and brown for 2 minutes per side. Transfer bison to a plate and set aside.

❷ Add onions and bacon to skillet and sauté for 5–7 minutes, until bacon is browned and onions are translucent.

❸ Add tomato paste and flour to skillet and stir until thick and pasty. Transfer tomato mixture and bison to a slow cooker, add broth, and stir until smooth. Add carrots, potatoes, and peas and cook on low for 7–8 hours, or high for 4–5 hours. Serve warm.

Snacks

SERVES 1	1500	2000	2500
Mochachia 2	recipe below	recipe below	recipe below
Grapes		1 cup (154 g)	1¼ cups (193 g)
Coconut water	1 cup		
Cantaloupe, chopped	¾ cup (120 g)		
Air-Popped Popcorn (page 287)		2 cups (16 g)	3 cups (24 g)
White mushrooms	5 (50 g)		
Sugar snap peas	½ cup (32 g)		
Vanilla Greek yogurt			½ cup
Blueberries			1 cup (145 g)

Mochachia ②

SERVES 1	1500	2000	2500
Vanilla almond milk	1 cup	1 cup	1 cup
Instant coffee	1 tsp	1 tsp	1 tsp
Cocoa powder	2 tsp	2 tsp	2 tsp
Honey	½ tsp	½ tsp	1 tsp
Chia Drink Base (page 286)	1 serving	1 serving	1 serving
CALORIES	213 KCAL	213 KCAL	224 KCAL

Put milk, coffee, cocoa, and honey into a large cup and mix well. Stir in chia drink base and serve over ice, if desired.

BASIC RECIPES

ROSEMARY
+
GRAPEFRUIT
+
WATER

BASIL
+
MANGO
+
WATER

BLOOD ORANGE
+
GINGER
+
WATER

MINT
+
LIME
+
WATER

RASPBERRY
+
LEMON
+
WATER

PEACH BITTERS
+
VANILLA
+
WATER

Grains

Buckwheat
MAKES 2½ CUPS
1 cup buckwheat
2 cups water

Bring buckwheat and water to a boil in a sauce-pan over medium-high heat. Cover, reduce heat to medium-low, and simmer for 10–15 minutes, until tender. Remove from heat, drain any excess liquid, and serve.

Quinoa
MAKES 3 CUPS
1 cup quinoa
2 cups water

Bring water to a boil in a saucepan over medium-high heat. Add quinoa, cover, reduce heat to medium-low, and simmer for 12–15 minutes, until liquid has absorbed. Remove from heat. Store in an airtight container in the fridge for up to 5 days.

Note: *1 cup dry quinoa yields 3 cups cooked quinoa.*

Wild Rice
MAKES 4 CUPS
1 cup wild rice
2¼ cups water

Bring rice and water to a boil in a large saucepan over medium-high heat. Cover, reduce heat to medium-low, and simmer for 35–40 minutes, until tender. Remove from heat, drain any excess liquid, and serve. If not consuming immediately, place in a resealable container and refrigerate for up to 5 days, or freeze for up to 6 months.

Chia Drink Base
MAKES ABOUT 1 CUP
3 Tbsp chia seeds
1 cup coconut water

Mix chia seeds with coconut water. Place in the refrigerator overnight.

Sauces and Seasonings

Balsamic Reduction
MAKES ABOUT 1 CUP
2 cups balsamic vinegar

Pour vinegar into a saucepan and bring to a boil over medium-high heat. Reduce heat to medium-low and simmer for 15–20 minutes, until vinegar is reduced by half and syrupy in consistency. (The reduction will continue to thicken as it cools, so you'll want to pull it from heat just before it reaches the ideal thickness.) Keep refrigerated for up to 1 month.

Note: *The odor through this process is very strong, so be sure to open windows and vent.*

Basil Pesto
MAKES 1½ CUPS
2 cups fresh basil, both leaves and stems
¼ cup roasted pine nuts
½ cup Parmesan cheese, grated
½ head Roasted Garlic (page 287)
⅔ cup good-quality olive oil

Put all basil, pine nuts, Parmesan, and roasted garlic into a blender or food processor. Pulse a few times to roughly chop. Turn on blender or food processor and slowly add the oil until pesto reaches your desired consistency (you may not end up using all the oil). Pesto will keep for up to a week refrigerated, and up to 4 months in the freezer.

Taco Seasoning
MAKES 1 CUP
½ cup chili powder
2 Tbsp cumin
2 Tbsp paprika
2 tsp garlic powder
2 tsp onion powder
1 tsp ancho chili powder
1 tsp oregano
1 tsp red pepper flakes
¼ tsp cayenne pepper

Mix all ingredients together in a small bowl and store in an airtight container for up to 6 months.

Dips

Hummus

MAKES ABOUT 1 CUP

1 (15-oz) can chickpeas, drained and rinsed well
½ head Roasted Garlic (see this page)
½ lemon, juiced
2 Tbsp tahini
¼ cup sesame oil
½ cup olive oil
Pinch of salt

Put chickpeas, roasted garlic, lemon juice, and tahini in a blender or food processor and blend until smooth. Turn speed to low and slowly pour in oils. Finish with salt.

Tzatziki

MAKES ⅔ CUP

½ cup plain Greek yogurt
½ head Roasted Garlic (see this page)
1 Tbsp chopped fresh dill
¼ cup peeled and grated cucumber
1 Tbsp lemon juice

In a medium bowl, whisk together yogurt, garlic, dill, cucumber, and lemon juice. Refrigerate for 30 minutes before using. (Letting it sit allows the flavors to meld.)

Stock

Chicken Stock

MAKES 8 CUPS

For the stock
1 chicken carcass, legs or wings chopped
2 large carrots, roughly chopped
2 celery stalks, roughly chopped
1 onion, skin on and roughly chopped
8 cups water

For the bouquet garni
3 sprigs thyme
5 whole black peppercorns
1 whole bay leaf
1 clove garlic, peeled
cheesecloth
twine

❶ Place the stock ingredients in a large stockpot. Put all the bouquet garni ingredients into a cheese-cloth, tie closed with twine, and place in stockpot.
❷ Bring to a simmer over medium heat. (Do not let the stock boil.) Simmer for 3–5 hours, skimming off any foam.
❸ Strain stock, discarding bouquet garni, and store in an airtight resealable container in the fridge. Freeze any stock that you will not use within 3–4 days.

Mix It Up: This recipe creates a light-colored chicken broth. For a darker broth, first roast the carcass on a baking sheet in a 350°F oven for 15–20 minutes.

Miscellaneous

Roasted Garlic

1 head garlic, excess skin removed
1 tsp olive oil

Preheat the oven to 350°F. Cut off top half of garlic head and brush with oil. Wrap head in tinfoil, place on a baking sheet, and bake for 15–20 minutes, until fragrant and caramelized. Squeeze cloves out of skin into a small bowl. Garlic will keep for up to 2 weeks refrigerated.

Granola

MAKES 2¼ CUPS

½ cup large-flake oats
¼ cup pumpkin seeds
3 Tbsp walnuts, chopped
2 Tbsp golden flaxseeds
2 Tbsp puffed quinoa
⅓ cup brown sugar
⅓ cup honey
¼ cup coconut oil, melted
1 tsp vanilla extract

❶ Preheat the oven to 325°F. Line a baking sheet with parchment paper and set aside.
❷ In a large bowl, combine oats, pumpkin seeds, walnuts, flaxseeds, puffed quinoa, sugar, honey, coconut oil, and vanilla and mix well. Evenly spread mixture on the prepared baking sheet and bake for 20 minutes, until slightly toasted and golden. (Keep a close eye on it so it doesn't burn.)
❸ Let granola cool completely and store in an airtight resealable container. One batch of granola will last you quite a few weeks and will keep for up to 2 months. You can also freeze granola for up to 4 months.

Air-Popped Popcorn

MAKES 6–8 CUPS

¼ cup popcorn kernels
1 brown paper bag

Place kernels in a brown paper bag. Fold bag over a few times at the top, leaving some room in the bag. Put bag in microwave for 2 minutes on high. Stop microwave when you hear popcorn stop popping (around 1:15–1:30). Carefully remove from micro-wave and shake bag to pop any kernels just on the verge of popping. Carefully open bag (watching out for steam) and pour into bowl.

Vinaigrettes and Dressings

For busy weeks, sometimes it's nice to have a few dressings on hand. Plus, it's super easy to do, and I love storing them in mason jars or old jam jars. Recreate my favorites below, or make your own combinations—just remember, the rule of thumb for any vinaigrette is a 2:1 oil-to-acid ratio, then you can add sweeteners, flavorings, and emulsifiers according to your taste preferences. (The nutritional values may change if you add one of these dressings to the existing recipes.) While other oils, such as olive, may be used, I recommend the following ones because of their rich omega-6 fatty acids.

Classic
MAKES ABOUT ¾ CUP
½ cup grapeseed oil
¼ cup balsamic vinegar
1 Tbsp honey
1 Tbsp Dijon mustard

Asian
MAKES ABOUT 1 CUP
¼ cup grapeseed oil
¼ cup peanut oil
¼ cup natural rice vinegar
2 Tbsp lime juice
1½ tsp brown sugar
1½ tsp grated ginger
1 tsp garlic paste
1 tsp peanut butter

Greek
MAKES ABOUT 1¼ CUPS
½ cup grapeseed oil
¼ cup white wine vinegar
½ tsp sea salt
1 Tbsp finely chopped shallots
½ head Roasted Garlic (page 287)
1 Tbsp chopped fresh parsley
1 Tbsp feta cheese

Italian
MAKES ABOUT ¾ CUP
½ cup grapeseed oil
¼ cup red wine vinegar
1 Tbsp honey
1 Tbsp parsley, dried
1 tsp oregano, dried

Ranch Dressing
MAKES ABOUT 1½ CUPS
1 cup mayonnaise
½ cup buttermilk
¾ Tbsp finely chopped fresh chives
½ tsp finely chopped fresh dill
2 cloves garlic, crushed
¼ tsp dried onion
Dash of salt and pepper

In a food processor, blender, or bowl, blend together acid, sweetener, and emulsifier until combined. While continuing to blend or whisk, slowly add oil to the mixture, until emulsified. Add flavorings and gently pulse or whisk to combine. Store in an airtight resealable container in the fridge for up to 1 week.

OILS
GRAPESEED
SAFFLOWER
SUNFLOWER

SWEETENERS
HONEY (MY GO-TO)
BROWN SUGAR
MOLASSES
AGAVE SYRUP
PURE MAPLE SYRUP

FLAVORINGS
FRESH HERBS
GINGER
GREEN ONION
PAPRIKA
TOASTED SESAME SEEDS
CORIANDER SEEDS
BLACK PEPPER
ONION POWDER
GARLIC POWDER
CAPERS
CITRUS ZEST
(LEMON, LIME, ORANGE)

ACID
BALSAMIC VINEGAR
RED WINE VINEGAR
WHITE WINE VINEGAR
RICE VINEGAR
APPLE CIDER VINEGAR
SHERRY VINEGAR
CHAMPAGNE VINEGAR
LEMON JUICE

EMULSIFIERS
DIJON MUSTARD
WHOLE GRAIN MUSTARD
ROASTED GARLIC
MAYONNAISE
HONEY
EGG YOLKS
MISO PASTE

MACRONUTRIENTS	DRI MALE	DRI FEMALE	1	2	3	4	5	6	7	8	9	10	11
Calories (kcal)			1567	1557	1496	1585	1589	1597	1551	1596	1583	1578	1586
Protein (g/%)	56/10–35%	46/10–35%	81/22	50/14	73/20	79/21	65/17	70/18	59/16	85/23	78/21	79/21	81/22
Carbohydrates (g/%)	130/45–65%	130/45–65%	208/45	232/50	196/46	212/46	220/46	217/47	217/49	204/44	218/47	207/46	218/48
Fibre (g)	38	25	39	47	32	39	46	37	39	40	40	38	38
Fat (g/%)	ND/20–35%	ND/20–35%	55/33	58/36	55/34	54/32	62/37	60/35	57/35	55/33	55/32	55/33	50/30
Saturated Fat (g)	ND	ND	14	18	15	16	14	18	19	13	15	13	16
Cholesterol (mg)	ND	ND	258	38	292	307	200	103	243	261	204	278	274
Omega-3 (g)	1.6	1.1	1.71	2.84	2.39	1.73	1.74	1.9	1.99	1.61	1.7	1.85	1.71
Omega-6 (g)	17	12	10.78	9.99	10.62	11.3	10.12	11	10.43	9.57	11.24	13.14	10.47
VITAMINS													
A (mcg_RAE) UL 3000 µg	900	700	2464	1442	3158	1080	1202	2325	1896	1817	1651	2584	979
B1 Thiamine (mg)	1.2	1.1	1.59	1.33	1.55	1.76	1.37	3.67	3.86	1.89	1.53	1.54	1.78
B2 Riboflavin (mg)	1.3	1.1	2.54	2.49	2.35	2.31	2.29	4.07	4.5	1.81	2.35	1.73	2.23
B3 Niacin (mg) UL 35 mg*	16	14	23.17	18.08	19.23	23.29	18.65	31.89	30.23	21.6	17.67	22.01	25.16
B5 Pantothenic Acid (mg)	5	5	6.51	5.96	8.53	6.02	5.81	5.71	7.88	5.66	6.46	6	6.14
B6 Pyridoxine (mg) UL 100 mg	1.3	1.3	2.8	2.29	2.83	3.04	2.69	4.99	4.73	2.56	2.68	2.18	3.2
Folate DFE (mcg_DFE) UL 1000 µg*	400	400	675.27	683	506.2	648.12	548.55	539	713	558	533	495	628
B12 (mcg)	2.4	2.4	4.98	5.07	5.42	5.19	4.64	5.95	7.06	4.46	6.22	4.6	7.27
C (mg) UL 2000 mg	90	75	328.4	228.11	191.08	509.23	230.72	322	257	285	395	280	250
D (IU) UL 4000 IU	600	600	138.91	173.51	105.86	158.52	412.65	147	176	150	320	146	386
Tocopherol / Alpha (mg) UL 1000 µg*	15	15	21.08	22.3	16.62	21.3	23.54	17.73	19.28	19.7	22.81	20.13	21.28
Vitamin E (IU)	22.5	22.5	28.98	29.3	23.46	28.45	31.96	23.8	25.45	26.73	30.7	27.59	28.43
K1 (mcg)	120	90	1814	925	685.43	412.59	852.41	400	544	916.49	1159.89	425.13	416
MINERALS													
Calcium (mg) UL 2500 mg	1000	1000	1304	1410	1022	1283	1169	1254	1327	1122	1423	1165	1224
Phosphorus (mg) UL 4000 mg	700	700	1489	1400	1341	1311	1237	1323	1174	1186	1377	1595	1488
Potassium (mg)	4700	4700	5021	5106	5615	4732	4909	5241	5043	4837	4769	4608	5294
Sodium (mg) UL 2300 mg*	1500	1500	1807	1223	1132	1454	1583	1296	1815	1516	1935	2166	1292
Iron (mg) UL 45 mg	8	18	17.96	18.3	17.97	20.76	18.55	18.21	18.34	18.89	18.3	18.48	18.4
Manganese (mg) UL 11 mg	2.3	1.8	7.91	8.66	5.33	7.16	7.27	8.09	6.32	6.77	8	7.67	6.43
Selenium (mcg) UL 400 mcg	55	55	107	67.58	99.01	95.54	77.89	71.36	91.85	107	111	75	99.74
Zinc (mg) UL 40 mg	11	8	11.41	11.98	12.88	11.12	10.98	12.63	12.25	12.03	11.97	11.86	10.95
Magnesium (mg) UL 350 mg age 19–30 / age 31–50	400/420	310/320	652	623	574	566	586	657	547	540	606	667	581

* only applies to synthetic forms

The analyses in this section were determined using NutriBase© Personal Plus Edition, v.11.73. While these numbers are accurate, there are many factors or variables that can change the precision of these numbers, such as products purchased, accuracy of measurements, ingredient substitutions, recipe revisions, assembly, and/or the season of the year. A perfect DRI intake for vitamin D is difficult solely from diet, and we advise you to discuss the supplement with your health care provider. In addition, sodium intake was attempted to be kept within the range of 1500 and 2300 mg. Health Canada has made it a goal to have everyone under 2300 mg a day, which can be a challenge when so many common products are high in sodium (bread, for one). We have given tips (see page 22) on how to lower your sodium intake. Needless to say, there is very limited room for adding sodium to dishes.

12	13	14	15	16	17	18	19	20	21	22	23	24	25	26	27	28	29	30
1582	1521	1546	1594	1595	1586	1586	1569	1566	1596	1588	1540	1533	1582	1582	1583	1583	1583	1597
75/21	75/21	62/17	72/19	72/19	89/24	87/23	78/21	75/19	83/22	80/21	69/19	65/18	86/23	80/22	85/23	73/19	72/19	79/21
240/54	197/44	219/49	215/46	215/46	207/45	205/45	208/45	218/46	210/45	215/46	206/45	217/47	207/45	204/44	207/45	223/47	209/46	211/45
47	39	39	40	40	38	39	41	39	39	38	44	44	40	41	41	46	38	41
39/25	56/35	57/35	59/35	60/35	51/31	52/32	57/34	59/34	54/32	55/33	56/35	57/35	54/32	56/34	54/33	56/34	58/35	58/34
12	14	19	15	15	15	14	17	13	16	21	15	17	13	10	13	16	12	17
163	308	94	217	210	373	385	280	166	306	156	283	301	275	273	377	99	222	157
1.59	1.59	1.82	1.58	2.66	1.76	2.61	1.74	2.86	1.92	1.72	1.8	1.68	2.95	3.14	1.9	2.04	3.23	3.96
10.07	15.96	9.81	10.55	10.32	9.85	10.08	11.07	10.03	11.32	10.22	10.09	9.92	14.21	21.24	12.35	13.45	14.81	10.52
1362	2632	1459	1444	1145	1791	1216	1097	1696	1477	987	1952	1160	1325	977	1264	1541	1332	1359
1.32	1.2	1.72	1.78	1.74	1.81	1.84	1.48	1.25	1.19	1.21	1.61	2.57	1.92	1.56	1.43	1.79	1.38	1.55
1.93	1.86	2.26	1.85	2.84	2.49	2.16	2.24	2.05	2.04	1.8	2.1	3.78	2.61	1.97	2.15	2.09	2.2	2.37
21.96	22.85	16.03	17.04	24.71	23.81	21.28	17.07	24	23.6	19.95	22.14	25.86	22.66	22.74	21.83	19.65	19.76	24.79
5.13	5.77	5.19	5.36	6.12	6.37	6.67	7.02	5.4	5.8	8.14	6.38	9.49	7.14	6.38	5.1	6.58	6.67	4.95
2.38	2.79	2.21	2.2	2.31	3.03	2.98	1.91	2.38	2.61	2.75	2.47	3.57	2.08	2.45	2.9	2.4	2.35	2.53
538	495	753	555	452.8	574.33	431.47	521.88	504.79	639.64	581.24	719	623.56	442.48	406.75	576.48	610.06	536.92	417.78
6.43	4.47	2.49	4.79	5.02	7.89	6.48	4.9	4.23	6.62	3.41	5.69	7.65	5.38	4.4	7.37	2.51	9.25	7.78
233	142.92	259	169.55	339.43	565.25	264.34	119.38	261.32	412.22	169.08	276	337.84	317.49	112.16	249.23	396.37	200.77	212.19
216	147.09	126	151.46	150.24	258.86	233.71	145.19	127.62	245.42	211.31	191	245.79	182.99	167.97	175.37	48.15	478.16	210.07
21.9	18.25	15.32	17.44	17.07	22.31	17.43	23.56	17.79	20.71	15.85	27.12	31.67	22.21	18.96	22.26	16.02	26.48	22.02
27.85	24.56	23.18	23.37	22.38	29.3	22.55	32.48	23.89	26.93	22.22	36.47	31.67	29.81	29.42	29.99	23.31	35.54	27.57
303	375	824.12	530	477.01	609.88	313.79	381.8	483.3	672.17	784.07	492	685.18	501.63	152.98	589.86	735.29	426.22	383.48
1363	1246	1103	1213	1184	1350.39	1405	1366	1295	1560	1319	1202	1701	1414	1369	1120	1015	1350	1464
1127	1169	1455	1308	1340	1441	1395	1520	1342	1174	1138	1106	1455	1331	1389	1300	1577	1152	1416
4785	4737	4996	4700	5004	5218	4679	5158	4724	5143	4806	4878	6543	4821	4967	4864	5332	4675	5220
2002	1446	2348	1927	1698	1624	1586	2112	2144	1424	1561	1759	1596	1970	1544	1468	2265	1873	1856
17.71	18.11	18	18.46	17.8	18.79	18.01	20.41	24.73	21.22	19.01	18.71	18.66	18.18	18.84	17.98	17.93	17.78	19.08
5.72	7.82	7.51	6.82	6.34	4.67	6.58	4.96	5.76	6.68	7.8	6.27	5.36	3.94	6.56	5.48	6.77	6.27	4.03
86.7	73.54	83	89.69	79.28	100.84	128.87	70.12	72.61	102.82	115.77	65.49	89.49	65.25	110.93	89.98	69.71	80.84	71.06
11.13	10.99	10.96	11.76	11.16	11.16	13.63	12.57	11.64	11.45	10.99	10.97	10.91	12.41	10.83	13.91	12.32	11.02	12.1
460	486	582	566	506	444	455	532	465	531	566	425	524	402	528	488	506	515	494

NUTRIENT ANALYSES
2000-CALORIE DIET

MACRONUTRIENTS	DRI		MEAL PLAN										
	MALE	FEMALE	1	2	3	4	5	6	7	8	9	10	11
Calories (kcal)			2008	2036	1968	1986	1993	2022	1984	1999	1999	2030	1969
Protein (g/%)	56/10–35%	46/10–35%	106/22	81/17	98/20	103/22	71/15	77/16	80/17	100/21	100/21	90/19	97/21
Carbohydrates (g/%)	130/45–65%	130/45–65%	273/47	284/48	271/49	265/46	290/49	285/49	271/48	259/45	263/45	278/47	277/50
Fibre (g)	38	25	44	53	38	50	53	45	39	46	47	51	44
Fat (g/%)	ND/20–35%	ND/20–35%	68/31	75/35	65/31	67/32	76/36	75/35	74/35	69/33	72/34	72/34	62/30
Saturated Fat (g)	ND	ND	17	26	21	19	16	27	23	16	23	15	21
Cholesterol (mg)	ND	ND	297	109	374	367	208	137	303	150	232	286	298
Omega-3 (g)	1.6	1.1	1.74	2.88	1.66	2.17	1.75	1.79	2.02	1.95	1.98	1.86	1.79
Omega-6 (g)	17	12	11.42	11.26	10.64	14.51	13.57	11	17.43	10.79	11.58	16.61	11.4
VITAMINS													
A (mcg_RAE) UL 3000 µg	900	700	2258	1838	3122	1266	1297	2578	2405	1609	1671	2709	1079
B1 Thiamine (mg)	1.2	1.1	2.02	1.56	1.96	2.05	1.63	3.76	4.02	2.26	1.79	1.86	1.88
B2 Riboflavin (mg)	1.3	1.1	2.81	2.95	3.01	2.79	2.66	4.45	5.25	1.8	2.58	2.36	2.71
B3 Niacin (mg) UL 35 mg*	16	14	30.52	29.78	24.17	30.27	21.2	35.85	31.9	25.99	22.86	24.69	26.66
B5 Pantothenic Acid (mg)	5	5	7.96	6.96	10.52	7.39	6.84	6.67	9.24	5.17	6.97	6.9	6.85
B6 Pyridoxine (mg) UL 100 mg	1.3	1.3	3.55	2.84	3.81	4.06	3.15	5.38	5.05	2.95	3.14	2.52	3.61
Folate DFE (mcg_DFE) UL 1000 µg*	400	400	578.51	724.15	558.32	767.69	610.76	568	778	689	565	584	705
B12 (mcg)	2.4	2.4	5.66	6.97	8.36	6.11	5.45	7.67	9.18	4.12	7.57	6.16	8.62
C (mg) UL 2000 mg	90	75	362.16	233.8	298.64	743.18	267.32	358	263	211	465	422	267
D (IU) UL 4000 IU	600	600	141.85	232.61	133.89	185.48	438.82	204	211	130	424	199	413
Tocopherol / Alpha (mg) UL 1000 µg*	15	15	20.27	28.72	18.35	25.74	27.86	23.08	25.73	18.81	22.64	31.58	23.21
Vitamin E (IU)	22.5	22.5	27.77	37.54	25.38	34.42	37.72	30.44	34.4	25.4	29.78	43.31	30.65
K1 (mcg)	120	90	1091.96	953.08	593.57	438.42	896.5	407	571	923.08	981.09	441.8	426
MINERALS													
Calcium (mg) UL 2500 mg	1000	1000	1331	1680	1350	1431	1259	1361	1566	1075	1468	1574	1575
Phosphorus (mg) UL 4000 mg	700	700	1997	1590	1609	1607	1390	1508	1498	1425	1753	1829	1814
Potassium (mg)	4700	4700	5404	6231	6936	5477	5462	5582	5425	5107	5347	5457	6044
Sodium (mg) UL 2300 mg*	1500	1500	1776	1912	1277	1577	1556	1359	2000	1658	2174	2267	1480
Iron (mg) UL 45 mg	8	18	18.16	21.37	23.2	22.79	18.4	19.61	18.18	17.81	21.54	21.59	19.85
Manganese (mg) UL 11 mg	2.3	1.8	9.03	9.5	5.83	8.65	7.05	7.91	5.98	7.05	8.88	8.88	7.18
Selenium (mcg) UL 400 mcg	55	55	132.21	84.51	134.13	108.97	77.72	80.39	115	113	124	78	115.9
Zinc (mg) UL 40 mg	11	8	13.1	14.64	17.47	13.63	12.06	14.86	13.99	13.64	14.98	14.39	13.17
Magnesium (mg) UL 350 mg age 19–30 / age 31–50	400/420	310/320	739	741	668	656	611	692	563	632	764	799	674

* only applies to synthetic forms

12	13	14	15	16	17	18	19	20	21	22	23	24	25	26	27	28	29	30
2015	1999	1983	1999	2026	1997	1995	1996	1987	1981	1999	1995	1989	2006	1995	1994	1994	2039	2003
89/19	96/20	83/17	87/18	95/19	101/21	101/21	94/20	94/19	100/21	94/19	94/20	86/18	103/21	95/20	101/21	84/17	91/19	92/19
312/55	267/47	277/49	270/47	268/45	256/45	263/47	272/46	267/45	244/43	259/46	258/45	276/46	257.45	282/49	263/45	282/48	276/48	265/45
61	42	44	41	47	42	40	51	46	38	36	47	55	44	51	47	50	45	49
52/26	71/33	73/34	74/35	76/35	72/34	66/32	74/35	76/35	75/35	74/34	72/35	74/35	72/34	64/31	70/33	74/34	72/33	75/35
18	15	22	18	19	20	20	23	17	23	25	21	21	21	12	18	22	19	22
176	335	287	292	277	396	440	287	202	334	185	337	354	298	343	399	116	276	196
2.38	1.59	1.91	1.66	2.7	1.96	2.65	1.82	2.91	3.36	1.79	1.71	1.7	2.98	3.18	1.8	2.21	3.25	4.05
10.7	27.08	16.53	16	10.81	15.28	10.4	15.27	14.46	17.72	15.87	11.71	11.8	18.75	23.38	14.13	15.62	15.01	10.99

12	13	14	15	16	17	18	19	20	21	22	23	24	25	26	27	28	29	30
1462	2772	1364	1690	1296	1815	1513	1023	1706	1176	1438	2301	1155	1249	1117	1124	1693	1458	1342
1.54	1.2	1.79	2.02	2.02	2.15	2.18	1.92	1.42	1.3	1.25	1.9	2.67	2.35	1.77	1.59	2.03	1.61	1.77
1.96	2.28	2.53	2.16	3.42	2.65	2.89	2.17	2.35	2.29	2.18	2.41	4.35	2.96	2.42	2.82	2.29	2.75	2.4
24.67	24.18	17.65	21.7	26.79	25.88	23.54	19.1	28.64	25.59	23.47	33.81	28.89	26.92	25.43	23.3	20.06	21.66	27.29
6.41	6.19	6.84	5.7	8.69	6.7	7.29	8.19	6.39	6.47	8.55	8.13	10.96	7.62	7.69	6.69	7	7.63	5.44
2.64	3.1	2.47	2.58	2.93	3.63	3.44	3.03	2.65	2.92	2.92	3.38	3.73	2.34	3.07	3.53	2.95	2.84	2.97
627	498	762	537	558.48	582.94	527.03	606.24	602.5	614.66	583.3	710.22	667.14	472.58	525.37	649.91	574.24	593.74	464.79
4.91	6.04	3.29	6.64	5.9	8.07	7.53	4.9	5.38	7.33	7.01	5.93	9.04	6.36	4.79	8.3	2.77	10.12	8.49
328	178.44	317	252.24	410.66	571.55	327.76	217.92	260.45	316.32	229.91	224.79	397.22	360.13	253.62	275.62	397.51	264.12	174.44
160.92	200.19	155	213.51	160.5	260.33	277.18	164.39	157.79	217.97	374.9	197.79	252.78	213.14	186.9	177.32	49.15	486.65	207.99
19.72	27.93	18.81	22.93	19.91	24.32	17.91	18.69	23.06	21.7	26.13	26.46	25.61	25.25	22.92	25.15	16.13	27.76	24.8
26.13	37.67	28.38	30.23	26.6	32.29	22.82	27.85	31.08	28.4	34.82	35.48	34.23	33.69	36.58	34.3	23.47	37.45	31.7
324	378	670	426	583.76	591.03	303.11	391.9	424.34	469.81	717.26	472.28	631.1	436.86	176.51	608.8	734.73	423.69	433.64

12	13	14	15	16	17	18	19	20	21	22	23	24	25	26	27	28	29	30
1256	1641	1265	1509	1443	1452	1403	1243	1574	1618	1834	1236	1719	1639	1500	1417	1139	1332	1436
1456	1230	1647	1391	1693	1646	1660	1699	1687	1470	1252	1370	1780	1581	1540	1574	1732	1510	1602
5471	5560	5568	4695	5786	5751	4919	6871	5001	5116	4825	6215	6996	4763	5934	6083	5784	4930	5131
2214	1733	2437	2039	2252	1759	1347	2252	2514	1573	1504	1966	1588	2118	1785	1975	2243	1902	1932
22.15	19.1	19.78	19.89	19.18	19.74	18.21	21.96	26	21.23	18.09	21.3	18.89	18.26	19.07	18.52	18.45	19.16	21.36
7.59	6.69	8.18	6.11	6.48	4.72	6.39	6.44	7.45	7.13	6.35	5.48	5.49	4.58	7.18	5.72	5.47	6.16	4.51
107.68	73.54	101	100.96	86.2	106.83	145.92	82.87	96.82	127.79	128.66	86.34	102	69.62	122.53	105.7	68.64	88.3	81.25
13.26	11.94	12.54	13.21	12.59	12.06	15.18	12.6	15.26	13.33	12.08	12.51	12.87	15.31	11.67	14.96	12.32	12.99	14.14
586	542	640	541	595	468	487	691	526	603	542	509	572	467	597	589	536	603	495

MACRONUTRIENTS	DRI MALE	DRI FEMALE	1	2	3	4	5	6	7	8	9	10	11
Calories (kcal)			2502	2491	2490	2447	2490	2546	2485	2500	2494	2471	2493
Protein (g/%)	56/10–35%	46/10–35%	111/18	98/16	122/20	133/23	87/15	102/17	100/17	118/20	114/19	114/19	112/19
Carbohydrates (g/%)	130/45–65%	130/45–65%	355/50	356/50	319/44	314/45	360/49	355/49	350/50	320/45	337/47	347/49	334/47
Fibre (g)	38	25	49	58	53	54	70	57	48	55	57	55	57
Fat (g/%)	ND/20–35%	ND/20–35%	87/32	91/34	94/35	82/32	96/36	94/34	90/33	92/35	91/34	82/31	92/35
Saturated Fat (g)	ND	ND	22	30	29	26	19	34	29	21	26	19	27
Cholesterol (mg)	ND	ND	298	107	400	600	163	211	344	153	243	429	277
Omega-3 (g)	1.6	1.1	2.5	2.9	1.84	2.63	1.73	1.95	2.47	2.01	2.07	3.06	1.82
Omega-6 (g)	17	12	15.45	14.61	13.24	15.59	14.24	13.25	19.35	14.68	17.55	18.48	17.03
VITAMINS													
A (mcg_RAE) UL 3000 µg	900	700	2276	1851	3921	1071	1326	2762	2551.7	1582	2345	2896	1034
B1 Thiamine (mg)	1.2	1.1	2.23	1.84	2.44	2.55	2	3.99	6.62	2.64	2.46	2.09	2.38
B2 Riboflavin (mg)	1.3	1.1	2.8	3.11	3.65	3.23	3.2	4.81	7.66	2.16	2.95	2.44	2.78
B3 Niacin (mg) UL 35 mg*	16	14	32.11	37.33	32.9	38.92	27.42	43.39	51.41	28.4	25.78	27.4	31.06
B5 Pantothenic Acid (mg)	5	5	8.85	7.96	12.14	9.64	8.75	8.17	10.46	6.32	7.87	8.6	7.45
B6 Pyridoxine (mg) UL 100 mg	1.3	1.3	3.86	3	4.3	5.01	3.8	5.9	8.05	3.34	4.24	3.15	4.28
Folate DFE (mcg_DFE) UL 1000 µg*	400	400	660.49	808.17	566.02	865.96	766.19	549	867	736	630	671	770
B12 (mcg)	2.4	2.4	5.72	6.2	9.62	6.5	5.23	8	11.59	4.57	7.65	6.91	8.45
C (mg) UL 2000 mg	90	75	461.54	405.75	403.06	928.82	351.01	516	401	313	527	440	268
D (IU) UL 4000 IU	600	600	141.85	206.48	163.35	189.27	436.66	216	218	130	426	223	411
Tocopherol / Alpha (mg) UL 1000 µg*	15	15	22.62	28.39	28.32	24.57	32.42	25.03	27.74	20.13	26.7	28.7	25.25
Vitamin E (IU)	22.5	22.5	31.27	37.72	39.57	33.33	44.69	33.35	37.39	27.37	35.83	38.95	33.69
K1 (mcg)	120	90	1097.94	936	419.34	224.62	937.31	163	495	870.57	1023.95	445.32	432
MINERALS													
Calcium (mg) UL 2500 mg	1000	1000	1346	1595	1336	1354	1365	1671	1623	1221	1578	1776	1530
Phosphorus (mg) UL 4000 mg	700	700	2171	2020	2048	1944	1725	1729	1731	1858	2060	2138	2130
Potassium (mg)	4700	4700	5426	6421	7387	5224	6444	6621	5806	5849	6558	5487	6729
Sodium (mg) UL 2300 mg*	1500	1500	1556	1642	1607	1718	1871	1789	1925	1674	2411	2138	1482
Iron (mg) UL 45 mg	8	18	21.66	26.74	25.17	24.59	22.38	21.88	19.02	22.21	24.28	24.37	23.54
Manganese (mg) UL 11 mg	2.3	1.8	10.44	10.92	6.3	9.93	9.16	6.95	6.51	7.67	9.66	10.5	9.14
Selenium (mcg) UL 400 mcg	55	55	136.1	95.98	158.75	160.83	100.14	103	121.22	123	131	104	127.29
Zinc (mg) UL 40 mg	11	8	14.71	16.97	20.25	15.91	14.57	15.99	16.61	16.63	16.36	16.78	15.39
Magnesium (mg) UL 350 mg age 19–30 / age 31–50	400/420	310/320	783	968	704	684	747	733	553	806	852	853	808

* only applies to synthetic forms

12	13	14	15	16	17	18	19	20	21	22	23	24	25	26	27	28	29	30
2503	2468	2575	2461	2500	2497	2488	2492	2500	2524	2498	2472	2488	2488	2498	2480	2495	2506	2479
111/19	103/17	96/15	106/18	115/19	123/20	134/22	109/18	105/17	135/22	115/19	114/20	107/18	127/21	119/20	124/21	107/18	107/18	126/21
352/49	335/48	377/52	335/48	329/35	319/45	310/45	347/48	346/48	311/43	323/45	322/45	351/48	317/45	323/45	320/45	345/47	330/47	323/45
68	50	54	52	52	50	43	62	51	44	49	56	67	47	55	54	62	46	56
80/31	94/35	91/33	91/34	94/35	92/35	88/33	92/34	98/35	93/34	96/35	91/35	91/34	91/34	94/35	92/35	93/35	95/35	89/34
23	19	27	20	28	29	26	30	21	26	34	26	30	22	16	20	32	24	28
257	347	320	302	299	417	512	303	385	393	211	357	462	329	383	414	131	317	270
2.49	2.27	2.16	1.72	2.73	2.48	1.91	1.87	3.09	3.51	1.89	1.79	1.76	3.07	3.32	1.88	3.25	4.83	4.1
21.09	35.83	18.36	18.15	11.92	18.11	12.52	15.33	20.86	22.81	17.37	15.89	12.26	26.26	36.31	18.3	17.14	15.67	11.18
1483	2939	1711	1683	1337	1837	1582	1399	1786	1301	1588	2376	1340	960	1166	1184	1638	1192	1565
1.89	1.42	2.16	2.43	2.35	2.48	2.99	2.1	1.89	1.66	1.56	2.14	3.51	3.26	2.31	1.88	2.03	1.68	2.07
2.08	2.59	3.38	2.34	3.55	3.04	3.22	2.27	2.65	2.53	2.4	2.54	5.42	3.44	2.65	2.59	2.42	3.17	2.77
32.11	27.23	21.16	23.32	33.56	28.93	29.62	23.79	30.02	33.93	27.3	35	33.7	33.3	31.29	24.27	20.74	28.55	33.97
7.78	6.52	8.05	6.73	9.76	7.9	8.45	9.01	7.86	7.42	9.13	8.5	13.4	9.31	8.87	6.6	6.5	10.05	6.68
3.57	3.34	2.91	2.84	3.07	4.05	4.56	3.34	3.42	3.74	3.44	3.92	4.99	3.02	4.32	3.68	2.9	3.73	3.67
701	583	850	649	647.67	625.99	580.29	697.28	485.11	648.1	720.88	737.52	790.67	467.7	572.87	656.97	581.91	670.19	495.65
5.27	6.26	7.23	6.64	4.77	8.73	8.12	5.06	5.44	7.48	7.51	5.94	10.62	6.63	4.87	8.3	3.27	12.36	9.35
345	297.13	438	347.19	481.18	652.97	398.38	337.1	299.48	364.26	367.73	269.69	455.19	272.72	287.92	253.25	398.02	206.87	195.72
178.36	202.19	315	213.51	112.2	261.89	294.75	165.39	161.37	279.54	434.54	197.79	285.62	221.33	187.27	202.52	65.95	637.81	210.22
23.79	32.1	26.71	22.03	17.89	25.1	18.8	21.56	23.6	23.92	27.43	29.09	27.85	27.88	26.86	28.31	17.24	32.15	26.65
32.17	43.89	37.62	28.89	24.92	33.46	24.15	32.13	32.54	31.7	36.77	39.41	37.57	37.61	42.46	38.55	24.69	44	34.46
342	509	682	449	619.71	608.91	309.66	413.83	384.87	501.11	719.94	507.9	642	493.85	231.72	640.49	755.08	472.06	464.94
1266	1583	1955	1799	1274	1683	1584	1393	1519	1756	1858	1450	2012	1676	1608	1689	1498	1361	1693
1646	1353	1929	1569	1971	2009	2140	2023	1937	1642	1582	1530	2238	1913	1876	1670	1930	1687	1907
5743	5108	6183	5212	6108	6448	5987	7303	5835	5775	5531	7076	8532	5338	7072	6138	6094	5411	6098
2297	1607	2556	2090	2244	1846	1532	2259	2542	1491	1870	2059	1749	2167	1849	1905	2323	1949	2271
24.37	18.1	20.77	20.9	22.48	23.27	22.01	26.16	28.32	20.76	18.94	23.52	22.7	20.06	21.76	20.34	21.64	18.2	24.24
8.35	5.91	7.26	6.78	7.46	7.1	6.59	8.28	7.75	6.94	6.31	5.55	6.64	5.37	7.72	5.89	7.13	6.04	5.08
126.73	74.24	108	104.02	91.88	112.09	182.12	96.16	118.6	144.78	132.45	84.48	123.15	81.23	138.02	95.04	66.23	101.44	103.48
14.76	12.26	14.74	14.75	13.77	13.71	18.1	15.17	16.3	14.03	13.31	12.98	15.24	17.3	13	16.06	14.11	13.5	16.74
593	512	681	597	656	574	591	773	568	639	648	569	712	523	692	555	623	615	556

REFERENCES

1. Washburn, Richard A. et al. "Does the Method of Weight Loss Effect Long-Term Changes in Weight, Body Composition or Chronic Disease Risk Factors in Overweight or Obese Adults? A Systematic Review." *PLoS ONE* 9, no. 10 (2014). Accessed July 17, 2017. https://doi.org/10.1371/journal.pone.0109849.

2. Swift, Damon L. et al. "The role of exercise and physical activity in weight loss and maintenance." *Progress in Cardiovascular Diseases* 56, no. 4 (2014): 441–447. Accessed July 17, 2017. https://www.ncbi.nlm.nih.gov/pubmed/24438736.

3. Warburton, Darren ER. et al. "A systematic review of the evidence for Canada's Physical Activity Guidelines for Adults." *International Journal of Behavioral Nutrition and Physical Activity* 7 (2010): 39. Accessed July 17, 2017. https://www.ncbi.nlm.nih.gov/pmc/articles/PMC3583166/.

4. U.S. Department of Health & Human Services. "President's Council on Fitness, Sports & Nutrition." Accessed April 16, 2017. https://www.hhs.gov/fitness/resource-center/facts-and-statistics/.

5. Ibid.

6. Dietitians of Canada. "Should I try a low carbohydrate diet to lose weight?" Accessed April 16, 2017. https://www.dietitians.ca/Downloads/Factsheets/Should-I-try-a-low-carbohydrate-diet-to-lose-weigh.

7. Health Canada. "Dietary Reference Intakes Tables." Accessed April 16, 2017. https://www.canada.ca/en/health-canada/services/food-nutrition/healthy-eating/dietary-reference-intakes/tables.html.

8. Heart and Stroke Foundation. "Position Statement: Sugar, Heart Disease and Stroke." Accessed April 16, 2017. http://www.heartandstroke.ca/-/media/pdf-files/canada/2017-position-statements/sugar-ps-eng. World Health Organization. "Guideline: Sugars intake for adults and children." (2015): 12–13. Accessed July 17, 2017. http://apps.who.int/iris/bitstream/10665/149782/1/9789241549028_eng.pdf.

9. Health Canada. "Dietary Reference Intakes Table."

10. Ibid.

11. PEN: Practice-Based Evidence in Nutrition. "Cardiovascular Disease: Evidence Summary." Accessed April 16, 2017. http://www.pennutrition.com/KnowledgePathway.aspx?kpid=2671&trid=3489&trcatid=42

12. Nutri-Facts. "Nutrients: Essential for healthy living." Accessed April 16, 2017. http://www.nutri-facts.org//en_US/nutrients.html.

13. Dietitians of Canada. "Vitamin D: What you need to know." Accessed April 16, 2017. https://www.dietitians.ca/Your-Health/Nutrition-A-Z/Vitamins/Vitamin-D--What-you-need-to-know.aspx.

14. Health Canada. "Dietary Reference Intakes Table."

15. Thomas, Diana M. et al. "Effects of dietary adherence on the body weight plateau: a mathematical model incorporating intermittent compliance with energy intake prescription." *The American Journal of Clinical Nutrition* 100, no. 3 (2014): 787–795. Accessed July 17, 2017. https://www.ncbi.nlm.nih.gov/pmc/articles/PMC4135489/.

16. Frankenfield, David et al. "Comparison of Predictive Equations for Resting Metabolic Rate in Healthy Nonobese and Obese Adults: A Systematic Review." *Journal of the American Dietetic Association* 105 (2005): 775–789. Accessed July 17, 2017. https://www.ncbi.nlm.nih.gov/pubmed/15883556

THANKS

Dave and Laura: This project would have never come to light if it were not for your investment in me and this endeavor. Art and Betty: This book would have taken an additional decade without your time and support. Thank you for all your prayers Ken, Marlene, Darlene, Derek, Elizabeth, Art, Tina, and Helmut, you are forever and always in my heart. All my love: Brittany, Luke, Ben, Annie, Jacob, Jason, Stacy, Micah, Olivia, Keira, Steve, Jodi, Aidan, Liam, and Morgan.

Katherine and Bev: Thank you for extending my life. I am always overwhelmed by your genuine care and concern for me.

To my mentors who have shaped me into the person I have become, I have such profound admiration for each of you. Susan, your guidance and friendship are tremendous gifts that I will always treasure. Neil, you will forever be in my heart. Sandy, you will always be one of my favorite people.

Thank you to all my friends who have not given up on me through this process: Alyssa, Kendall, Courtney, Amy, Sarah, Lauren, and countless others.

A huge thank you to the Figure 1 team, this book could not have happened without your genuine belief in me and this project. The talents of your entire team compare to none!

Thank you, Lindsay, for helping us create such a beautiful book.

Last, but furthest from the least, thank you Janine and Ashlee for joining me on this whirlwind journey. Your belief in me and my crazy vision from the start of this journey means more than you will ever know. I will forever cherish your friendships.

I would like to express my sincere appreciation to the countless number of others who have invested in making this dream become a reality. I am truly humbled by all the support, encouragement, and genuine excitement for this project.

CONVERSION CHART

VOLUME

Imperial	Metric
⅛ tsp	0.5 ml
¼ tsp	1 ml
½ tsp	2.5 ml
¾ tsp	4 ml
1 tsp	5 ml
½ Tbsp	8 ml
1 Tbsp	15 ml
1½ Tbsp	23 ml
2 Tbsp	30 ml
¼ cup	60 ml
⅓ cup	80 ml
½ cup	125 ml
⅔ cup	165 ml
¾ cup	185 ml
1 cup	250 ml
1¼ cups	310 ml
1⅓ cups	330 ml
1½ cups	375 ml
1⅔ cups	415 ml
1¾ cups	435 ml
2 cups	500 ml
2¼ cups	560 ml
2⅓ cups	580 ml
2½ cups	625 ml
2¾ cups	690 ml
3 cups	750 ml
4 cups / 1 qt	1 L
5 cups	1.25 L
6 cups	1.5 L
7 cups	1.75 L
8 cups	2 L

WEIGHT

Imperial	Metric
½ oz	15 g
1 oz	30 g
2 oz	60 g
3 oz	85 g
4 oz (¼ lb)	115 g
5 oz	140 g
6 oz	170 g
7 oz	200 g
8 oz (½ lb)	225 g
9 oz	255 g
10 oz	285 g
11 oz	310 g
12 oz (¾ lb)	340 g
13 oz	370 g
14 oz	400 g
15 oz	425 g
16 oz (1 lb)	450 g
1¼ lbs	570 g
1½ lbs	670 g
2 lbs	900 g
3 lbs	1.4 kg
4 lbs	1.8 kg
5 lbs	2.3 kg
6 lbs	2.7 kg

LIQUID MEASURES

Imperial	Metric
1 fl oz	30 ml
2 fl oz	60 ml
3 fl oz	90 ml
4 fl oz	120 ml

LINEAR

Imperial	Metric
⅛ inch	3 mm
¼ inch	6 mm
½ inch	12 mm
¾ inch	2 cm
1 inch	2.5 cm
1¼ inches	3 cm
1½ inches	3.5 cm
1¾ inches	4.5 cm
2 inches	5 cm
2½ inches	6.5 cm
3 inches	7.5 cm
4 inches	10 cm
5 inches	12.5 cm
6 inches	15 cm
7 inches	18 cm
10 inches	25 cm
12 inches	30 cm
13 inches	33 cm
16 inches	41 cm
18 inches	46 cm

BAKING PANS

Imperial	Metric
5- × 9-inch loaf pan	2 L loaf pan
9- × 13-inch cake pan	4 L cake pan
11- × 17-inch baking sheet	30- × 45-cm baking sheet

CANS & JARS

Imperial	Metric
6 oz	170 g
28 oz	796 ml

OVEN TEMPERATURE

Imperial	Metric
200°F	95°C
250°F	120°C
275°F	135°C
300°F	150°C
325°F	160°C
350°F	180°C
375°F	190°C
400°F	200°C
425°F	220°C
450°F	230°C

TEMPERATURE

Imperial	Metric
90°F	32°C
120°F	49°C
125°F	52°C
130°F	54°C
140°F	60°C
150°F	66°C
155°F	68°C
160°F	71°C
165°F	74°C
170°F	77°C
175°F	80°C
180°F	82°C
190°F	88°C
200°F	93°C
240°F	116°C
250°F	121°C
300°F	149°C
325°F	163°C
350°F	177°C
360°F	182°C
375°F	191°C

INDEX

A

acorn squash
    beans and, chicken with, 250
    bowl, turkey sausage soup in, 266
    ring, eggs in, 60
    stuffed, with tahini sauce, 162, *163*
    in vegetable bake, 234
almond butter, apples with, 155
almond flour
    –crusted Arctic char, 80
    in pop-up pancakes, 246
    for pork schnitzel, 242
almond milk, original. *See also* chocolate
    almond milk; vanilla almond milk
    in apple pie chia pudding, 262
    in mulberry puffed quinoa cereal, 278
    in pop-up pancakes, 246
almonds. *See also* almond butter, apples
    with; almond flour–crusted Arctic
    char; almond flour; almond milk,
    original; chocolate almond milk;
    vanilla almond milk
    in berry and Boursin® salad, 78
    in popcorn trail mix, 91
apple(s)
    with almond butter, 155
    pie chia pudding, 262, *263*
    in stuffed pork roast, 186
applesauce, in apple pie chia pudding, 262
apricots, dried, in popcorn trail mix, 91
Arctic char with wild rice, corn salad, and
    beet greens, 80
arugula
    in baked potato with spinach salad, 128
    in BBQ chicken salad, 280
    in portobello and prosciutto pizza, 62
    in portobello mushroom sandwich, 248
    in roasted balsamic tomato bowl, 272
    in roasted vegetable salad, 96
    in side salad, 98
    in watermelon, goat cheese, and beet
    salad, 210
Asian dressing, 288
Asian lettuce wraps, 200, *201*
asparagus
    in grilled vegetables, salmon with, 274
    pork schnitzel with, 242
    in roast chicken with vegetables, 88–89
    in roasted vegetables, sole with, 178
avocado
    in BBQ chicken salad, 280
    in bocconcini salad, 54
    in breakfast burrito, 270
    in chicken and mango summer roll, 104
    in chicken chimichurri melt, 256

    in chicken fajitas, 72
    in Cobb salad, 232
    and goat cheese toast, 76, *77*
    in lentil taco lettuce wraps, 224
    in side salad, 160
    in spinach and egg salad, 168

B

bacon
    in bison stew, 282
    in pork and bean chili, 106
    in potato and leek soup, 56
    in stuffed pork roast, 186
    in sweet potato frittata, 254
bagel, chia-flax, spicy egg salad on, 184, *185*
baked potato with spinach salad, 128, *129*
baked quinoa, halibut with, 218, *219*
balsamic reduction, 286
balsamic tomato bowl, 272, *273*
banana
    in all smoothies except pumpkin-
    cinnamon and vanilla-cinnamon
    (p. 235). *See* smoothie
    parfait, 214, *215*
    in tropical dollar pancakes, 230
    in yogurt parfait, 45
barbecue sauce
    in BBQ chicken salad, 280
    for mango BBQ chicken pizza, 160
basil
    in baked potato with spinach salad, 128
    in bocconcini salad, 54
    on breakfast pizza, 238
    in chimichurri sauce, 250
    in marinara sauce, 234
    paste, in cauliflower cottage pie, 98
    pesto, 286
    pesto, in spaghetti squash bowl, 194
    pesto, tomato, and ricotta toast, 86
    in roasted balsamic tomato bowl, 272
    in vegetable bake, 234
BBQ chicken
    mango pizza, 160, *161*
    salad, 280, *281*
bean. *See also* black beans; edamame;
    green bean(s); white bean(s)
    and pork chili, 106, *107*
    quinoa, and buckwheat salad, 70, *71*
beet
    greens, Arctic char with, 80
    in side salad, 146, 194, 266
    watermelon, and goat cheese salad, 210, *211*
bell peppers. *See* orange bell pepper,
    in chicken fajitas; red bell pepper;
    yellow bell pepper

berries. *See* blackberries; blueberry(ies);
    mulberry puffed quinoa cereal;
    raspberry(ies); strawberry(ies)
berry and Boursin® salad, 78, *79*
bison, 278
    spinach, and sweet potato salad, 64, *65*
    stew, 282
    taco salad, 258
black beans
    in BBQ chicken salad, 280
    in bison taco salad, 258
    in breakfast burrito, 270
    in lentil taco lettuce wraps, 224
    in quinoa taco bowl, 192
    in Southwest crustless quiche, 44
blackberries
    in berry and Boursin® salad, 78
    for coconut and flaxseed French toast, 68
    in creamy berry farina cereal, 198
    with lemon-ricotta crepe, 182
    with vanilla chia crepes, 134
blueberry(ies)
    with apple pie chia pudding, 262
    in banana parfait, 214
    in Cobb salad, 232
    with coconut and flaxseed French toast, 68
    in creamy berry farina cereal, 198
    dried, in green bean, feta, and pomegranate
    salad, 144
    with lemon-ricotta crepe, 182
    with mulberry puffed quinoa cereal, 278
    with pop-up pancakes, 246
    vanilla chia pudding, 52, *53*
    in yogurt parfait, 177, 259
bocconcini
    in grilled squash salad, 240
    salad, 54
Boursin® Garlic & Fine Herbs
    and berry salad, 78
    in bison, spinach, and sweet potato salad, 64
    with Britt's Brussels, 174
    in sweet potato breakfast stack, 222
bran. *See* oat bran; wheat bran, in mulberry puffed
    quinoa cereal
bran buds, in mulberry puffed quinoa cereal, 278
bread, in recipes. *See also* French toast;
    sandwich; toast
    in stuffed pork roast, 186
    for turkey sausage and zucchini pizza loaf, 202
breakfast burrito, 270
breakfast pizza, 238
breakfast quesadilla, 110
breakfast sandwich, 142
breakfast stack, sweet potato, 222, *223*
breakfast summer roll, 84, *85*

Page numbers in italics refer to photos.

Britt's Brussels, 174, *175*

broccoli
    and mushrooms, with vegetable bake, 234
    in sweet potato frittata, 254
    in Thai chicken, quinoa, and veggie bowl, 48

Brussels sprouts
    Britt's, 174, *175*
    in kale slaw, 130
    in side salads, 208, 226, 266
    with stuffed pork roast, 186

buckwheat, 286
    quinoa, and bean salad, 70, *71*
    salad, potato and leek soup with, 56

burrito, breakfast, 270

buttered popcorn, 209

butter lettuce
    in Asian lettuce wraps, 200
    in lentil taco lettuce wraps, 224

buttermilk
    in mango, ginger, and white chocolate scones, 150
    in prosciutto, cheese, and caramelized onion scones, 94

butternut squash
    pancakes, 158
    in potato and leek soup, 56
    and spinach salad, 122, *123*

c

cabbage. *See* Napa cabbage, in grilled vegetables; red cabbage

cacao nibs
    in banana parfait, 214
    in chocolate chia pudding, 166

candied ginger, mango, and white chocolate scones, 150

carbonated water
    in chia and fruit fizz, 199
    in tropical fizzy chia drink, 239

carrot juice
    in chia and fruit fizz, 199
    in red smoothie, 111
    smoothie, 90

carrot(s). *See also* carrot juice
    in Asian lettuce wraps, 200
    in bison stew, 282
    cake French toast with cream cheese syrup, 118
    in cauliflower cottage pie, 98
    in chicken and mango summer roll, 104
    in chicken noodle soup, 170
    in chicken pot pie, 226
    in chicken stock, 287
    in grilled vegetables, salmon with, 274
    in instant noodles, 120
    in kale slaw, 130
    roast chicken with, 146
    in roast chicken with vegetables, 88–89
    in roasted vegetables, sole with, 178

in side salad, 106, 194
with stuffed pork roast, 186
in Thai chicken, quinoa, and veggie bowl, 48
in turkey sausage soup, 266

cauliflower
    cottage pie, with quinoa salad, 98, *99*
    mash, roast chicken with, 88–89

cereal
    creamy berry farina, 198
    granola, 287
    mulberry puffed quinoa, 278, *279*

cheddar
    in BBQ chicken salad, 280
    in bison taco salad, 258
    in breakfast burrito, 270
    in breakfast sandwich, 142
    in cheese and onion crustless quiche, 126
    in chicken fajitas, 72
    in Cobb salad, 232
    in quinoa taco bowl, 192
    in Southwest crustless quiche, 44
    on spicy Hawaiian pizza, 264
    in spinach and egg salad, 168
    in turkey crepe sandwich, 176
    in vegetable bake, 234

cheese. *See* bocconcini; Boursin® Garlic & Fine Herbs; cheddar; cottage cheese; cream cheese syrup; feta; goat cheese; Gruyère-chicken crepe; mozzarella; Parmesan; provolone; ricotta

cheese and onion crustless quiche, 126

chia
    apple pie pudding, 262, *263*
    in butternut squash pancakes, 158
    chocolate pudding, 166, *167*
    drink base, 286
    -flax bagel, spicy egg salad on, 184, *185*
    and fruit fizz, 199
    jam, strawberry-mango, 102, *103*
    in mochachia, 247, 283
    tropical fizzy drink, 239
    vanilla blueberry pudding, 52, *53*
    vanilla crepes, 134, *135*

chicken
    in bocconcini salad, 54
    butternut squash and spinach salad with, 122, *123*
    chimichurri melt, 256, *257*
    chimichurri, with beans and squash, 250, *251*
    fajitas, 72
    fingers with fries and tzatziki, 138
    ground, in Asian lettuce wraps, 200
    -Gruyère crepe with shiitake-truffle sauce, 216
    mango pizza, 160, *161*
    and mango summer roll, 104
    noodle soup, 170
    pot pie, 226, *227*

quinoa, and veggie bowl, Thai, 48, *49*
roasted, with potatoes, carrots, and spinach salad, 146, *147*
roasted, with vegetables and cauliflower mash, 88–89
salad, BBQ, 280, *281*
stock, 287
in watermelon, goat cheese, and beet salad, 210

chickpeas
    in hummus, 287
    in quinoa, buckwheat, and bean salad, 70

chili, pork and bean, 106, *107*

chimichurri
    chicken melt, 256, *257*
    chicken with beans and squash, 250, *251*
    sauce, 250

chocolate. *See also* cacao nibs; cocoa powder; dark chocolate; hot chocolate; milk chocolate
    -banana smoothie, 73, 105
    chia pudding with strawberry sauce, 166, *167*
    hazelnut spread, in banana parfait, 214
    steamer, 55
    vanilla, and banana smoothie, 127, 143
    -vanilla smoothie, 183
    white, mango, and ginger scones, 150, *151*

chocolate almond milk
    in chocolate chia pudding, 166
    in hot chocolate, 81
    in warm chocolate steamer, 55

chowder, creamy corn, ham, and roasted red pepper, 154

cinnamon
    in apple pie chia pudding, 262
    in apples with almond butter, 155
    in breakfast summer roll, 84
    in carrot cake French toast, 118
    -pumpkin smoothie, 225
    -sugar popcorn, 97, 127, 217, 239
    in vanilla-almond steamer, 271
    -vanilla milk, 217, 235
    -vanilla smoothie, 209, 235
    -vanilla steamer, 177, 258

classic dressing, 288

Cobb salad, 232, *233*

cocoa powder
    in chocolate chia pudding, 166
    in hot chocolate, 45, 81, 91, 111, 119, 159, 191
    in mochachia, 247, 283
    in smoothies, 73, 105, 127, 143, 183, 217, 259
    in vanilla-almond steamer, 271
    in warm chocolate steamer, 55

coconut. *See also* coconut milk; coconut milk beverage; coconut water
    in banana parfait, 214
    in breakfast summer roll, 84
    in cinnamon-sugar popcorn, 127
    -crusted Arctic char, 80
    and flaxseed French toast, 68, *69*

and lemongrass poached halibut with collard greens, quinoa, and wild rice, 114, *115*

-lime mojito, 119, 139, 143

in mulberry puffed quinoa cereal, 278

in tropical dollar pancakes, 230

coconut milk
in Arctic char with wild rice, corn salad, and beet greens, 80

and lemongrass poached halibut, 114, *115*

in potato and leek soup, 56

coconut milk beverage
in breakfast summer roll, 84

in tropical smoothie, 191

coconut water
in banana-flax smoothie, 259

in butternut squash pancakes, 158

in carrot juice smoothie, 90

in chia and fruit fizz, 199

in chia drink base, 286

in chocolate-banana smoothie, 105

in coconut-lime mojito, 119, 139, 143

with lime, 73, 81, 97

in morning smoothie, 171

in red smoothie, 111

in tropical fizzy chia drink, 239

in tropical green smoothie, 44, 155

in tropical mango smoothie, 271

in tropical smoothie, 55, 191, 247

in vanilla, chocolate, and banana smoothie, 143

in vanilla green smoothie, 61

in vanilla wheat germ smoothie, 217

coffee, instant, in mochachia, 247, 283

collard greens
in Greek wrap, 152

halibut with, 114, *115*, 218, *219*

in prosciutto cup, 190

in Thai chicken, quinoa, and veggie bowl, 48

corn
in bison taco salad, 258

ham, and roasted red pepper chowder, 154

in lentil taco lettuce wraps, 224

in quinoa taco bowl, 192

salad, Arctic char with, 80

salad, BBQ chicken with, 280, *281*

in Southwest crustless quiche, 44

corn tortillas
for chicken fajitas, 72

for fish tacos, 130

cottage cheese
in prosciutto cup, 190

in sweet potato frittata, 254

cottage pie, cauliflower, 98, *99*

couscous, in Greek wrap, 152

cream cheese syrup, 118
carrot cake French toast with, 118

vanilla chia crepes with, 134

creamy berry farina cereal, 198

creamy corn, ham, and roasted red pepper chowder, 154

cremini mushrooms
in buckwheat salad, 56

in spinach and egg salad, 168

in turkey sausage and zucchini pizza loaf, 202

crepe. *See also* pancakes
chicken-Gruyère, 216

lemon-ricotta, 182

sandwich, turkey, 176

vanilla chia, 134, *135*

cucumber
in Asian lettuce wraps, 200

in bocconcini salad, 54

in Greek wrap, 152

in quinoa, buckwheat, and bean salad, 70

for salad, with tuna quinoa bake, 208

in turkey crepe sandwich, 176

in tzatziki, 287

D

dark chocolate
in chocolate-banana smoothie, 105

in chocolate chia pudding, 166

in hot chocolate, 81, 111

in popcorn trail mix, 91

in warm chocolate steamer, 55

dill, in tzatziki, 287

dollar pancakes with mango syrup, 230, *231*

dressings, 288. *See also individual salads; sauce*

drink. *See also* smoothie; steamer; vanilla almond milk
base, chia, 286

chia and fruit fizz, 199

hot chocolate, 45, 81, 91, 111, 119, 159, 191

mochachia, 247, 283

mojito, 119, 139, 143

tropical fizzy chia, 239

E

edamame
with Asian lettuce wraps, 200

in instant noodles, 120

in side salad, 128, 226

eggplant
in grilled squash salad, 240

in vegetable bake, 234

egg(s). *See also* French toast; quiche
in breakfast burrito, 270

on breakfast pizza, 238

in breakfast quesadilla, 110

in breakfast sandwich, 142

with Britt's Brussels, 174

on butternut squash pancakes, 158

in Cobb salad, 232

in goat cheese and avocado toast, 76

in pop-up pancakes, 246

in prosciutto cup, 190

in a ring, 60

salad on a chia-flax bagel, 184, *185*

soft-boiled, and soldiers, 206, *207*

and spinach salad, 168, *169*

in sweet potato breakfast stack, 222

in sweet potato frittata, 254

F

fajitas, chicken, 72

farina berry cereal, 198

feta
in baked potato, 128

in breakfast quesadilla, 110

in Greek dressing, 288

in Greek wrap, 152

green bean, and pomegranate salad, 144, *145*

in grilled vegetable and hummus flatbread, 46

in roasted corn salad, Arctic char with, 80

fish
Arctic char with wild rice, corn salad, and beet greens, 80

halibut with baked quinoa and collard greens, 218, *219*

halibut with collard greens, quinoa, and wild rice, 114, *115*

salmon with grilled vegetables and wild rice, 274, *275*

sole en papillote with roasted vegetables, 178, *179*

tacos with kale slaw and mango salsa, 130, *131*

tuna quinoa bake, 208

fizzy chia drink, 239

flatbread, grilled vegetable and hummus, 46, *47*. *See also* pizza

flax(seed)
in banana parfait, 214

in berry and Boursin® salad, 78

in butternut squash pancakes, 158

in carrot cake French toast, 118

-chia bagel, spicy egg salad on, 184, *185*

in Cobb salad, 232

and coconut French toast, 68, *69*

in granola, 287

in mango, ginger, and white chocolate scones, 150

in mulberry puffed quinoa cereal, 278

in prosciutto, cheese, and caramelized onion scones, 94

in side salads, 128, 160, 194, 226

in smoothies, 61, 73, 90, 97, 105, 111, 155, 259

in turkey crepe sandwich, 176

in yogurt parfait, 45, 259

French toast
carrot cake, 118

coconut and flaxseed, 68, *69*

fries, chicken fingers with, 138

frittata, sweet potato, 254, *255*. *See also* quiche

G

garlic
  in Asian lettuce wraps, 200
  in Britt's Brussels, 174
  in cheese sauce, for vegetable bake, 234
  in chimichurri sauce, 250
  in marinara sauce, for vegetable bake, 234
  roasted garlic, 287
  roasted, in basil pesto, 286
  roasted, in Greek dressing, 288
  roasted, in hummus, 287
  roasted, in tahini sauce, 162
  roasted, in tzatziki, 287
  in tuna quinoa bake, 208
ginger
  in Asian dressing, 288
  in Asian lettuce wraps, 200
  in instant noodles, 120
  mango, and white chocolate scones, 150, 151
  in Thai chicken, quinoa, and veggie bowl, 48
goat cheese. *See also* feta
  and avocado toast, 76, 77
  on breakfast pizza, 238
  in buckwheat salad, with potato and leek soup, 56
  on portobello and prosciutto pizza, 62
  in roasted balsamic tomato bowl, 272
  in roasted butternut squash and spinach salad, 122
  in roasted vegetable salad, 96
  on vegetables, roast chicken with, 88–89
  in warm green bean salad, 112
  watermelon, and beet salad, 210, 211
goji berries, in mulberry puffed quinoa cereal, 278
granola, 287
  in apple pie chia pudding, 262
  in banana parfait, 214
  in yogurt parfait, 177
Greek dressing, 288
Greek wrap, 152, 153
Greek yogurt, plain. *See also* vanilla Greek yogurt
  in breakfast quesadilla, 110
  in butternut squash pancakes, 158
  in cheese and onion crustless quiche, 126
  in prosciutto cup, 190
  in smoothies, 61, 97, 105, 111, 127, 143, 235, 259, 271
  in Southwest crustless quiche, 44
  in tropical dollar pancakes, 230
  in tzatziki, 287
  in yogurt parfait, 45
green bean(s)
  feta, and pomegranate salad, 144, 145
  salad, 112, 113
  in turkey sausage soup, 266
grilled squash salad, 240, 241

grilled vegetable and hummus flatbread, 46, 47
grilled vegetables, salmon with, 274, 275
Gruyère-chicken crepe, 216

H

halibut
  coconut and lemongrass poached, 114, 115
  in fish tacos, 130
  poached, with baked quinoa and collard greens, 218, 219
ham. *See also* prosciutto
  on breakfast pizza, 238
  corn, and roasted red pepper chowder, 154
Hawaiian pizza, 264, 265
hearts of palm
  in berry and Boursin® salad, 78
  in instant noodles, 120
  in red smoothie, 111
  in side salads, 106, 146, 216, 226, 266, 146
  in tropical green smoothie, 155
  in white bean and kale salad, 136
hemp seeds
  in breakfast summer roll, 84
  in side salad, 106
  in yogurt parfait, 45
hot chocolate, 45, 81, 91, 111, 119, 159, 191. *See also* warm chocolate steamer
hummus, 287
  with chia-flax bagel, 184
  in Greek wrap, 152
  and grilled vegetable flatbread, 46, 47

I

instant noodles, 120, 121
Italian dressing, 288
Italian turkey sausage, in stuffed squash with tahini sauce, 162

J

jam, strawberry-mango chia, 102, 103

K

kale
  in breakfast quesadilla, 110
  in instant noodles, 120
  slaw, fish tacos with, 130, 131
  in slaw, with pork and bean chili, 106
  in tropical green smoothie, 44
  in turkey sausage soup, 266
  and white bean salad, 136, 137
kefir
  in tropical smoothie, 55
  in tuna quinoa bake, 208
kiwi, in breakfast summer roll, 84
kohlrabi
  in kale slaw, fish tacos with, 130
  in side salad, 146, 194

L

"lasagna," vegetable, 234
leek
  in cauliflower cottage pie, 98
  and potato soup, 56, 57
lemon
  in chimichurri sauce, 250
  in hummus, 287
  -ricotta crepe, 182
  for salad, with tuna quinoa bake, 208
  in tahini sauce, 162
  in tzatziki, 287
  in vanilla blueberry chia pudding, 52
lemongrass and coconut poached halibut, 114, 115
lentil(s)
  in quinoa, buckwheat, and bean salad, 70
  taco lettuce wraps, 224
  in white bean and kale salad, 136
lettuce
  for salad, with tuna quinoa bake, 208
  wraps, 200, 201, 224
lime
  in Asian dressing, 288
  -coconut mojito, 119, 139, 143
  coconut water with, 73, 81, 97
  in mango salsa, fish tacos with, 130
  popcorn, spicy, 259
loaf, turkey sausage and zucchini pizza, 202, 203

M

mango
  with apple pie chia pudding, 262
  in banana-flax smoothie, 259
  BBQ chicken pizza, 160, 161
  in breakfast summer roll, 84
  in carrot juice smoothie, 90
  in chia and fruit fizz, 199
  and chicken summer roll, 104
  ginger, and white chocolate scones, 150, 151
  in morning smoothie, 171
  with mulberry puffed quinoa cereal, 278
  salsa, fish tacos with, 130
  smoothie, 271
  -strawberry chia jam, 102, 103
  in sweet potato breakfast stack, 222
  syrup, tropical dollar pancakes with, 230
  in tropical fizzy chia drink, 239
  in tropical green smoothie, 44, 155
  in tropical smoothie, 191, 247
  in vanilla green smoothie, 61
  in yogurt parfait, 259, 267
maple
  salmon with grilled vegetables and wild rice, 274, 275
  sugar, in creamy berry farina cereal, 198
  sugar, vanilla almond milk with, 239
  syrup, in apple pie chia pudding, 262
  syrup, in cream cheese syrup, 118, 134
marinara sauce, 234
melt, chicken chimichurri, 256, 257

milk chocolate
    in hot chocolate, 91
    in warm chocolate steamer, 55
mint, in mojito, 119, 139, 143
mochachia, 247, 283
mojito, 119, 139, 143
morning smoothie, 171
mozzarella. *See also* bocconcini
    in baked quinoa, halibut with, 218
    in butternut squash pancakes, 158
    on mango BBQ chicken pizza, 160
    in prosciutto, cheese, and caramelized
        onion scones, 94
    spaghetti squash bowl with, 194
    on spicy Hawaiian pizza, 264
    in stuffed squash with tahini sauce, 162
    in turkey sausage and zucchini pizza loaf,
        202
mulberry puffed quinoa cereal, 278, *279*
mushroom(s). *See* cremini mushrooms;
    portobello mushroom(s); shiitake
    mushroom(s); truffle; white mushrooms

N
Napa cabbage, in grilled vegetables, 274
navy beans, in pork and bean chili, 106
noodles
    and chicken soup, 170
    instant, 120, *121*
    rice, in chicken and mango summer roll,
        104
not-your-average Cobb salad, 232, *233*
nutritional yeast
    in cauliflower cottage pie, 98
    in cauliflower mash, 88–89
    in cheese sauce, for vegetable bake, 234
nuts. *See* almonds; peanuts, in Asian lettuce
    wraps; pine nuts; pistachios, in warm
    green bean salad; walnuts. *See also*
    seeds

O
oat bran
    in red smoothie, 111
    in tropical smoothie, 55
    in yogurt parfait, 45
oats. *See also* oat bran
    in granola, 287
    in mulberry puffed quinoa cereal, 278
    in tropical dollar pancakes, 230
onion
    caramelized, prosciutto, and cheese
        scones, 94, *95*
    and cheese crustless quiche, 126
orange
    in chia and fruit fizz, 199
    in morning smoothie, 171
    in tropical green smoothie, 44
    in tropical smoothie, 55
orange bell pepper, in chicken fajitas, 72

P
pancakes. *See also* crepe
    butternut squash, 158
    pop-up, 246
    tropical dollar, 230, *231*
panko crumbs, for pork schnitzel, 242
papaya, in smoothies, 55, 61, 90, 191, 247, 259
parfait
    banana, 214, *215*
    yogurt, 45, 177, 259, 267
Parmesan
    in basil pesto, 286
    in cheese sauce, for vegetable bake, 234
    in chicken noodle soup, 170
    in corn, ham, and roasted red pepper
        chowder, 154
    in quinoa, buckwheat, and bean salad, 70
    in roasted vegetables, sole with, 178
peanut butter
    and almond milk smoothie, 97
    in Asian dressing, 188
peanuts, in Asian lettuce wraps, 200.
        See also peanut butter
peas. *See also* snow peas; sugar snap peas
    in bison stew, 282
    in quinoa, buckwheat, and bean salad, 70
pesto, basil, 286
    spaghetti squash bowl with, 194
    tomato and ricotta toast, 86, *87*
phyllo dough, for chicken pot pie, 226
pie
    cauliflower cottage, 98, *99*
    chicken pot, 226, *227*
pilaf, shiitake-truffle, pork schnitzel with,
    242
pineapple
    in breakfast summer roll, 84
    in mango salsa, fish tacos with, 130
    in smoothies, 44, 171, 191, 271
    on spicy Hawaiian pizza, 264
pine nuts
    in basil pesto, 286
    in quinoa, buckwheat, and bean salad, 70
pinto beans, in pork and bean chili, 106
pistachios, in warm green bean salad, 112
pita, for grilled vegetable and hummus
    flatbread, 46
pizza. *See also* flatbread, grilled vegetable
    and hummus
    breakfast, 238
    loaf, turkey sausage and zucchini, 202, *203*
    mango BBQ chicken, 160, *161*
    portobello and prosciutto, 62, *63*
    spicy Hawaiian, 264, *265*
poached halibut with baked quinoa and
    collard greens, 218, *219*
pomegranate
    butternut squash and spinach salad with,
        122
    green bean, and feta salad, 144, *145*

popcorn, 287
    buttered, 209
    cinnamon-sugar, 97, 127, 217, 239
    spicy lime, 259
    trail mix, 91
poppy seeds, in carrot cake French toast,
    118
pop-up pancakes, 246
pork. *See also* bacon; ham; prosciutto
    and bean chili, 106, *107*
    roast, stuffed, 186, *187*
    schnitzel with asparagus and shiitake-
        truffle pilaf, 242, *243*
portobello mushroom(s)
    and broccoli, with vegetable bake, 234
    and prosciutto pizza, 62, *63*
    sandwich, 248, *249*
    in spinach salad, pizza loaf with, 202
    in wild rice, 80
potato(es)
    baked, with spinach salad, 128, *129*
    in bison stew, 282
    in chicken pot pie, 226
    in corn, ham, and roasted red pepper
        chowder, 154
    fries, chicken fingers with, 138
    and leek soup with buckwheat salad, 56,
        57
    roast chicken with, 146, *147*
    in roasted vegetables, sole with, 178
    with stuffed pork roast, 186
pot pie, chicken, 226, *227*
prosciutto
    butternut squash and spinach salad with,
        122, *123*
    cheese, and caramelized onion scones,
        94, *95*
    in cheese and onion crustless quiche,
        126
    in Cobb salad, 232
    cup, 190
    and portobello pizza, 62, *63*
    on spicy Hawaiian pizza, 264
    in spinach and egg salad, 168
    in sweet potato breakfast stack, 222
    in turkey crepe sandwich, 176
    in warm green bean salad, 112
provolone
    in chicken chimichurri melt, 256
    in portobello mushroom sandwich,
        248
    in tuna quinoa bake, 208
pudding
    apple pie chia, 262, *263*
    chocolate chia, 166, *167*
    vanilla blueberry chia, 52, *53*
puffed quinoa
    cereal, mulberry, 278, *279*
    in granola, 287
pumpkin-cinnamon smoothie, 225

pumpkin seeds
    with Britt's Brussels, 174
    in buckwheat salad, potato and leek soup
        with, 56
    in butternut squash and spinach salad, 122
    in carrot cake French toast, 118
    in chia-flax bagel, 184
    in granola, 287
    in mulberry puffed quinoa cereal, 278
    in popcorn trail mix, 91
    in side salads, 106, 128, 154, 266
    in spinach and egg salad, 168
    in warm green bean salad, 112
    in yogurt parfait, 45

Q
quesadilla, breakfast, 110
quiche. See also frittata, sweet potato
    cheese and onion crustless, 126
    Southwest crustless, 44
quinoa, 286
    in bison taco salad, 258
    in bocconcini salad, 54
    in breakfast summer roll, 84
    buckwheat, and bean salad, 70, 71
    chicken, and veggie bowl, 48, 49
    halibut with, 114, 218
    puffed, cereal, mulberry, 278, 279
    puffed, in granola, 287
    in roasted balsamic tomato bowl, 272
    salad, cauliflower cottage pie with, 98
    in Southwest crustless quiche, 44
    in stuffed squash with tahini sauce, 162
    taco bowl, 192, 193
    in tropical dollar pancakes, 230
    tuna bake, 208
    in turkey sausage soup, 266
    and wild rice, Arctic char with, 80

R
ranch dressing, 288
    in BBQ chicken salad, 280
    in bison taco salad, 258
raspberry(ies)
    in banana parfait, 214
    in berry and Boursin® salad, 78
    in breakfast summer roll, 84
    in chia and fruit fizz, 199
    for coconut and flaxseed French toast, 68
    in creamy berry farina cereal, 198
    with lemon-ricotta crepe, 182
    with pop-up pancakes, 246
    in red smoothie, 111
    in tropical mango smoothie, 271
    with vanilla chia crepes, 134
    in yogurt parfait, 267
red bell pepper
    in breakfast quesadilla, 110
    in butternut squash and spinach salad, 122
    in chicken fajitas, 72
    corn, and ham chowder, 154

in mango salsa, fish tacos with, 130
on portobello and prosciutto pizza, 62
in roasted corn salad, Arctic char with, 80
in sole en papillote, 178
in stuffed squash with tahini sauce, 162
red cabbage
    in chicken and mango summer roll, 104
    in kale slaw, fish tacos with, 130
    in red smoothie, 111
    in slaw, with pork and bean chili, 106
red chili, in coconut and lemongrass
    poached halibut, 114
red leaf lettuce, for salad with tuna quinoa
    bake, 208
red smoothie, 111
rice. See rice noodles; rice paper, for summer
    rolls; wild rice
rice noodles
    in chicken and mango summer roll, 104
    instant, 120
rice paper, for summer rolls, 84, 104
ricotta
    -lemon crepe, 182
    in spaghetti squash bowl, 194
    in stuffed pork roast, 186
    tomato, and pesto toast, 86, 87
roast chicken
    with baby potatoes, baby carrots, and
        spinach salad, 146, 147
    with vegetables and cauliflower mash,
        88–89
roasted balsamic tomato bowl, 272, 273
roasted butternut squash and spinach
    salad with chicken, prosciutto, and
    pomegranate, 122, 123
roasted corn salad, Arctic char with, 80
roasted garlic. See under garlic
roasted red pepper, corn, and ham chowder,
    154
roasted vegetable salad, 96
roll. See breakfast burrito; chicken fajitas;
    Greek wrap; summer roll
rotini, in chicken noodle soup, 170
rutabaga, in turkey sausage soup, 266

S
salad
    BBQ chicken, 280, 281
    berry and Boursin®, 78, 79
    bison, spinach, and sweet potato, 64, 65
    bison taco, 258
    bocconcini, 54
    buckwheat, 56, 57
    butternut squash and spinach, 122, 123
    green bean, feta, and pomegranate, 144,
        145
    grilled squash, 240, 241
    kale slaw, fish tacos with, 130, 131
    not-your-average Cobb, 232, 233
    quinoa, buckwheat, and bean, 70, 71
    quinoa, cauliflower cottage pie with, 98

roasted corn, Arctic char with, 80
roasted vegetable, 96
side, 106, 154, 160, 216, 226, 266
spicy egg, on a chia-flax bagel, 184, 185
spinach and egg, 168, 169
spinach, 128, 129, 146, 147
warm green bean, 112, 113
watermelon, goat cheese, and beet, 210, 211
white bean and kale, 136, 137
salmon with grilled vegetables and wild rice,
    274, 275
salsa
    in bison taco salad, 258
    in breakfast burrito, 270
    in lentil taco lettuce wraps, 224
    mango, fish tacos with, 130
    in quinoa taco bowl, 192
sandwich. See also toast
    breakfast, 142
    chicken chimichurri melt, 256
    portobello mushroom, 248, 249
    turkey crepe, 176
sauce
    balsamic reduction, 286
    basil pesto, 286
    cheese, 234
    chimichurri, 250
    dressings, 288
    hummus, 287
    marinara, 234
    shiitake-truffle, chicken-Gruyère crepe
        with, 216
    strawberry, 166
    tahini, 162
    tzatziki, 287
sausage. See turkey sausage
schnitzel, pork, 242
scones
    mango, ginger, and white chocolate, 150, 151
    prosciutto, cheese, and caramelized onion,
        94, 95
seeds. See chia; flax(seed); hemp seeds;
    poppy seeds, in carrot cake French toast;
    pumpkin seeds; sesame seeds; sunflower
    seeds. See also nuts
sesame seeds. See also tahini
    in Asian lettuce wraps, 200
    in breakfast summer roll, 84
    in chicken and mango summer roll, 104
    in grilled vegetables, 274
shiitake mushroom(s)
    in breakfast quesadilla, 110
    in grilled vegetables, salmon with, 274
    in side salad, 98
    -truffle pilaf, 242
    -truffle sauce, chicken-Gruyère crepe with,
        216
    in vegetables, roast chicken with, 88–89
slaw
    kale, 130, 136
    with pork and bean chili, 106

slow-cooked bison stew, 282
slow-cooked chicken fajitas, 72
slow-cooked chicken pot pie, 226, *227*
slow-cooked pork and bean chili, 106, *107*
smoothie
    banana-flax, 259
    carrot juice, 90
    chocolate-banana, 73, 105
    chocolate-vanilla, 183
    morning, 171
    peanut butter and almond milk, 97
    pumpkin-cinnamon, 225
    red, 111
    tropical, 55, 191, 247
    tropical green, 44, 155
    tropical mango, 271
    vanilla, banana, and chocolate, 127, 143
    vanilla-cinnamon, 209, 235
    vanilla green, 61
    vanilla wheat germ, 217
snow peas
    in grilled vegetables, salmon with, 274
    in instant noodles, 120
soft-boiled egg and soldiers, 206, *207*
sole en papillote with roasted vegetables,
    178, *179*
soup. *See also* chili, pork and bean; stew, bison
    chicken noodle, 170
    creamy corn, ham, and roasted red pepper
        chowder, 154
    instant noodles, 120
    potato and leek, 56, *57*
    turkey sausage, 266
Southwest crustless quiche and tropical
    green smoothie, 44
spaghetti squash bowl with sun-dried
    tomatoes, mozzarella, and pesto, 194, *195*
spicy egg salad on a chia-flax bagel, 184, *185*
spicy Hawaiian pizza, 264, *265*
spicy lime popcorn, 259
spicy maple salmon with grilled vegetables
    and wild rice, 274, *275*
spinach
    in BBQ chicken salad, 280
    in berry and Boursin® salad, 78
    bison, and sweet potato salad, 64, *65*
    in bison taco salad, 258
    in bocconcini salad, 54
    in breakfast burrito, 270
    in buckwheat salad, potato and leek soup
        with, 56
    and butternut squash salad, 122, *123*
    on chia-flax bagel, 184
    in chicken and mango summer roll, 104
    in chocolate-banana smoothie, 73
    in Cobb salad, 232
    and egg salad, 168, *169*
    in grilled squash salad, 240
    in quinoa salad, cauliflower cottage pie
        with, 98
    in roasted vegetable salad, 96

    in side salads, 106, 128, 146, 154, 160, 194,
        202, 216, 226, 266
    in smoothies, 44, 61, 90, 155
    in stuffed squash with tahini sauce, 162
    in sweet potato breakfast stack, 222
    in Thai chicken, quinoa, and veggie bowl,
        48
    in turkey crepe sandwich, 176
    in watermelon, goat cheese, and beet
        salad, 210
squash. *See* acorn squash; butternut
    squash; pumpkin-cinnamon smoothie;
    zucchini
steamer
    vanilla-almond, 271
    vanilla-cinnamon, 177, 258
    warm chocolate, 55
stew, bison, 282
stock, chicken, 287
strawberry(ies)
    in berry and Boursin® salad, 78
    in breakfast summer roll, 84
    in creamy berry farina cereal, 198
    with lemon-ricotta crepe, 182
    -mango chia jam, 102, *103*
    with pop-up pancakes, 246
    sauce, chocolate chia pudding with, 166
    in smoothies, 55, 90, 111, 155
    in yogurt parfait, 45, 259
stuffed pork roast, 186, *187*
stuffed squash with tahini sauce, 162, *163*
sugar-cinnamon popcorn, 97, 127, 217, 239
sugar snap peas
    in butternut squash and spinach salad,
        122
    in side salad, 208
    in Thai chicken, quinoa, and veggie bowl,
        48
summer roll
    breakfast, 84, *85*
    chicken and mango, 104
sun-dried tomato(es)
    in baked potato, 128
    in BBQ chicken salad, 280
    on breakfast pizza, 238
    in Cobb salad, 232
    in prosciutto cup, 190
    in side salad, 154
    spaghetti squash bowl with, 194
    in spinach and egg salad, 168
    in spinach salad, turkey sausage and
        zucchini pizza loaf with, 202
    in sweet potato breakfast stack, 222
    in sweet potato frittata, 254
    in tuna quinoa bake, 208
sunflower seeds
    in berry and Boursin® salad, 78
    in bison, spinach, and sweet potato
        salad, 64
    in buckwheat salad, potato and leek soup
        with, 56

    in butternut squash and spinach salad, 122
    in carrot cake French toast, 118
    in chia-flax bagel, 184
    in Cobb salad, 232
    in mulberry puffed quinoa cereal, 278
    in popcorn trail mix, 91
    in quinoa, buckwheat, and bean salad, 70
    in quinoa salad, cauliflower cottage pie with,
        98
    in side salads, 106, 128, 154, 160, 194, 202,
        216, 226, 266
    in Thai chicken, quinoa, and veggie bowl, 48
    in warm green bean salad, 112
    in white bean and kale salad, 136
sweet potato
    bison, and spinach salad, 64, *65*
    breakfast stack, 222, *223*
    frittata, 254, *255*
Swiss chard
    in Thai chicken, quinoa, and veggie bowl, 48
    in tropical green smoothie, 44
syrup. *See also under* maple
    cream cheese, 118, 134
    mango, tropical dollar pancakes with, 230

T

taco bowl, quinoa, 192, *193*
taco lentil lettuce wraps, 224
taco salad, bison, 258
taco seasoning, 286
    in bison taco salad, 258
    in chicken fajitas, 72
    in lentil taco lettuce wraps, 224
tacos, fish, 130, *131*
tahini
    in hummus, 287
    sauce, stuffed squash with, 162
Thai chicken, quinoa, and veggie bowl, 48, *49*
toast. *See also* French toast
    for Britt's Brussels, 174
    goat cheese and avocado, 76, *77*
    with prosciutto cup, 190
    soft-boiled egg and, 206
    with strawberry-mango chia jam, 102
    tomato, ricotta, and pesto, 86, *87*
tomato(es). *See also* sun-dried tomato(es);
    tomato paste; tomato purée
    in baked potato, 128
    in BBQ chicken salad, 280
    in bison taco salad, 258
    in bocconcini salad, 54
    bowl, roasted balsamic, 272, *273*
    in breakfast sandwich, 142
    in cauliflower cottage pie, 98
    in chicken chimichurri melt, 256
    in Cobb salad, 232
    in Greek wrap, 152
    in grilled vegetable and hummus flatbread,
        46
    in lentil taco lettuce wraps, 224
    on mango BBQ chicken pizza, 160

in pork and bean chili, 106
in portobello mushroom sandwich, 248
in quinoa, buckwheat, and bean salad, 70
ricotta, and pesto toast, 86, *87*
sauce, in baked quinoa, 218
in side salads, 128, 154, 160, 216, 226
in Southwest crustless quiche, 44
in turkey crepe sandwich, 176

tomato paste
in bison stew, 282
in marinara sauce, for vegetable bake, 234
in portobello and prosciutto pizza, 62
on spicy Hawaiian pizza, 264
in turkey sausage and zucchini pizza loaf,
202
in turkey sausage soup, 266

tomato purée
on butternut squash pancakes, 158
in prosciutto cup, 190
in spaghetti squash bowl, 194
in sweet potato breakfast stack, 222
in tuna quinoa bake, 208

tortilla
for breakfast burrito, 270
for breakfast pizza, 238
for breakfast quesadilla, 110
for chicken fajitas, 72
for fish tacos, 130
for mango BBQ chicken pizza, 160
for spicy Hawaiian pizza, 264

trail mix, popcorn, 91
tropical dollar pancakes with mango syrup,
230, *231*
tropical fizzy chia drink, 239
tropical green smoothie, 44, 155
tropical mango smoothie, 271
tropical smoothie, 55, 191, 247

truffle
oil, in wild rice, Arctic char with, 80
-shiitake pilaf, 242
-shiitake sauce, chicken-Gruyère crepe
with, 216

tuna quinoa bake, 208

turkey. *See also* turkey sausage
in cauliflower cottage pie, 98
crepe sandwich, 176

turkey sausage
soup in an acorn squash bowl, 266
in stuffed squash with tahini sauce, 162
and zucchini pizza loaf with spinach salad,
202, *203*

tzatziki, 287
chicken fingers with, 138
in Greek wrap, 152
for salad, with tuna quinoa bake, 208

V

vanilla. *See also* vanilla almond milk; vanilla
Greek yogurt
-almond steamer, 271

in apple pie chia pudding, 262
banana, and chocolate smoothie, 127
blueberry chia pudding, 52, *53*
in breakfast summer roll, 84
in carrot cake French toast, 118
chia crepes with cream cheese syrup,
134, *135*
chocolate, and banana smoothie, 143
in chocolate-banana smoothie, 105
-chocolate smoothie, 183
-cinnamon milk, 217, 235
-cinnamon smoothie, 209, 235
-cinnamon steamer, 177, 258
in cream cheese syrup, 118, 134
in granola, 287
green smoothie, 61
in pop-up pancakes, 246
wheat germ smoothie, 217

vanilla almond milk. *See also* almond milk,
original; chocolate almond milk
in apple pie chia pudding, 262
in banana parfait, 214
in cinnamon-vanilla milk, 217
in cream cheese syrup, 118, 134
in creamy berry farina cereal, 198
in hot chocolate, 45, 91, 111, 119, 159, 191
with maple sugar, 239
in mochachia, 247, 283
in smoothies, 61, 73, 97, 105, 127, 143, 155,
171, 183, 209, 217, 225, 235, 259
in vanilla-almond steamer, 271
in vanilla blueberry chia pudding, 52
in vanilla chia crepes, 134
in vanilla-cinnamon milk, 235
in vanilla-cinnamon steamer, 177, 258

vanilla Greek yogurt. *See also* Greek yogurt,
plain
in all puddings. *See* pudding
in banana parfait, 214
in carrot cake French toast, 118
in coconut and flaxseed French toast, 68
in smoothies, 90, 143, 171, 191, 209, 225,
247
in yogurt parfait, 177, 259, 267

vegetable(s). *See also individual vegetables*
bake, 234
chicken, and quinoa bowl, 48, *49*
grilled, and hummus flatbread, 46, *47*
grilled, salmon with, 274
roast chicken with, 88–89
roasted, sole with, 178
salad, roasted, 96

W

walnuts
in granola, 287
in green bean, feta, and pomegranate
salad, 144
with lemon-ricotta crepe, 182
in side salad, 160

in watermelon, goat cheese, and beet salad,
210
warm chocolate steamer, 55
warm green bean salad, 112, *113*
water chestnuts, in Asian lettuce wraps, 200
watermelon, goat cheese, and beet salad,
210, *211*
wheat bran, in mulberry puffed quinoa cereal,
278
wheat farina berry cereal, 198

wheat germ
in apple pie chia pudding, 262
for Arctic char, 80
in banana parfait, 214
in butternut squash pancakes, 158
in mochachia, 247
in pop-up pancakes, 246
in smoothies, 44, 55, 73, 90, 97, 105, 111, 127,
143, 155, 171, 183, 209, 217, 225, 271

white bean(s)
and kale salad, 136, *137*
quinoa, and buckwheat salad, 70
and squash, chicken with, 250

white chocolate, mango, and ginger scones,
150, *151*

white mushrooms
in side salad, 154
in Thai chicken, quinoa, and veggie bowl, 48

wild rice, 286
Arctic char with, 80
halibut with, 114
salmon with, 274
in shiitake-truffle pilaf, 242

wrap. *See also* summer roll
Asian lettuce, 200, *201*
breakfast burrito, 270
chicken fajitas, 72
Greek, 152, *153*
lentil taco lettuce, 224

Y

yeast. *See* nutritional yeast
yellow bell pepper
in chicken fajitas, 72
in grilled squash salad, 240
in sole en papillote, 178
yellow squash, in grilled squash salad, 240
yogurt. *See* Greek yogurt, plain; vanilla
Greek yogurt
yogurt parfait, 45, 177, 259, 267

Z

zucchini
in grilled squash salad, 240
in grilled vegetable and hummus flatbread,
46
in roast chicken with vegetables, 88–89
in roasted vegetables, sole with, 178
and turkey sausage pizza loaf, 202, *203*
in vegetable bake, 234

CONTRIBUTORS

JANINE ELENKO

Janine Elenko is a registered dietitian (RD) with a bachelor of science (B. Sc.) degree in Human Nutrition and is currently working towards a master's degree in Public Health. After a dietetic internship in Ontario, Janine went on to work in stroke rehabilitation. Her passion lies in advocating social change within communities.

ASHLEE GILLESPIE

A Red Seal chef who specializes in pastry, Ashlee adopted a love for raw and fresh ingredients during her work in Australia and New Zealand. Ashlee also developed tremendous insight into gluten-free cooking after she was diagnosed with celiac disease.